MW00720244

Cardboard Ocean

Also by Mike McCardell

Cardboard Ocean

A MEMOIR

Mike McCardell

HARBOUR PUBLISHING

Harbour Publishing Co. Ltd.
P.O. Box 219, Madeira Park, BC, V0N 2H0
www.harbourpublishing.com

Cover photograph by Nick Didlick
Interior photographs are from the author's collection, with the following
exceptions: Page 43—refurbished ice cream truck photo courtesy Harry
Wilkinson, Bungalow Bar Ice Cream Truck; Page 243—Jackie Robinson of
the Brooklyn Dodgers, 1954, photo by Bob Sandberg, Library of Congress;
Page 302— Jackie Robinson comic book cover, 1951, Fawcett Publications;
Page 305—postcard of Ebbets Field in Brooklyn, NY, created by Acacia
Card Company, circa 1930-45, Boston Public Library; Page 352—abandoned
Bungalow Bar Ice Cream truck, 1973, photo by Arthur Tress, National Archives
(412-DA-5440).
Edited by Lacey Decker Hawthorne
Dust jacket design by Anna Comfort O'Keeffe
Text design by Mary White
Printed and bound in Canada

Canada Council   Conseil des Arts
for the Arts   du Canada

BRITISH COLUMBIA
ARTS COUNCIL
An agency of the Province of British Columbia

Harbour Publishing acknowledges financial support from the Government of
Canada through the Canada Book Fund and the Canada Council for the Arts,
and from the Province of British Columbia through the BC Arts Council and
the Book Publishing Tax Credit.

Cataloguing data available from Library and Archives Canada
978-1-55017-664-3 (cloth)
978-1-55017-665-0 (ebook)

This special book is dedicated to my wife, Valerie.
I met you after I left my life on the street in this story.
You have been my life since then.

Contents

B.C. – Before Computer Games

First, and most importantly before you start reading, I want to thank you. You who have this book in your hands. Yes, you. You, or your friends or your relations or some schmuck you know who was shovelling chicken droppings or someone else who saved some ducks crossing the street or helped a woman crossing the street, you have given me a wonderful life. Thank you.

I have written stories about you, or your friends. They are average, everyday stories, but to me they are better than Greek dramas or Broadway musicals.

And now I would like to tell you about my favourite story. This one beats everything because this is what made me whatever I am. You all lived through the years when you were eight and nine and ten and eleven, just before and just when the juices started to run inside you and the world flipped over on its back. And there you were trying to figure out which way was up and no matter which way you pointed, you were wrong.

This is when I swam in the cardboard ocean. You had

adventures just like this in different places and different times. But it was all the same. It was wonderment.

This is what helped create us all before video games. Everything in here is true. It all happened over three or four years but in my memory, as with most kids, it all happened at once.

As in my other books, start anywhere, each chapter is a story. And if you don't want to start at the beginning, read the chapter called "World War" (page 285).

This was your life as well as mine.

Love to you all,

Mike

Always Tell the Truth

"Honest, Miss Johnson, me and all the kids on my street, we go swimming in the Mediterranean every summer."

That was in the 1950s in P.S. 54 in Queens, New York. Don't worry if you have no idea where that is. Most New Yorkers don't know either. It is not the part of New York that has big buildings. It is not the famous part. It is like East Vancouver, or Whalley. They are in greater Vancouver, but a universe away.

Miss Johnson looked down at me. She wore a long skirt. She always wore a long skirt and told us she would never get married because we were her family. If she married she would have to quit teaching because that was the law. So she did not get married. I thought that was terrible because she would never have sex, which I knew you should have because it made you happy.

Actually, it did not make you happy if you were married because married people I knew were always yelling at each other so I thought they could not have sex because they were not happy. This was one of the things I did not understand. You had to get married to have sex and sex made you happy, unless you were married, then you were not happy. We wished Miss Johnson would get married so she would have sex, even if it would make her unhappy.

"Don't lie to me," said Miss Johnson. "It is good to have imagination, but don't lie."

"Honest, we are going swimming in the Mediterranean like we did last summer. I can still remember how some stuff in the ocean tastes."

"Mickey, if you lie again I will send you to the principal."

"But Miss Johnson, I am not lying."

"Have you ever been on an airplane?" she asked.

"No."

I did not see what that had to do with it.

"Have you ever been on a boat?"

"No."

This was plain silly now.

"Have you ever met a Greek?"

Okay, now we're talking. Things were going to go my way.

"We know lots of Greeks. They are right next to the Mediterranean," I said.

"What do they look like?"

Miss Johnson was getting angry. I could tell because she was breathing deeply and the bumps underneath her blouse were getting bigger. We all liked it when Miss Johnson got angry.

"They are hairy," I said. "And they wear heavy winter coats all summer long—"

"That does it, Mickey. You're not only lying, you are making fun of me. Go see Miss Flag right now."

Darn, darn and worse. I am going to be held in again, and that would mean I would miss a game on the street and worse, I would miss a swim in the ocean, which was the Mediterranean even if she did not believe me. And at the end of the summer the ocean would be gone and I hated to miss even a half hour of swimming.

"Go sit in the corner," said old Miss Flag, when I arrived at her office.

I had been there before.

"What's it for this time?" she asked.

I said, "Miss Johnson said I should see you because she said I was lying, but I was not lying."

"Well, stay there until you decide to tell the truth."

So I went over to the big chair in the corner – at least it was not facing the corner – and I sat. I liked the chair. It was smooth and hard and all wood and I could look at the grains and follow them with my fingers, but it was still a prison. I had to sit and sit and sit while people came in to see Miss Flag, and they would wait in the outer room with me until she would see them and I would sit and they would go in her office and close the door and time would pass very slowly and they would come out shaking their heads and walk away and I was still sitting.

Or sometimes they would come out and shake Miss Flag's hand and say they would try harder. Then someone else would come and sit on the bench across the room from me and look at me and say nothing, and then go in to see Miss Flag. And I would sit. Then they would come out of her office and go home. They hardly noticed me when they left. I was just part of the furniture.

About five o'clock, Miss Flag walked out of her office with her coat on and noticed me and said, "Are you still here? Go home and next time, do what your teacher says."

I shot out of the chair and banged through the office door and I prayed to God I didn't break the glass on the door and ran down the hallway and pushed the panic bar on the inside of the outside door. It flew open and I jumped down the entire flight of stairs. That was a great jump. I never did it during the day because

I might fall at the bottom and the other kids would laugh at me. But now I was in a hurry and no other kids were there.

It was still light out, just heading into summer, and I ran down the street. The elevated train, the El, was running overhead and I loved the sound because it was loud and I tried to run underneath it as fast as I could, trying to keep up with it.

The B.C. Years: Before Computer Games

"Kar!"

I flattened myself against a fender. The game had already begun and I took over as pitcher because Johnny had to go to the bathroom.

"Kar, Kar!"

I had two strikes against Jimmy Lee and one ball but every time a car came by, he would say I only had one strike.

This is why I love the East Side of Vancouver. It is like the East Side of New York. Kids on the street making up games and making up how to play them while they were playing them. This is life before computers when skill of playing and skill of cheating were equal skills.

"Kar!"

Later in life I learned how a crow sounds. It says "Kar!" But on the street in the third inning of the ball game, it was just another car that was as much of a pain as crows are in other places.

The car came and went. Damn, that was close. I think he was trying to hit me. The street was narrow, but that was really close.

"You bum," I shouted at the car. "And your 'kar' is a piece of junk."

Sometimes the cars stopped and the drivers got out and we had to run because you're not allowed to have fights with adults. That was one of the rules.

"I'm still up," said Jimmy Lee. "I got three balls and one strike."

"Do not," I said. "You got two strikes."

"One strike."

"Two."

"It's a do over, I don't remember what he got," said Tommy. Tommy was catching for both teams. We had one extra guy, and Tommy was a good catcher, but he couldn't remember which foot to place in front of the other if he was walking.

He was also a terrific fighter, but sometimes he forgot which side he was on. One time he punched me in the face while we were fighting another gang.

"Tommy!? I'm on your side. Those are the other guys."

"Oh." It looked like he had just been told a super big secret, and he thumped three guys in a row, all unlucky members of the other guys.

"Kar," said Vinnie.

Oh, man. This was not like the middle of summer when we could get in three or four pitches in a row. Then traffic was light because some people had vacations, but now the factories were working overtime and the cars and trucks were messing up our games.

I flattened myself against a parked car again. This time a '48 Chevy went right down the middle of the street and gave us plenty of room. I liked the '48 Chevys because they had big fenders and you could hop up on them and sit and play bongo drums between your legs until the owner came out and tried to play the drums on your head.

"Truck," said Vinnie. Vinnie was on Jimmy Lee's team today. He had hit a single and was waiting at first base for Jimmy Lee to get a hit. It would be closing time for the factories in a few minutes and then the trucks would really screw up the game.

We would have to quit and read comics or something but it would be another game Jimmy Lee would swear he won. His record so far this season was ten or twenty wins and no losses.

"Truck," Vinnie said again.

"I'm giving up," I thought. By now Jimmy Lee would have the count at 3 and 0.

The truck was coming toward second base, from Jamaica Avenue, and going to the factories and we knew the Chevy going the other way would have to squeeze over almost rubbing the paint off the parked cars. It was fun to watch because the trucks did not care who they hit.

"I quit," said Jimmy Lee. "We can't get any more game in today. We'll just say we won."

"Did not," I shouted. "You were losing, you always do that."

He grabbed the bat and started walking off the street. When he stepped on the sidewalk I knew the game would be over. You can't get to the sidewalk and change your mind. That would be like giving in.

"I'm pitching anyway," I said. "If you're not there, you lose."

I grabbed the Spalding rubber ball in my fingers and wound up. I stood at the crack in the middle of the street, the same crack everyone used facing the sewer plate in the middle of the street which was home plate.

My arms were up, the ball was above my head when Jimmy Lee ran back to the sewer and held up the bat. I let go of the pink ball, he swung and bam!

Damn. Even with the fat pin that we stuck in it to keep it

from flying too far, the ball was really flying. It was over the wires heading over the elevated train, which meant a home run. Vinnie took off from first, which was the fender of the car parked where first base should be, and he was running for the pothole that was second and then rounding the bases for third, which was the unlucky other car that was parked where third base should be. By the time you got to third you always slammed into it, so the fenders on that side of the street were pretty scratched up, usually from the rivets of our Levi's.

Jimmy was strutting toward first. He knew it was a homer. It was the only way he could hit a ball because he was so slow that if he hit a grounder he would be tagged out. But a home run was his territory.

"See," he said as he touched the first base fender and strutted past me. "See, we won."

The game went on, briefly. "Kar," shouted Buster. Buster was on our team. He was playing first. He later joined the Marines so you knew from the beginning that he was tough and if you tried to reach first base while he had the ball, it was better that you turned around before you got there.

The game today did not much matter. There was no end of the season results. They won because there was too much traffic for us to go on. Tomorrow we would have another game and half the kids would be on the other team. It would be game number one hundred before the summer actually started. Or maybe it was game two hundred. It depended whether you counted games that only went a couple of innings before being called off due to cars.

It was like playing street hockey in Vancouver. That is, street hockey before computer games were invented. In the B.C. years, Before Computer years, the streets were filled with hockey sticks and kids. Not now.

The closest I saw of street games in Vancouver after computer games was a group of girls who made the longest hopscotch game in the world. At least that is what they called it and it probably was. It was near Nat Bailey Stadium, two blocks from Main Street, and they made a game with chalk on the sidewalk that went on for five blocks, no six blocks, no, "come around the corner," one of the girls said to me. Seven blocks, without stopping. You don't get that on computers.

But the best part of the game for me, and the worst for them, was when the neighbourhood boys started playing and using their own rules.

"NO! You're cheating," said the girls.

The boys were skipping numbers, and throwing the pebble off to the side, and then running ahead. Rotten boys. Just like Jimmy Lee. Bless them.

Back to Jimmy Lee.

He stuck his tongue out at me and grabbed the bat and bounced the end of it on the street and it bonged and bounced up into his hand. That was a neat trick. You could do it if you banged the stick down just right. It would shoot up like a ball. But if you were slightly off when you slammed it down, it would crash like a stick hitting the ground and you would look like a dumb-ass kid who could not bounce a stick.

"I got to get this back to my mom before she sees it's missing," said Jimmy.

He ran up the steps to his house which was across the alley from my house and if he was quick enough he would get the stick jammed back into the broom before his mother caught him. She said he was not allowed to use it anymore after he broke the last one – she had to buy a new broom and she said she could not afford that.

Fifty years later in Vancouver, my daughter said she wanted to show me something.

"You lived for stickball, right, Dad?" she said. "You've got to see this."

She was holding her daughter's hand when she led me down Granville Street.

We went into Restoration Hardware, which does not sell hardware. But they do sell stuff that you say, oh man, I gotta have that, followed by, oh boy, I can't afford that.

She took me past the silver candlesticks and the gold picture frames to a pile of long boxes with stickball bats inside. They were not for sale, they were ON SALE.

Each box had written on it: "From the Bronx and Brooklyn the asphalt field of dreams spreads out to the world."

The bats were a handcrafted maple wood stick with electric tape wrapped at one end. The tape was to make it look authentic. Sticker price, $29.

My baseball goodness god. I was now living in a city of street hockey. You need nothing but old hockey sticks, a ball and kids to play. But you never paid for the stick. They were pulled out of the garbage cans behind some skating arena and the broken pieces were taped back together and they started a new life on the rink that was made of black asphalt.

The sticks in stickball came when your mother turned her back and you unscrewed it from the broom.

Now they were manufactured with electric tape and sold in a box with dreamy words written on the side.

The bat was 75 percent off because, get real, nobody in Vancouver grew up playing stickball.

I picked up a box with the stickball bat inside. At 75 percent off, they were almost giving it away.

I stood in line. I thought of the games I had as a kid with my friends who would stay forever in the streets of my mind. I remembered the thrill of being ten and eleven years old.

"Will that be cash or charge, sir?"

"Never mind," I said. I put it back. Things are not as real as memories, and fancy things that pretend they are something they are not, are not like the kids who lived in your past. I walked down the sidewalk holding my granddaughter's hand. "Someday," I told her, "I'll teach you to play stickball, with a broomstick we swipe from your mother."

"What about your story of swimming in the Mediterranean," my daughter said. "Was that better than stickball?"

My head went into a dream. "The Mediterranean was so beautiful. I took the train to get there."

My daughter shook her head. "No wonder Miss Johnson said you were lying. You can't take a train from New York to get to Greece."

"Of course you can," I said. "That's when my mother ran away from my father."

That's a scary story. My father used to come home drunk every night and my mother and me would push the dresser in front of the bedroom door and lean against it while he banged on the other side.

"Don't worry," she said. "Your uncle will be home in the morning and everything will be okay then."

My Uncle John was a cop. He wore a suit to work with guns underneath it, so actually he was a detective. He kept his bullets in the top drawer of his dresser and I had to use a kitchen chair to climb up there to take one out of the box.

Don't get upset when your kid sticks her finger in the fan. She has to find out what it does and chances are the fan is made so little fingers can't touch the blades. Fan makers have kids, too.

The bullet was different. They were made before childproof packaging was thought of. I brought it outside and me and a friend spent a while hitting it with a rock to make it go off.

"What are you doing?" my mother asked when she leaned out the window.

"Nothing," I said. We covered up the bullet. I knew we shouldn't be doing this but I wasn't sure why.

My mother must have seen what we were doing because she suddenly ran out the front door and grabbed the bullet off the sidewalk.

"You are crazy! Your uncle will kill you."

See, there are worse things than killing yourself.

In the mornings, Uncle John would come home from work with his friends who were also detectives and they would laugh and joke and my mother would make them breakfast. My father, who was my uncle's brother, was still sleeping.

My mother would put out plates of bacon and eggs and pots of coffee and I would sit under the kitchen table and look at the guns they had strapped to their legs and listen to the stories of the night before.

"He was running across the rooftop, but I got him, grabbed him and slammed his head into the edge of the roof. You know, the part that's all metal."

I wanted to be a cop, like my uncle, and after his friends left I would say to him, "Can I be a junior policeman?"

"You're a little young," he would say. "Maybe in a few years, but meanwhile, take care of your mother."

Then he got up from the table, walked into his bedroom at the back of the apartment and I didn't see him again until night.

"You think someday Uncle John will make me a junior policeman?" I asked my mother.

"You should leave him alone for now, he is very tired."

She looked like she liked him very much.

At night, before I went to bed, I would go into his room and watch him get ready for work. He took the bullets out of his top drawer and loaded them into one pistol that he put into a holster under his arm.

Then he would check the bullets in another gun that he put into a holster and strapped to his right calf.

Then he picked his blackjack off the top of his dresser.

"Feel this, Mikey."

It was easy-to-grip rubber and only a little bigger than my hand, but it was so heavy. I opened my left hand and hit it like a ball.

"Owww." Oh, it hurt.

"It'll crack open a head. Almost kill someone," said my uncle. "It's my favourite little toy."

Then he straightened his tie and told me to take care of my mother and he left for work.

The next morning I was waiting for him outside on the front stoop. He was alone and he was banged up. I knew this because his tie was pulled over to the side and he had a bruise on his face and bandages on his knuckles.

"Can I be a junior policeman today?" I asked.

He stopped and looked down at me for a long time. At least it seemed like a long time. Then he said, "Why not? Today would be perfect to swear you in on the force. We need more kids."

He told me to come with him. He said good morning to my mother as she stood in the kitchen, cooking, and the two of us walked down the hallway to his room. Inside he took a card out of his wallet. I could not read, but I knew it was real because it had a police shield on one side. He wrote something on the back.

"Hold up your right hand," he said.

I did.

"Repeat after me. I swear to uphold the law."

I did not know what the law was, but I said, "I swear to uphold the law."

"And I swear to be good."

I said, "I swear to be good."

23

"And this is most important of all," said my uncle. "I swear to take care of my mother."

I raised my hand up higher and said, "I swear to take care of my mother."

Uncle John wrote something on the back of the card then leaned forward and put it in my shirt pocket.

"By the power invested in me, I hereby make you a junior policeman," he said. "And now I'm going to bed."

I jumped straight up. I ran down the hallway to my mother who was still in the kitchen.

"I'm a junior policeman," I said. "Uncle John made me a junior policeman. I'm a junior policeman."

"Well, I hope you thanked him," she said.

I had not, but his door was closed. I pulled the card halfway out of my pocket so that the badge showed. Then I got my plastic six-shooter and went outside.

This was when a six-year-old could go outside alone and walk around the block even in Brooklyn, so long as he did not cross the street. And six-shooters are not bad, so long as they are plastic.

Today there are daycares in Vancouver that will not allow boys to shoot each other with sticks they find in the park. Those boys will grow up to be judges and social reformers who will remember wonderful childhoods, until their sticks were taken away.

When I ran outside with my six-shooter that day, the first person I saw was Mrs. Ruzzito. She was taking a newspaper from her neighbour's stoop. I spoke to Mrs. Ruzzito.

Then I saw an old man coming out of the bar where my father hung out. He opened a pack of cigarettes and dropped the paper on the sidewalk.

I pulled up my badge and spoke to him. "Mister, you are not supposed to do that."

And then I saw the most terrible thing of all. Spike, who lived across the street, was letting his dog go to the bathroom on the sidewalk.

I knew you were supposed to curb your dog. There were pictures on signs along the street with a dog by the curb and words above the picture for those who could read. "Curb your dog," it said, even though that looked like black marks to me.

I pulled up my card, checked my gun, then looked both ways and crossed the street.

Can you break the law to enforce the law? It's a problem for six-year-olds and governments.

I spoke to Spike. He had tattoos. He was scary, but I was a junior policeman, with a card that had a badge on it. "That's not nice," I said. I was shaking. He just stared at me then walked away. "You're under arrest," I said. I saw him laugh, but he did not turn around.

The next morning I was sitting on the front stoop waiting for my uncle.

It is funny that only in New York do you call it a stoop. We played stoopball, throwing a ball against a stoop and catching it. If it bounced once it was five points, if you caught it on the fly it was ten, and if it was a pointer which shot out like a home run blast after hitting the edge of a step, it was twenty-five points. Not many of us caught a pointer, but we all learned to count.

In the rest of America, and the world, it is called the front steps, and you climb them to get into the house.

I was sitting on the stoop, waiting.

My uncle got out of a car along with three of his police buddies. My heart was pounding.

"Well, junior policeman, how are you doing?"

He remembered. He did not forget. He said it right in front of real policemen with real guns. I could not believe it. I stood up.

"I arrested some people," I said.

His friends started laughing. I did not feel bad. Of course they would laugh. It was my first day on the job.

"You what?" asked my uncle.

"I arrested some people and told them to come here this morning and you would take them to jail."

While his friends were snickering, Uncle John sat down on the stoop, picked me up and put me on his lap. I had the feeling I did something wrong.

He squeezed me tightly. I felt his gun next to my cheek, but he kept squeezing.

"You know, Mikey, what I really wanted to be, more than a policeman, was a cowboy. Do you think you could teach me how to be a cowboy?"

I knew I did something wrong. I wasn't sure what, but I knew it was wrong and I had done it. But my Uncle John was not yelling at me, not like my father. My face was hurting because he was still squeezing me against his gun, but he was not yelling.

"Do you think you could make me a junior cowboy?" he asked.

He let me have room to breathe.

"I think so, Uncle John. I think you could be a real cowboy, even more than a junior cowboy."

"I don't know, I've never ridden a horse before. Someday could you teach me?"

"Sure," I said.

He let me slide off his lap and his friends were still laughing as they walked in the front door. He was the last to go in and he turned to me and winked. My uncle winked at me. I would do anything for him.

I waited until the door closed and waited and waited until I figured they were in the kitchen and then I ran in through the front door. It did not have a lock. Can you imagine a door in Brooklyn that did not have a lock?

I sneaked down the hallway past them and they were too busy

eating to notice me. In my corner of the room which was the room where my mother and father slept, except they did not sleep together – my mother slept with me at night and my father slept in the day with his snoring and woke up with his hangover – I got out my wooden horse.

It was just a stick with a horse's head, but it was my horse. And I got out my cowboy hat, which was now too small for me because I got it when I was younger, and I put my police card with the badge in my cigar box. The box had my penknife and some buttons and coins, and now my official membership as a junior policeman.

Then I sneaked back down the hallway and out the front door. I would have to practise riding if I was going to teach my uncle how to be a cowboy. I still had my six-shooter, every cowboy needs that, and my hat. I pulled the string up real tight so it stayed on my head, and I rode down the street.

It felt good to be out on the range without having to worry about crime. I was looking for lost cattle.

Twenty-five years later, just after I got out of the Air Force, I was a police reporter at the New York *Daily News.* Those were the last days of the old-fashioned newspaper when the rewrite men, even if they were women, wore green visors on their heads and their sleeves were held up by rubber bands and they wore a headset while talking to the reporter on the street.

There was a murder on Canal Street. Stitch McCarthy, the old Irish heavy-drinking, always-in-debt reporter, was on the scene. He scribbled notes in pencil on some folded paper then went to a pay phone.

"Hey, Dick."

There were three writers at the *News* when I worked there named either Dick or Henry: Two names, three writers. Dick Lee, Henry Lee and Dick Henry. If you were young like me and went to the wrong one with whatever you were going with, he would explode and rip you apart, making you wish you had gone into accounting or surveying or anything except news.

"Hey, Dick. There's three dead and they are mobsters and this is how they got gunned down."

Dick would take a drink of his beer and begin to write.

"Copy!"

The copy boy pulled the paper out of the typewriter. It had one sentence on it. He ran to the city desk where the city editor checked it for whatever he checked it for, libel, accuracy, then sent it to the news desk where they would find a place to put it in the paper. Then the single line went to the copy desk.

That was the old-fashioned desk like you have seen in old movies about newspaper offices. It was shaped like a horseshoe and the slot man in the middle would give the line out to one of the editors who might change a word, and might not. They were brilliant editors.

Then the paper would go down a conveyer belt to the composing room one floor down on the sixth floor. That was like a vision of hell with a hundred fires burning below pots which were melting ingots of zinc that would be turned into lines of type on the Linotype machines.

"Excuse me," said my daughter. "What the heck does this have to do with taking a train to Greece?"

"Everything!" I said. "Everything leads to something. That may sound dumb, but much, much later in life I am with a cameraman for CTV, a very nice station I may add, and it is snowing and he says, 'Which way should we go?'"

I point my fingers in opposite directions. He goes to Queen Elizabeth Park and we find a little girl building her first snowman. And the nose keeps falling out.

"Oh, story god in the heavens, thank you." The little girl

looks at the pebble which is a nose and it is on the ground. She picks it up and puts it back. She smiles. Then it falls out again. She does not give up. A two-year-old is facing a problem and conquering it.

On television it is beautiful. How did we find it? Simple, it does not matter where you go because everywhere leads to somewhere. Life happens that way. Just follow it.

"Go on," said my daughter, not sure if we were talking about noses or newspapers.

All the Linotype machines were going at once and printers were picking up the hot metal lines of type from each machine and putting them into trays that would be squeezed into metal forms on heavy metal trays which would become a story in a newspaper. Meanwhile Stitch McCarthy, who badly wanted a drink, was still on the phone next to the murder scene and Dick Henry's typewriter was still writing the story, one line per page.

By the time Stitch hung up, the last line of the story was being set into type. By the time the police brass were arriving at Canal Street because this was a big murder, the metal type had been pressed into a heavy cardboard, and then the cardboard filled with more melted zinc and formed into a plate that was bent like half a circle.

By the time the coroner was arriving at Canal Street, the metal plate was on the presses and the paper was feeding through at a blurring speed.

By the time the coroner was counting the bullet holes, the newspapers were on a truck heading for Canal Street.

Bam. The papers were thrown in a bundle on the sidewalk and the wire holding them together was cut open by a paper seller.

"Read all about it. Mobsters gunned down on Canal Street. Get tomorrow's news tonight."

Some of the cops would buy the paper to see their names in it because they all knew Stitch, and whatever information they could get, they would give to him.

That was when newspapers beat CNN.

Another day I was in the morgue, what is now called the library of the *News*. They had information on everything. Reporters were supposed to have contacts with the church and underworld and police and judges and what information they had, they would file in the morgue because information was sacred.

As a fluke I looked up my name, which is what people do now on Google.

McCardell.

"My God, there's a file on McCardell," I said to myself.

A big file.

"No, it's not on me. It's on John McCardell."

I pulled the paper and pictures out of the manila folder. They were undercover surveillance photos of my uncle. He was going into stores. He was getting something in the stores. He was coming out with bags, sometimes brown paper bags, sometimes sports type bags.

More pictures of the same.

There were notes behind the picture: Suspect in bribery scandal; Policeman out of uniform collecting payoffs; Protection money.

When he was not catching crooks, my uncle was a crook. He was collecting cash from shopkeepers, mostly bars, and bringing the money back to the station house to split with the lieutenant and captain. Uncle John wore a badge but he was a criminal, a crooked cop.

Some years before that I once asked my mother what happened to Uncle John after he simply disappeared.

"He retired early and went to Florida," she said.

But he was a thief, a rotten no-good man who did not uphold the law and did not do what was good.

On the other hand, what the heck. When I retire I will still rent a horse somewhere on some tourist ranch. I only sat on a horse once before in my life, but I will do it again and take his memory for a ride and teach him to be a cowboy. We all make mistakes.

"So what about taking the train to get to Greece?" my daughter asked again.

"It's coming. First we have to get to the train."

Getting There

My mother told me the first game I learned to play was "fall down drunk like daddy." I don't remember that. I just remember my mother hiding my father's shoes and locking him in the back room and him climbing out the bedroom window and walking down the street in his socks and shaking his fist back at my mother.

It was what I thought was a typical family.

Sometimes when he was supposed to be babysitting me while my mother went to work, he would take me to the bar at the corner. That was on Ovington Avenue in Brooklyn. He would put me up on a bar stool at the end of the bar and get me a Coke and I would draw circles in the water on the dark wooden bar.

All I remember hearing of the men was "I killed a lot."

"Yeah, well, I killed a lot, too. Almost got killed myself, too."

I had seen one picture of my father with a helmet and a pistol and a canteen on an island. He said all the enemy were gone by the time he got there.

The only other conversation I remember was the men talking about the boy who was killed by a car around the corner. It was one of those cars from the late 1940s or maybe just the early 1950s that had a rocket ship bullet-like projection in the front to make it look fast and powerful, or something like that. To be honest, I never thought of what it was supposed to be.

But the men said that the bullet had gone right through the kid's head. "Killed him dead. Smashed him right through the brain."

I kept drawing circles in the water on the bar and ate another peanut and wondered what it was like to have a big bullet go through your head. It was one of those questions of childhood.

One night my mother woke me up while it was still dark.

"Shhhhh . . . "

I was still in my pajamas. She had a suitcase and my coat. We quietly walked down the hallway and out the front door.

That's when we got on the train. It was the longest train ride I had ever taken. We went from one side of Brooklyn to the middle of Queens where the subway went above ground and became the elevated train, the El, and when we got off the El the sun was up.

We walked down 125th Street from Jamaica Avenue toward the railroad yards. My cousin, who I did not remember ever seeing before although I was told he visited at least once, was sweeping the sidewalk.

I had never seen anyone sweeping outside before.

"Why are you sweeping?" I asked.

He looked friendly. "Because my mother told me to, because today was special because you are coming."

We would live there while my mother found another apartment. What my aunt did not like about us coming was that it put her son out of his room. We moved into it. What my cousin liked about us coming was that we put him out of his room. He moved out into the hallway at the top of the stairs, outside his parent's apartment. He was about twelve years old and living on his own, even if it was just a few steps to their front door. He was the happiest kid I have ever known. We lived there for more than a year. The best year ever for him.

He walked with me on the first day to my new school, P.S. 54, in which Miss Flag was the principal and Miss Johnson was teaching.

The El passed by half a block from the school and made so much noise that education came only between trains.

"Children, today we will learn that Columbus . . . "

But the train was coming and it took five seconds to go from an approaching rumble to a total drown-out of words.

My cousin Dick, my mother and me, after we left Brooklyn and went to live with him and his parents in Queens. He was very tall, he still is. I always looked up to him.

Rumble. Drown out. Rumble. Fade away.

Until I left for basic training in the Air Force, every conversation, every radio and television program was drowned out every few minutes by the trains. It was worse during rush hour. But even at night on the radio we never knew whether Superman saved the earth or not because just as he was going to stop it from spinning and turn back time to undo the evil that was going to happen, the train went by. We could only guess he saved the world because the next thing we heard was "Be with us next week for the next exciting adventure of Superman."

" . . . and that is why we have an America now," said the teacher.

But we didn't know why. We could only see her mouth moving while the train went by.

One day we went on a field trip. The teacher told us we did not need our coats. We followed her out of the classroom and then downstairs to the basement and then through a big metal door that we had never been through before. This was very exciting.

It was warm in the sub-basement and there were pipes and boilers. We went down metal steps and I held on to the banister even though I thought only girls did that, but it was a long way down.

At the bottom the janitor told us to make a circle around the furnace. It was hot even back where we were standing.

He opened the front grating and we saw a giant circle of fire.

"Those are the blue flames that keep us warm," he said.

Then he shut the grating and we went back to our classroom and I forgot all about it.

Fifty years later my wife and I were babysitting our granddaughter, Ruby, who was four, and we were sweeping outside. I should have known that was special because any time with her was special. She was holding onto the broom and helping me.

My wife opened the door and said the house was cold, do something. Wives say things like that.

I took Ruby down to the basement and opened the grating on the front of the furnace. It had gone out. I lit it and a circle of flames jumped up and Ruby jumped back.

"Those are the blue flames that keep us warm," I said to her.

She looked at me with her beautiful granddaughter eyes and said, "Now can we have some ice cream?"

But I know that fifty years from now she will be with her grandchild and something like that will happen. They will have some kind of heating, even if it is nuclear flames pretending to be real.

She will light it and she will say to her grandchild, "Those are the blue flames that keep us warm." And then she will say, "My grandfather told me that."

And I will have a connection with a child I will never know, thanks to a janitor in P.S. 54.

"But what about swimming in the Mediterranean?" my daughter asked. "Your story is not bad, but you keep promising to tell me how you got to Greece."

"We took the train, the El, the Jamaica Avenue El train. The noisy train that blocked the sun from the street. The train we took when we moved to our new home on 132nd Street, just off Jamaica Avenue. There was the ocean."

She was getting a bit impatient. You are probably getting the same way, but we are there now.

When my mother and I moved to a new apartment of our own, we got off the train at 132nd Street. The ocean was around the corner.

Finally, There

Our back windows looked out onto the Long Island Rail Road commuter tracks. They were close enough to almost read the headlines on the newspapers except the trains went by so fast the news was all a forgettable blur, like watching television news now.

At rush hour, the trains in the back passed by every ten minutes. There were four sets of tracks. The El on the corner of the street also passed by every ten minutes.

"My God," said an uncle who helped us move in. "How are you ever going to be able to sleep?"

Then there were the airplanes of Idlewild Airport, which was nearby. They took off over our street. This was long before President Kennedy was killed and they changed the name to JFK.

"What noise? You get used to it," said Joey, a kid I met the first morning on the new street.

"What's your name?" he asked.

"Mike," I said.

"Okay, Mickey, I'll show you around."

For the next twenty years I was Mickey.

"This is where we go swimming," he said.

We had gone around the corner to 131st Street, and there was a beautiful sight, a factory that turned out ice cream.

"We climb up there and jump in," said Joey.

We were standing near a fenced-in compound two stories high filled with cardboard boxes.

"Here, follow me," he said.

We climbed up the chain-link fence to the top.

"We usually get on the roof, then jump in."

Joey crawled off the top of the fence onto the flat black tar roof of the factory and I followed and wow, how else could it be described? It was wonderful up here. You could watch the El passing by but now I was looking straight at it instead of straight up. And when I turned around I was looking straight at the commuter train. I was on top of the world.

"Follow me."

He jumped into the boxes and sunk to his chest. I jumped and did the same.

"Now you dive down and you can swim all day."

I followed him and I was pulling my way through the boxes but no way near as fast as Joey.

"It's like swimming," he said, "except I don't know what swimming is. I never did it."

He stopped swimming and I caught up to him. This was amazing, incredible, even neat. We were about halfway down the pile, pushing boxes aside and pulling ourselves forward. The deeper we went, the harder it got and some of the boxes were sticking in my back. I struggled forward and one of them hit me in the face. This was before cardboard was flattened when it was thrown out.

"Mickey, look at this."

"What?"

Joey had crawled ahead of me and the boxes closed in behind him. All I could see was a bumpy wall of brown.

"Come here, over here, where I am, you brought us luck."

"Where?"

"Here!!"

I didn't know if the voice was coming from below or above me, so I started to pull myself straight through the cardboard. I pushed aside one box when a foot came shooting back and the heel kicked me in the face.

"Owww!"

"Sorry, I was coming back to get you."

I tried to pull my hand back through the cardboard to wipe the sting off my cheek but I couldn't move because my arm was wedged between a box and the fence.

"I'm stuck."

"You can't be stuck. Nobody gets stuck here and besides I gotta show you this."

I pulled myself forward and crawled up next to Joey who had his head inside a box.

"Look at mif. I's gret."

I couldn't understand him.

He struggled to get out but couldn't move back because when he pushed against the box that was by his knees, the box went into my stomach and I yelled.

He turned his head in the box so he could look out at me.

"There's wafers here. Look at how many."

He used one hand to pass back to me about a dozen broken chocolate wafers that go on the outsides of ice cream sandwiches.

"There's lots in here," he said as his head went back inside the box.

I could hear him crunching on them. I took a bite. They were so good. The chocolate filled my mouth and made me want more.

I heard later in life that chocolate is the only thing besides crack cocaine that is instantly addictive. I wanted more.

I shoved a second and third one into my mouth before I swallowed the first. I tried to get some of them down my throat so I could fit more into my mouth. This was better than anything I had ever done in my life, although I had not done very much.

"Wan' mor'?" Joey mumbled with his mouth full and his head in the box.

"Yeah, let me see how much there is," I said.

Then came a crashing from above us. It was not like someone jumping into the water because I didn't know what that sounded like, but it was like cardboard boxes getting crushed and crumpled and then I felt the boxes crushing and crumpling into my back.

"Joey," someone yelled. "You got wafers, I know you got wafers."

"Tommy," sputtered Joey while he tried to swallow. "I don't have any wafers," Joey shouted.

"Do so, I could hear you eating."

"You didn't hear me eating, and I wasn't eating."

His mouth was almost cleared out.

"He heard you," Joey said to me. "You gotta be quiet when you find wafers. You can hear things far away in the ocean. Here."

He shoved a pile of wafers at me and grabbed two handfuls for himself.

"Follow me."

He started pulling through the boxes, going level and then diving. He could not grab the boxes because his hands were full, so he used his arms and feet to move through the boxes. There were more crashes from above.

"Joey, we're coming for you."

"That's Jimmy Lee," said Joey, "and that means Johnny will be there too. Maybe Dorothy. And if she's here . . . "

More crashes. More boxes crunching around us.

" . . . the little kids are here, too," he finished.

I could not keep up with Joey. He was a fish, okay, maybe a slow-moving fish, but he was moving like a fish and I could barely crawl.

"Who are you?"

I turned my head. I was ten feet down under a pile of cardboard boxes and a pretty girl was talking to me. I don't think a girl had ever talked to me before.

"Mickey," I said. I was surprised. I had never called myself that before.

"You new around here?"

I couldn't answer. She had hair, and eyes.

"Well, are you new? And who beat you up?"

"No one," I said because I didn't want her to think anyone could beat me up.

"Well, you sure look like it," she said. "But let's get Joey, he has wafers."

She started swimming away. I said, "I have wafers, too."

She crawled backwards. There was commotion around us, above us, to one side of us and below. Boxes were crushing down and the whole world under the cardboard was moving. Then the boxes started moving underneath us.

"Those are the little kids," she said, sort of gesturing with her head down below. "They try to get under Joey and wait until he drops some."

"Joey said the little kids come with you." My gosh, I had said something, more than just I have wafers.

"But I do have wafers," I said and held out one hand filled with crushed brown pieces.

"No, those are yours. I want Joey's. He always gets a lot."

She began swimming away.

"Wanna come?"

"Yes," I said very loudly, louder than I planned on saying it. I don't know why I said it like that, but yes, I want to go with you more than I want chocolate.

She was off, almost sliding through the pile of brown boxes. She was wiggling and gliding. I tried to follow, but my elbows got in the way.

She stopped and I pulled myself up closer and saw she was wrestling under the boxes with Joey. I didn't even know her and I wanted to be the one wrestling with her.

"Okay," Joey muffed through his stuffed mouth. "Have them all." He held out a chocolate covered hand to her.

"There's only crumbs," said the girl. "You didn't even save me any."

"I shared them with the new kid."

They saw half my face staring at them from between two boxes.

"Did you punch him?" the girl asked Joey.

"No, he just put his face in my foot. I'll see you at the top."

They started climbing and I tried to follow, but no way could I keep up with them. They knew which boxes would hold them and they put their feet on them and climbed almost like on a ladder. I stepped on a box and it collapsed and the edge of it banged into my shin and then the other boxes caved in on top of me.

"Owww," I tried to keep it quiet, but the girl looked down. I could just barely see her face. She was more than a full body length ahead of me.

"Come on, Mickey. Let's go lay on the beach," she said when I finally got to the top.

Looking out from the roof of the ice cream factory, my eyes felt relaxed. I never had that feeling before. Always before there was something in front of me, not far away. At most, a building was across the street, but mostly things were just a few steps away. Your eyes got used to seeing close up. But up here you could see forever, almost. And it was so high. If I was at the end of the roof near the El I could throw a ball and bounce it off one of the trains.

And when the big passenger trains were not racing by, like right this second, you could see over the tracks almost to the end of the world. Those trains were on a hill the same height as the factory, but this hill was endlessly long. It was built so that when the trains came to a road they were already up high and could cross over the cars on a trestle. The train stopped for nothing.

And down below us on the street were the ice cream trucks. They clogged the road. No other traffic could get through but there was no other traffic, only the white trucks with boxes on the back and pretend chimneys on top of the boxes. They were getting loaded up with small boxes of ice cream pops and sandwiches and blocks of dry ice that were steaming in the air.

This newer Bungalow Bar truck is a Chevrolet from 1960, when the swimming was long behind us. I have to say that because some old guys will say, "Hey, that's a 1960 Chevy and he said they were '53s." Never get your truck years mixed up.

And there were the bells. They hung out over the top of the windshields and the drivers would test them and it sounded like Christmas was supposed to sound until a train went by. Then we could see the bells moving, but they were not making any noise.

The poor drivers I later learned, made their living from the bells. But they had to ring them while they were driving which meant one hand was pulling a cord attached to the bells while their other hand was shifting gears while their other hand was steering.

The trucks were 1953 Chevy pickups, with a big cooler in the back and on top of the cooler was a peaked shingled roof with a make-believe chimney.

It looked like a bungalow, and so the company was called Bungalow Bar.

"What's a bungalow?" I asked.

"Don't know," said the girl. "I think it's where people in the country live."

"Is your name Dorothy?" I asked.

She looked like that was a dumb question.

"Go stand over there and I'll tell you."

I stood where she said. Then she came flying at me and hit me with two hands on my chest and knocked me backwards and all I thought was "I'm two stories up and I'm going to fall on the sidewalk and get killed, and I was not sure she was Dorothy . . ."

Then I hit the boxes.

"Owww."

My head, my back, I thought I was being beaten. I fell backwards onto the boxes and the boxes had sharp points.

"Yes, it's Dorothy," she shouted down to me.

That is a good way to remember.

I tried to stand in the cardboard, but each time I got up I fell down. The boxes moved like boxes thrown on top of other boxes. Everyone was laughing. Okay, I made it funny for them. I hurt but I would not tell them.

"Mickey, come back out of the ocean. This is our beach, and we all push each other in the water."

Dorothy was talking to me and there were almost a dozen kids up there, three of them small, like eight years old. They were playing by themselves, but the rest were bigger kids like us.

I looked at Dorothy. It seemed like I looked at her for an hour or two.

"How old are you?" I asked.

"Almost eleven," she said, and my world collapsed. I was almost ten.

"How old is Joey?" I asked.

She looked at Joey who was with Jimmy Lee and Tommy stretched out on the black tar roof using the metal edge of the roof as a pillow.

"He's almost twelve," she said.

The rest of my world and my eternity and everything I had ever hoped to achieve blew apart like an atom bomb hitting it, and we knew all about atom bombs.

We were the kids of the real atomic age, when death was only a flash away, but losing a girl because of a year was something that could really upset your day.

Staying Alive

We had practised duck and cover in class almost every day.

"Children, if you see a bright flash through the windows, what do you do?"

"Duck and cover," we all said.

"Right. Cover the backs of your necks," said Miss Johnson. "The Russians will try to kill us but we will beat them."

Miss Johnson said we lived in a great country where we could have meat three times a day.

"In Russia they only have it once a year."

We did not want to be Russians.

But I might as well be because Dorothy was almost eleven. And I was almost ten.

"Let's go down on the street," said Joey one day while we were standing on the factory roof. There are days when the surf is calm and you don't feel like swimming. "Maybe we can play some stickball."

So everyone followed and slid over the edge of the roof and grabbed hold of the fence and climbed down. They all did it like they knew every hand-hold. I followed them but I gripped tight. It was high when you are up there looking down.

"Who are those kids?" I asked Dorothy who was climbing just below me.

She looked down the street.

"There's going to be trouble," she said.

There were about seven boys coming toward us, weaving their way through the parked ice cream trucks.

Joey jumped from the fence before he got to the bottom. He did not wait for anyone to catch up. He started walking straight at the newcomers. The other ones on the fence dropped to the ground and ran to him.

There were only a handful of big boys on our side and three little ones. I didn't count Dorothy and me. I did not know what was going to happen, but I could guess. And my guess was not good.

"That's Rocky," said Dorothy. She said nothing else.

Joey, Jimmy Lee and Tommy stopped in front of the other gang. The little kids on our side ran up behind him.

"Hit him, Joey," one of them shouted.

Jimmy Lee turned around. "Shut up."

Dorothy was off the fence now and running to join Joey. I walked up to them. I was too new to be running like I knew what was going on, but I knew I should be there.

"We want your swimming pool and we're going to take it," said the guy in the front of the new gang.

"Over my dead body," said Joey.

"That can be arranged," said Rocky.

"You try it and I'll smack you," said Joey.

Then Joey stepped toward Rocky. He was not afraid. I watched. My heart was racing.

One of the little kids ran up to one of the other gang and kicked him in the shin then ran away. The kid who got kicked yelled, grabbed his shin and then grabbed another little kid from our side and hit him.

Joey moved in and grabbed hold of the intruding kid and picked him off the ground. I had never seen anyone so strong. No wonder Dorothy hung around him.

The leader of the other gang hit Joey and all hell broke loose. Everyone was pounding on everyone, even Dorothy, who was hitting as fast as she could swing her fists. I wasn't going to stand in the background, even though I had never been in a fight before. But a fist came out of nowhere and hit me in the nose.

"Owww!" That was all I was saying. It stung like stink.

It was Tommy.

"I'm on your side," I said.

"Sorry."

Tommy turned around and hit someone from the other side.

One of the little kids was hitting and punching and kicking even though he was not doing any damage.

"Stop fighting."

The voice was loud. I looked up with my tear-filled eyes and saw a huge man with a thick, white winter parka and hair all over his face standing over us.

"Stop," he said again.

His eyebrows went down to his moustache and his moustache went down to his chin.

"Stop, or I'll kill you all."

He raised a curved ice pick like an axe.

Most stopped fighting.

"Stop!"

Everyone stopped.

"Go on, get out of here. If you kids can't play nice I don't want you here," he said. He talked funny, the words not sounding like normal people's words.

"It's our street," said the leader of the other guys.

"No, it's ours," said Joey.

The giant snowman waved his ice hook between them.

"It's neither of your street. Now get out of here."

"No," said the other kids.

The snowman turned his ice pick until the point was pointing at the kid's face.

"Go."

The kid looked at the point, then turned and started walking away.

"We'll be back."

The snowman turned to us.

"I know you kids play here, but there can't be fighting, so go away now."

We turned around and started leaving.

"You good kids, I know. But no fighting," he shouted at us.

We walked around the corner with the little kids laughing and pushing each other.

"I got them good," said one of them. "I just about knocked out one of them."

Joey and Dorothy and Jimmy Lee and Tommy were walking ahead. I was way behind. Queens, I thought, was a lot tougher than Brooklyn.

"Where's your brother?" Dorothy asked Joey.

"Home. Sick today."

Then she came back and walked with me and told me that Joey's little brother had cerebral palsy and Joey usually carried him everywhere. That's why he was so strong. Then she told me Jimmy Lee's little brother also had cerebral palsy, but he never came outside. That's a lot of cerebral palsy, I thought, whatever that was.

Later that night when my mother got home from work, she looked at my face.

"Were you in a fight?"

"No," I said. "I just banged into some boxes."

She did not ask me to explain.

"Do you like your new neighbourhood?" she asked.

"It's okay."

"What'd you do today?"

"Nothing much. Just hung around."

Later I lay in bed listening to the elevated train, and then the commuter train. I could see the lights of its cars outside my window, and then I listened to the elevated train and then watched the commuter train and then it was morning and I opened my eyes and could see a train racing by outside my window.

This was a very exciting place.

Gone Fishing

"Buster got a fish."

I had been on 132nd Street for a week and learned that no one had a pet.

"You're not having a dog," said Tommy's mother. "If we can't afford meat for us, how are we going to feed a dog?"

Can't argue with that.

But Buster got a fish.

We ran in a pack to Buster's door.

"Can we see your fish?" we shouted through the wood while we beat on it.

"What do you think it looks like?" Tommy asked.

"Don't know," said Vinnie. "We had fish last night. The pope said we got to eat fish on Fridays, like Jesus. But it always looks like a piece of white with onions on it."

"I don't like fish," said Tommy. "It stinks."

Buster opened the door.

"Shhhhh," he said. Then he pointed to a soup bowl on the kitchen table. "There it is, but be quiet."

We sneaked up on it.

"Is it alive?" asked Vanessa. "It's not moving."

"Of course it's alive. Do you think my mother would bring home a dead fish? It's just sleeping."

"It's not sleeping," said Tommy. "Its eyes are open."

"I know, but it sleeps with its eyes open," said Buster.

We looked down in the soup bowl at one goldfish going glob, glob, glob. Or at least that's what we thought it was doing. It wasn't swimming. We expected to see a fish swimming, but really, it had nowhere to swim to. It just stayed in the middle of the bowl going glob, glob, glob.

"How'd you get it?" someone asked.

"My mother won it at bingo," said Buster.

"What do you do with a goldfish?" asked Tommy.

"Don't know," said Buster. "I guess you just look at it."

So we leaned further over the bowl and looked.

"You think it's hungry?" asked Dorothy.

"What do you feed a fish?" asked Tommy.

"Probably lettuce," said Vanessa. "That looks like seaweed."

So Buster opened the refrigerator and found a couple of lettuce leaves. He tore off a few pieces and we broke them into tiny bits and dropped them onto the water.

The fish still went glob, glob, glob.

"Maybe it needs some fresh air," said Vanessa.

Vanessa was prettier than Dorothy, and she had bumps on her chest.

Buster picked up the bowl and carefully slid one foot in front of the other, not lifting them off the floor as he carried the bowl to the front door. We opened it for him and he went outside.

"Careful you don't trip," we said.

"My mother would kill me," said Buster.

He got to the sidewalk, holding the bowl and we all looked down. The fish was still going glob, glob. It waved its little fins faster but it did not move.

"I hope it doesn't die," said Buster. "My mother would blame me for killing it. I think she thinks I killed my little brother, but I didn't. He just died in his crib and I found him that way."

"Don't worry, Buster," said Dorothy. "We know you didn't kill your brother. And the fish will be okay. Let me see."

She leaned over and stared. "I think I saw it eat something," she said.

"What you got there?"

The voice of Rocky again.

"What are you doing on this block? This is our block," Tommy said.

We had been concentrating so much on the fish we did not see Rocky and his gang coming down the block.

"We want to finish that fight."

Rocky stepped up to Tommy. Rocky was bigger than Tommy.

"This is our block," said Dorothy.

It was one of those rules – you did not go on a block that was not yours. You could pass by another gang's block on the way to school, but you did not walk on the block.

This continued into teenage years. A week after I graduated from high school, which I did in February because I was slow, I was out clearing my lungs in the cold air. I had been painting the old apartment next to the railroad tracks that my mother and I still lived in. We used oil-based paint then and my throat was raw.

I had gone out onto the grey snowy street to have a cigarette and walked several blocks from home. I hardly realized I walked into another neighbourhood. I passed under the railroad tracks that went over the street – there was a new gang there, which was the remains of Rocky's gang.

It had now been taken over by Sanchez. The ethnics had changed, but not the gang. I turned to go the other way but faced more gang members coming at me from that direction. I ran across the street but they caught and surrounded me.

"We owe you," said Sanchez.

"For what?" I was getting pretty old for this.

"One of our guys got beat up by your guys."

"I don't even see my guys anymore," I said. "I go to work every day."

I had been working in the taxi cab garage, pumping gas into a fleet of cabs, and had hardly seen anyone on my street for more than a year. I had just gotten a new job at the *Daily News*, in the mail room and was supposed to start work in two days.

"Don't care," said Sanchez. "We owe you."

Some of them grabbed my arms and Sanchez started hammering me in the face with his fist. He was bigger than me, but that did not stop him. I would have punched back but my arms were being held by two other guys who did not let go of them.

In short, I got smashed.

"There," they said, and left.

I looked down at the snow and it was red. Then I felt a hole in my teeth with my tongue. I went home and went back to painting. When my mother woke up from a nap she called the police.

"We cannot have this kind of thing go on in our neighbourhood," the police said.

Eventually they arrested Sanchez and he pleaded guilty to assault and went to jail for a few months.

I had to go to the dentist and he put a temporary cap on one tooth. This was in the days when the patient in a dentist office sat up straight and the dentist bent over. The drill was run on pulleys and I watched the thick strings go around and around while I smelled the smoke of my next good tooth getting ground down.

Two days later, I went to work in my new job in the mail

room of the *Daily News*. I joined a bunch of rejects because to get assigned to the mail room you did not need much education. I brought my lunch in a brown paper bag. I had made a salami sandwich on Levy's Real Jewish Rye, which was standard eating for most people, both rejects and executives.

We went to the locker room to eat. I took a bite of my sandwich but Levy's Real Jewish Rye is very meaty bread. My new temporary cap and adjoining new temporary false tooth got stuck in the bread and separated from my gums.

I had a mouth full of rye bread and salami with teeth embedded in it inside my mouth. I could not swallow it because my teeth were in it. I could not open my mouth to ask where the bathroom was because now I had a hole in the front of my mouth plus a wad of half-chewed bread and salami with teeth stuck in it inside my mouth. That would have made a bad impression.

So I sat there, in the locker room, in silence, not eating, holding my sandwich, listening to the others, with a glob of teeth and bread and salami in my mouth until lunch was over. When they finally got up and went back to work, I spit the sandwich out into my hands and pulled out the teeth and stuck the teeth back into my mouth and went back to work.

I had to keep my mouth shut the rest of the day because I was afraid my teeth would fall out. So I said nothing, even when they asked me if I knew which mail went where. I nodded, then guessed.

I think they thought I was strange.

So when Rocky showed up on our block when we had the fish, I had a feeling that was just the beginning of the troubles.

Pow. That was Tommy hitting one of Rocky's gang. Tommy did not wait for something to start. He started it. Then Vinnie punched someone.

It was time I was part of this gang. I hit the guy closest to me. It was Rocky. I hit him hard. He looked surprised. I was new. He hit back and I hit again and grabbed him around the neck and tried to pull him down but he would not go down.

Darn.

This was not a good position to be in. I was holding him around the neck and that takes two arms which leaves his two arms and fists free and he started to pound on me.

"My fish!" shouted Buster. "My fish is gone. My mother's going to kill me!"

Buster was standing over the sewer with the bowl in hand. It was empty. He had been pushed and the bowl tipped and for reasons only known to God, he was standing over the steel grating that covered the hole that went ten feet down into the blackness of sewer water.

Buster was crying. The fighting stopped.

"What are you talking about?" said Rocky.

"My fish," shouted Buster. "My mother's fish. You made me lose it."

Buster dropped the bowl and ploughed head and fist first into Rocky's gut. Buster was half his size but his world was over and dying was nothing compared to facing his mother.

He hit Rocky so hard he knocked him over. He punched and pounded and Rocky was on the ground and Buster was on top and it was a strange scene. The little kid was kicking the stuffing out of the gang leader.

Some of Rocky's friends grabbed Buster and dragged him off their leader and that was it for the fight. This was too much to understand. They lost, again. They backed off a few steps.

"We'll be back and show you who's boss," said Rocky. And then they left.

"My fish is gone," said Buster. He was looking down into the blackness of the sewer which was steel grating flush with the asphalt. There were five long slots open and his fish had gone down one of them. Buster fell to his knees.

"My mother will kill me."

Dorothy put her arm around his shoulder. I fell in love at that moment. Dorothy was kind and loving and understanding and she had her arm around someone else, and I was jealous for the second time in my life and over the same girl all in one week.

"My uncle knows about fishing," Dorothy said to Buster. "We'll get your fish back."

She left and ran down the street and I saw Buster trying not to cry, but he was not doing a good job of it.

"Don't worry," said Jimmy Lee. "Dorothy is good at fixing things and we'll get your fish back."

We sat around the sewer without saying anything. This was much more exciting than leaning against a dresser while my father was beating on the door on the other side.

When Dorothy came back, she brought a ball of string and some safety pins.

"This is all we need," she said. "You tie the pin to the string and lower it in the water and the fish will bite on it. My uncle said it always works."

We dropped the pins slowly down through the sewer grating and could feel when they hit the water. That was when the string went limp.

"Just pull it up and down," said Dorothy. "This is fishing."

We pulled and dropped and pulled and dropped.

"I got it. I got the fish," said Jimmy Lee. "I have it."

He pulled, with the string piling up on the asphalt. "It's big," said Jimmy Lee.

"I see it," said Tommy. "It's right below the metal."

He squeezed his hand through the opening.

"I can reach it. I can get it."

"See, Buster, it'll be okay," Dorothy said.

"Yuck," said Tommy. He pulled his hand back up through the grating and threw a blob of squishy plastic that looked like a balloon onto the street.

"What's that?" I asked.

We all looked at this long, ugly fat piece of clear plastic. We all came to the same conclusion at the same time.

"Ugh," said Dorothy.

"It's so big," said Jimmy Lee.

We all thought the same thing. It was huge and we knew we were not. We did not know how anyone would ever have something large enough to fill that.

"Put it back," said Dorothy. "I don't want to look at it."

"But if we put it back we'll have to fish it out again before we get the fish," I said.

Dorothy rolled her eyes and looked at the sky, which you could see between the buildings and the elevated tracks.

"I'm going home. I'm not going to touch those things," she said. "Good luck, Buster."

I watched her walk away and I did not stop looking. She was going and I was still there and I did not want to be there. I wanted to be going with her even if she was a year older than me.

Buster and Jimmy Lee and I sat around the sewer until dark and Buster cried a lot. He figured his mother would yell at him for half the night and then kill him in his sleep.

"She's coming," he said.

He saw his mother walking down the stairs after a train pulled out of the station.

"If only I had left the fish in the kitchen like she said."

His mother walked over to us.

"What are you doing?" she asked. She seemed nice.

"Trying to get the fish back," said Buster. He did not look up. "It fell down the sewer."

"What fish?" she said. "Oh, that silly goldfish. Good, I was thinking of flushing it down the toilet anyway," she said.

Buster looked up with the question mark of a tilted head.

"We can't keep a fish in the house," his mother said. "I would've had to get another bowl to put it in because we need the soup bowl and then it would die and we'd have a bowl we don't need. You didn't lose the bowl, did you?"

Buster shook his head.

"Come on in and have supper," she said.

Buster jumped up like it was the happiest day of his life. He carefully lifted the bowl from the sidewalk and ran after his mother.

"How come the bowl didn't break when it fell?" I asked Jimmy Lee.

He shrugged. "Maybe the ghost of his dead brother saved it," he said.

I thought that was a good possibility.

"Dead brothers and sisters always hang around to help. My grandfather told me that," he said.

Jimmy Lee and I went fishing over that sewer almost every night through the summer and into the fall until it got too cold to sit on the ground. We talked about everything that happened during the day, and he told me that his little brother screamed a lot because he was in pain. He wished his brother would die, but he never said that to his mother because she always wished he would get better. He had cerebral palsy. But his was very bad. He never got out of his crib, even though he was ten.

The next spring we took up fishing again. Sometimes when we were sitting on the street over the sewer someone would try to park their car there.

"Hey kids, get off the street, I want to park my car there."

We would both look up at the driver. We both just stared and shook our heads. This was our fishing hole. Nobody was going to park a car over it. The driver would honk, sometimes leaning on the horn, but we kept on shaking our heads.

A couple of times they would drive up slowly and push against us with their bumpers but we still wouldn't move.

"Are you kids crazy? I'm going to run you over."

But we still did not move, and the driver took off, leaning on his horn. We weren't really scared because this was our spot and we didn't think they would kill us just to have a place to park.

When Jimmy Lee was sixteen he met a girl, a real girl, not one from the neighbourhood. He got accepted into her neighbourhood because he told them he was a fisherman and a semi-professional ball player and a champion swimmer. They had never known such a person before. He sounded like he was very tough and knew things that no one else knew about.

He got married when he was seventeen, with the consent of his parents. We all were in the wedding: Tommy, Vinnie, Joey, Buster, Johnny, Dorothy and Vanessa. I don't know what the girls did, because the bride had her own wedding friends. But the boys had to get a shave from Augie the barber.

Augie's assistant barber, Alfonse, was not able to come to work for a few weeks because he was being charged with statutory rape of the daughter of the lunch counter people next to the barber shop. We all knew Alfonse was going out with their daughter, but we didn't think he was raping her, we just thought he was making love to her. But we were told that since she was not yet sixteen and he was old, like in his twenties, that it was not making love but rape. We thought rape was bad and love was good, but we really didn't know much of anything.

Anyway, since Alfonse was not working, Augie had to shave all of us himself. None of us had ever had a shave before in the barber shop, just haircuts. I waited my turn and got soaped up and then Augie dragged the straight razor over my face. It scratched, but it did not feel bad.

It was just one year before that when I told Augie I wanted sideburns like Elvis, but he said I would have to wait until I started shaving. Now I was shaving and he was shaving off my sideburns.

"You can't have sideburns at a wedding," he said. "If you looked like Elvis they would throw you out."

That night I did not sleep. I spent eight hours rubbing my face on the pillow trying to take away the burning. I did not like shaving.

Five years later while I was in the Air Force, I got a letter that Jimmy Lee had died of a heart attack while he was jogging. He had two kids. When the hearse took his body through the old neighbourhood it rolled over home plate where he had scored the winning run, and past the cardboard ocean where he ate chocolate wafers and it drove by the fishing hole where we had become friends.

His widow and children riding in the car saw only the old neighbourhood where he grew up, nothing else. They did not see the stickball games or the fist fights or the telephone Jimmy Lee and I had between our windows. They might have loved him more if they knew real stories.

Cell Phones Without Batteries

*I*n his back room, Jimmy Lee passed the crib where his brother with cerebral palsy was screaming. Alex always screamed. I could hear him next door in the summer when the windows were open.

That was the summer when Jimmy and I put a long string between two tin cans and ran it from our back windows across the alley. Then we tied knots in the string and hooked the string over nails that we hammered in the outside of our windows.

"Hey, Mickey," Jimmy shouted at me through my back window. He threw pebbles at the glass until I woke up.

"Hey, you want to talk on our phones?"

I got out of bed. My mother had gone to work. I was alone in the apartment. Jimmy was the first face I saw in the morning.

"Yeah, wait 'til I pee."

"I'll go back home and talk to you," he said.

I went to the bathroom which was dark and next to the refrigerator. The bathroom was really a disaster. I knew that even then, because the window on the air shaft that was supposed to let in light and air had been painted over many times before we moved in.

There were air shafts all over the city. They were supposed to bring the heavens into the ground floor apartments, but they only brought in the garbage that was dropped from the top floor apartments and the mice from down below that lived off the garbage.

We lived on the bottom floor so the garbage was piling high. Since there was no way of stopping the downflow of banana peels and newspapers, the only solution was to paint and seal the windows that were meant to let in air and light.

But the really bad part was the ceiling, which was cracked from one end to the other. I said I could fix it, I told my mother. But I did not know much about fixing ceilings.

When your mother sneaks away from your father when you are eight and raises you alone, you do not learn much about fixing ceilings. The only tool in the apartment was a screwdriver for chipping the ice from the freezer when it had to be defrosted twice a year because there was not enough room left in it to squeeze in some frozen peas.

I got some pieces of plasterboard and nailed them over the cracks. I did not do a good job. So I got some plasterboard powder and mixed it with water and tried to fix it.

"What are you doing today?" my mother asked once before she went off to work.

"Trying to fix the ceiling."

"Don't try," she said. "Maybe the landlord will do it."

No. The landlord would not do it. The landlord was upstairs smoking and typing, sending out overdue notices for rent. I knew he was smoking because I found his typewriter in a pile of junk in the basement many years later. It was an Underwood, the same model that had been used in the Lindbergh baby kidnapping case. That's what everyone told me when I showed it to them, because that typewriter had become the most famous machine in the most famous kidnapping case in history.

But the landlord's typewriter was not part of the crime. I knew that, because the key that had J on it was yellow from the nicotine that had been on the landlord's right index finger from too much smoking and the yellow had oozed and soaked through the plastic of the key and stained it forever.

I said that was cool. He was a real smoker, not someone who used filters. I would be like him, I said, a real smoker.

When I finished peeing, I leaned out the back window.

"Jimmy Lee," I shouted across the alley. "We can talk now."

He stuck out his head. His brother was screaming behind him.

"Talk in your can," Jimmy Lee said.

I picked up my can from the nail and he did the same on his side. Then we both leaned out and pulled the string tight.

"Can you hear me?" he shouted into the can.

I tried to lean forward because his brother was making so much noise that I couldn't hear anything except the screaming. The string went slack.

"I can't hear anything," I shouted into the can.

Jimmy leaned further to get away from his brother.

"What did you say?" he shouted into the can, with the string hanging down toward the ground.

"I said 'what did you say?'"

"I can't hear you," he said.

He held up his can and looked at me.

"We have to hold the string tight," he said.

Then he pulled it, but I was not ready and he pulled it out of my hands and my can went flying down to the ground where it banged and rolled.

"I'll get it," Jimmy Lee said.

He pulled up his string, like a fishing line. He swung one can back and forth then tried to throw it to me. But I missed.

"What do you want to talk about when you catch it?" he shouted.

He pulled it back in again and threw it, but a bed sheet fell on his head. Mrs. Belimeyer hung out her back window above Jimmy Lee putting out her laundry, but we know she dropped that on purpose just to hit him.

"You rotten kids," she shouted. "You're getting my sheets dirty. I'm telling your mothers."

She would have raised her fist to us as she always did, but her hands were full with her next sheet.

"Forgetaboutit," I shouted to Jimmy Lee. "I just wanted to tell you Miss Johnson still doesn't believe we are swimming in the Mediterranean."

"What'd you say?" said Jimmy Lee.

He pushed the sheet aside and swung the can again. I caught it, pulled the string tight and shouted into it:

"Miss Johnson doesn't believe we swim in the Mediterranean."

Mrs. Belimeyer looked down at us.

"You kids are good for nothing," she said. "And you should drown if you ever went swimming, and you don't know how to swim anyhow."

Then she put another sheet on the line. This one also hit Jimmy Lee on the head.

"Ahh, forget about the cans. You going to play stickball later?" he shouted.

"Yeah," I shouted back.

"And when you drown you are going to hell," said Mrs. Belimeyer, not bothering to look at us this time.

"And after that we'll go for a swim," said Jimmy Lee.

Rooftop Rated XXX

I walked down the street and met Buster and Joey and Vinnie and Tommy. That was unusual for them to be standing around doing nothing in the middle of the block. Usually they were standing around doing nothing at the end of the block.

"Want to come with us tonight? We're going to watch Vanessa undress," said Joey.

My heart sputtered. Actually, I don't know what my heart did. Some other mysterious part of me sputtered.

"What? How?" I said.

"When she gets ready for bed she undresses by her window," said Buster. "I've seen her."

"When?" I asked.

"About ten, or maybe later."

Ten was bad, but later was pushing it. I could easily stay out in the winter until nine. Nine thirty was beginning to be a problem. Later was a big problem, but to see Vanessa naked, oh my gosh, for that, I could stand a screaming at.

We broke up and went home early because it was already getting dark and it was suppertime for most. If any of us were late for supper, then we would be in deep trouble, and if we got into trouble we would not be allowed out. And if you are not allowed out and miss seeing Vanessa naked, you might as well kill yourself.

"We meet at Buster's house at nine fifteen, all of us," said Joey.

That was enough. I went home and waited for my mother and had hot dogs and potato salad and tomato for supper. We ate at the kitchen table and said nothing and I washed the dishes and tried to be nice.

We all tried to be nice. Can you imagine getting into an argument at home and being kept in the house, being locked in and told no way are you leaving and you are going to put out the garbage and then do your homework even if you don't have any homework, and then clean your room, and then you have to go to bed, while your friends are watching Vanessa undress and you are staring at the ceiling?

So we went home on time and tried to be as polite as could be. "Yes, ma'am, I would like some spinach." "No thank you, I don't care for any more bread."

"What's the matter?" asked Tommy's father. "I think you did something wrong."

"No, sir, not me," said Tommy. "I didn't do nothing wrong, not me, no sir," he said while thinking of Vanessa naked and worried that if he looked guilty his father would find some reason to keep him in. He better act normal.

"On second thought I don't want any spinach."

His father looked relieved.

At nine o'clock, half a dozen boys told their parents that they were going out to play basketball.

"The schoolyard's locked," said Tommy's mother.

"We're going to play at the end of the street," said Tommy.

"There's no place to play basketball at the end of the street," said Tommy's father.

"We're going to make a basketball hoop," said Tommy.

"It's dark," said Tommy's mother.

"We'll play under the street light," said Tommy.

"Be back by ten so you can do your homework."

"Don't have any homework."

"You better have some or I'll give you something else."

It was the same in every apartment. We would take the consequences. We wanted out.

At nine fifteen, a half-dozen boys were squeezing their way between the cold cinder-block garages behind Vanessa's apartment.

"How do you know she gets undressed?" I asked Buster.

"Sssshhh. If they hear us they'll call the cops."

"But how do you know?" I whispered.

"I've seen her. They're not very big, but she has them. And I saw her touch them."

"What'd they look like?" asked Joey, who did not believe Buster had really seen what he said he saw.

"This big," said Buster.

He held his hands together like he was holding something much bigger than an apple but smaller than a basketball.

"They were nice," he said.

"But how'd you see them?" I asked again, and I was getting anxious to hear the answer because I wanted an answer before I got in trouble for trying to see them. I wanted to know that he had really seen them.

"I was climbing on the roof because I thought maybe I could see her. I saw from the street that her lights were on and her shade was not pulled down and I wanted to see if I could see, so I climbed up there and I saw them. I really did and they were this big."

He held his cupped hands together again, but this time what he was not holding was bigger.

We all believed. At nine twenty, in the dark and with the cold autumn air working through our jackets, half a dozen boys climbed onto a garage roof and then made a flying leap across three arm lengths of space to the roof of the factory.

"Wow, that was close," said Vinnie.

The rest of us had jumped the entire way and landed on our feet. Vinnie was hanging off the edge of the factory roof, holding onto the metal edge. He pulled himself up. Vinnie was strong, but he was not a jumper.

"It's good you didn't fall," said Tommy.

"Shhh," said Buster.

Tommy whispered. "It's good you didn't fall or you would have made a lot of noise."

"I might have been killed too," said Vinnie.

"Yeah, but you would have made noise and then none of us could see her," said Tommy.

We crawled along the roof, bending low like cats on the cold tar and gravel. We knew no one was inside the big factory except the night watchman and he could only take our names if he caught us, and the chances were very slim that he could catch even one of us.

We were giddy as we got across from Vanessa's back windows.

At nine twenty-five, half a dozen boys lay side by side on the roof with heads propped up on hands, staring at the back of a dark apartment window.

"I bet she's beautiful with no clothes on," said Tommy.

"I once saw a naked girl, but she was my cousin," said Vinnie.

"That doesn't count," I said.

We lay there for ten minutes saying nothing before Tommy said, "I'm so cold I can't feel my thing anymore."

"You will when she shows up," said Vinnie.

"Suppose we get caught," said Johnny. "They could arrest us as Peeping Toms."

"We'll just say we lost a ball on the roof," said Tommy.

"So why are we trying to find it at night?" asked Johnny.

"Because I got it for my birthday," said Tommy, "and if we don't find it, I'll be in trouble."

Ten more minutes and we were clenching our teeth to keep them from chattering.

"If she doesn't come soon I'm going to have to go home," said Vinnie.

We all had that same problem, but Tommy said he didn't care. He would get in trouble to see Vanessa.

It was ten after ten. We knew the time because we could see the Sealtest Milk Company clock if we looked the other way across the tracks. We could also read "Any Time Is The Right Time For Milk." None of us ever got a watch, not even a cheap one for Christmas or our birthdays because of that clock. And none of us wanted to look at the clock because it would mean that we had to go and more importantly, we might be looking the wrong way when Vanessa came into her room.

Then suddenly, out of the blackness, the light came on in the window and we went rigid. Buster was right. We could see right into her bedroom. It was going to happen. Vanessa walked in and started combing her hair. We gasped. She began braiding her hair. We crawled closer to the edge of the roof.

"Can you see that?"

"Look at that!"

"Holy cow!"

We were all whispers while Vanessa combed in silence.

Then in answer to all our hopes and wishes and dreams and secret prayers, she started to unbutton her shirt.

"Oh, God." It was a gasp. It was going to happen.

She took off her shirt and we saw a white bra for almost a full second before her sister walked into the room and went to the window and pulled down the shade.

"She knows we're here," said Tommy in less of a whisper and more of a panic.

"No way, she can't," said Vinnie.

But we knew we had been spotted. Why else would she have pulled the shade so fast and so firmly? We fell over each other trying to get off the roof before we were caught. We jumped to the garage roof and then down to the ground. Even Vinnie jumped and Vinnie can't jump.

There must be a god who cleaned away the broken bottles and cinder blocks and garbage cans from our landing pad because we didn't look before we leaped. We hit the ground and just kept running.

"Did you see her?" shouted Vinnie as he ran. "I mean, did you see her bra?"

"She was almost naked," Johnny said, while the night air blew past his face and his feet pounded.

When we stopped running we fell over each other laughing and talking and describing how much nakedness we had seen.

"I swear she almost had her bra off. I swear I saw it," said Jimmy Lee.

"I saw her naked. I mean I saw it, just before the shade went down. Didn't you see her?" That was Joey who sat on the curb with a smile and faraway look.

We all went home that night with an excitement in our bodies that we had not known before. It was a blissful feeling.

"How'd the basketball game go?" Tommy's father asked.

"Fine, really fine," Tommy said.

"Maybe tomorrow night I'll come down and see what you've accomplished," said his father.

Tommy had the curse of having a father who kept trying to see what Tommy was doing instead of spending his time in the bar like normal fathers. Tommy always said the other kids were lucky.

The Greatest Game Ever Played

The next morning on the way to school Tommy and Vinnie and Johnny and Joey and Buster and I gathered at the end of the block and tried to figure some way of turning the street into a basketball court. We had a ball, which we had stolen from the school – we were mad because we had to learn basketball, which we didn't understand.

"You do not get your hands dirty, do you understand?"

No, we didn't understand.

That was the gym teacher, who was also the history teacher in P.S. 54, which is still on 127th Street, just off Jamaica Avenue where the trains still rumble by.

"This is called basketball. It's what's played all over America, and this is America so we will play it. And you don't get your hands dirty. If I see dirty hands you're out."

We looked at our hands. They were dirty. We had not begun and we were already finished.

"You use your fingertips, that's all, and you bounce it, like this."

He bounced the big ball using his fingertips and we watched and we got bored and started fighting.

"Hey, you kids. Stop that or you're going to the principal's office."

We stopped. He bounced.

"This is purely American. It's as American as apple pie. Do you kids know what apple pie is?"

To be honest, none of us had ever had a piece of apple pie. I know that's hard to believe, but most of our mothers said if they were ever asked, "Do you know how long it would take me to make the crust? I haven't got all day. I'm a busy woman."

"I didn't think so," said the gym teacher when he saw a row of blank stares. "Well, this is American and you will learn it."

He did not tell us that it was invented by a Canadian, who was trying to figure out a way to keep kids playing something when it was too cold to play outside. The Canadian gym teacher was working in Springfield, Massachusetts, where you can't do much of anything outdoors in winter.

"Do any of you dummies know what soccer is?" our gym teacher asked.

We all stared blankly.

"Soccer is a game they play in Europe. Do any of you know where Europe is?"

We all raised our hands and shouted, "That's where we bombed and killed the Nazis!"

"But where is it?" he asked.

We all stared. We knew where.

"Over there," we said because that was what we had been told, over and over.

"Well, it's far away and none of you are ever going to get there.

But they play something called soccer there and they kick a ball like this."

He held up the basketball.

"They kick it with their feet and they can't use their hands."

We stared blindly. We were trying to learn about basketball and now he was telling us about something called soccer, which sounded impossible. We were trying to imagine how you don't use your hands. All sports use hands, even though we only knew one sport, baseball, and your legs were for running, and maybe kicking in a fight, but not for kicking a ball.

"Well, some guy in America invented this to replace soccer in the winter. Don't worry if you don't understand. You don't under-stand anything anyway."

He still never mentioned the Canadian.

Then he started bouncing the ball and we stared. "You use your fingertips to control it."

We steal it to control it, we thought.

There was a new metal hoop with a backboard put up outside the door of the school in the concrete playground. He took us outside and said we would throw the ball at the hoop and if we scored that was a basket.

"I thought it was supposed to be played indoors," said Tommy.

"Don't be a wise guy," said the gym teacher. "That was when they invented it, but we're playing it now. Besides, we don't have a gym in the school."

Education was so confusing.

"When you get the ball through the hoop, you get a basket."

We had heard that before, but we did not know what it meant. None of us had ever seen a basketball game. It was not on tele-vision and even if it was, only Vinnie said he had a television but we never saw it.

There was Warren and Brian who lived down the street

from us when we lived with my father in Brooklyn. They had a television.

Every night, the other neighbours and my mother and I would carry folding metal bridge chairs down the street to Warren and Brian's house. And we would sit in a room that had linoleum on the floor and watch the television. Mostly it had wrestling. But the kids tried to get there early to watch Howdy Doody. That was the greatest show ever on television, with Buffalo Bob. I wanted Buffalo Bob to be my father and Howdy to be my friend.

But we didn't see basketball.

"Now let's see some of you hoodlums try to get a basket," said the gym teacher.

We had no idea what he was talking about.

"Why is it a basket if it's a hoop?" someone asked.

This is the street where we grew up—132nd Street and Jamaica Avenue in Queens, New York. It was our corner of heaven where we hung out and where we fed Stumpy the pigeon (his story is on page 106). I see only magic here.

"Because it's basketball," he said. "You really are stupid."

That was the day we stole the ball. After we went back inside to go to spelling lessons, we watched where the teacher put the ball. It was never seen again. The next day the teacher taught us to do push-ups, like they do in the Army.

"You little jerks will pay for that."

On 132nd Street, we gathered with our basketball.

"We need a backboard. How do we get a backboard?"

Johnny said he could do that. Johnny could do anything with nails and wood. He built forts in the alley. They were made from wood he found around the factories and with nails he found on the street.

He told us to look for wood for the backboard and soon we came back with a couple of pallets that had fallen off delivery trucks.

"We need nails," Johnny said.

We searched around the factories and came back with handfuls of bent nails.

"We need some tools," Johnny said.

It was the first time I saw Johnny happy. Mostly he hung around with the rest of us playing stoopball waiting for his father to come home.

"I got a hundred and fifty," said Johnny, catching a pointer off the edge of the stoop.

"You can't have that much," said Vinnie, who was not a good catcher. "You're cheating."

"I don't cheat," said Johnny, who was a very good catcher.

He threw the ball against the stoop. It bounced coming back to him.

"Five."

He threw again, and he caught it on the fly.

"Ten," he said. "That's one sixty-five."

"Cheater," said Vinnie, who was reading a comic while waiting for his turn.

Johnny threw again and the ball hit the pointed edge of a concrete step. It flew back like a homer smashed by a stick on the street. This came so fast Johnny jumped. He had good reflexes. He stuck his arm up and grabbed the ball before it went into the street.

"Twenty-five," he shouted. "That's one ninety," he said after a pause to add it up.

We all learned to count from stoopball, just like we learned odds from the cleaner who was a bookie.

"That'll be eight to five on the number five horse in the fifth," we heard the customers say.

"My mother wants this cleaned and pressed, and don't miss the spots, she said to tell you," I said.

"Five to one on number six in the seventh," said the old man in line after me.

"What's five to one?" I asked the man behind the counter after the man behind me had passed over a dollar without getting any clothes in return and I waited to ask because I wanted to learn the mysteries of dry cleaning.

The man behind the counter held his ball of thread and needles and said, "He gets five dollars if his horse comes in, but it won't because it's a nag. And I didn't say that, all I do is mend clothing, you got that, kid?"

I nodded and left. Five to one means just that. And if you add those calculations to the five, ten and twenty-five points of stoopball you got all the math you need to know. Let them give me a test. Five to one you are not going to get a pointer worth twenty-five. Math was just the world of stoopball and a visit to the cleaners.

And then what usually happened was Johnny saying, "My father's coming."

We knew what that meant. We left. I watched Johnny watching his father stagger down the street from the bar. I wanted to tell him that I knew what it was like to watch your father stagger like a drunk because he was what your mother called a stupid drunk, but I did not get the chance because Johnny wanted us to leave him alone.

He grabbed his father's arm and steered him into the house.

I remember the first time I saw Johnny when I was new on the street. He was reading comic books but I did not know why.

"Johnny had a dog," Dorothy told me.

"He found it wandering the street and he put a rope around its neck and Johnny was so happy. They ran down the street and then back up the street.

"Johnny's mother would not let him keep it inside and Johnny's father hated dogs. So Johnny built a house for it by the railroad tracks and he bought milk for it and gave it cookies and every day Johnny would spend all day with it.

"And then Johnny was running one day and the rope slipped out of his hand and the dog kept running and went out into the street and a car was going by and the dog ran right in front of the car and was killed."

That was when Dorothy stopped talking. She was crying.

"The dog just was splattered in the street and Johnny hugged it but it wouldn't come back to life and Johnny went home. The dog was there the next day and the day after and the day after and it rained and water went around it and the cigarette butts got caught in its fur and it just stayed there."

Dorothy was talking but she was not looking at me. She was looking straight ahead like she was looking at something, but not at me.

"I passed it going to school and then coming home from

school and then when I went back to school the next day. Poor Johnny. He didn't go to school for three days until the garbage truck came and the men shovelled his dog up and threw it in the back."

Dorothy looked at me. I thought she was beautiful.

"Johnny just read comics after that for a long time."

That was when I met him, a couple of days after I moved in. He was in the back alley sitting on the ground with his back against a wall reading comics.

"Can I read some of your comics?" I asked.

He looked up.

"I'm new here. I live a couple of doors away," I said.

He didn't say anything. He just looked, then nodded and pointed to a stack of comics on the ground next to him.

I sat down and looked through them. Lots of Archie and some Donald Duck and Superman and some with war stories. I took one of the Archie and Jughead, even though I couldn't read so well, but I looked at the pictures.

"My name's Mickey," I said.

He nodded and kept reading. I kept reading. A few minutes later he said his name was Johnny.

"I used to have a dog," he said.

"What happened to it?"

"He got killed. Here, you can read my Superman. I just finished it."

But today with the basketball backboard it was different. Johnny was happy.

"We need some tools," he said.

Buster and Vinnie both came back with crowbars. They both got them from underneath their older brother's beds.

"What do they use crowbars for?" I asked.

"Work," they both said.

"My brother works at night and says he needs the crowbar for moving things."

"Mine too," said Vinnie.

Johnny used the crowbars like a hammer to straighten the nails on the ground. Then he tore the pallets apart and put the pieces back together to make a solid board. I had never seen anyone work with tools before.

I remember once my mother showing me an electric socket that was sticking half out of the wall with wires hanging down.

"That's the kind of work your father does," she said.

Beyond that I did not know how things got put together. But Johnny was putting everything together and the board was finished and he said we have to get it up on that pole.

Johnny was a good climber, so we bent over and he got up on our backs until he could reach the spikes that were hand-holds in the pole. He had a crowbar hooked over his belt and a pocket full of nails and he climbed halfway up, just below the wires and just under the street light.

"We need a rope," said Johnny.

Two little kids ran home and came back dragging a ratty piece of rope behind them. Tommy tied some of the thin parts of it together then threw it up to Johnny. Johnny lowered one end and we tied it to the backboard.

Then Johnny hung the rope over a spike and lowered the other end back down to us. A bunch of us pulled down on the rope while the backboard went up on the other end. I had never been part of anything that was being done by anyone before. Being together was fun.

Johnny hammered the nails through the backboard while we held the rope that held the board. Then Johnny put in more nails. It looked like the whole centre of the board, up and down the pole, was a solid line of nail heads.

He climbed down. Something was missing.

"We need a hoop," said Dorothy.

Darn. You forget the most obvious stuff. The hoop that was a basket even though it didn't look like a basket but was the reason the game was called basketball, even though there was no basket.

The only wire we could think of was coat hangers. We got a few, twisted them together and wrapped them around the ball. We knew the ball had to fit through it, and it could.

Johnny climbed down and got the hoop then climbed back up the pole to nail the hoop into the backboard. I did not think I could even climb the pole and there was Johnny climbing and making something. I watched Dorothy watching him and wished I could do things like that.

We chose sides. I wound up on Dorothy's team. I did not care who else was on our side. Joey was on the other team. I would get the ball, bounce it with my fingertips, throw it up and get a basket and Dorothy would love me.

We started the game. Some of the parents and old folks on the street came out to watch. This was different than stickball. This was new. This was as American as apple pie even though many of the old folks could only speak Italian or Slavic and had no idea what apple pie was.

Most of them had never seen a basketball game. It was getting dark and the street light came on right above the backboard. We bounced and threw the ball to each other and then I got it and threw it up at the hoop. It hit the outside of the hoop and bent the wire.

Then Buster got the ball and threw it and also hit the wire, which was now half flattened against the backboard.

Three more shots at the basket and there was no hoop left.

"I got closest," said Jimmy Lee. "Our side won."

We stopped playing. There was nothing left to throw at and we wandered off in small groups. Most went home, a few of us sat on the curb and talked about the Dodgers, who were doing very well this season.

Forty years later I went back to New York for a visit. I told my wife I wanted to go to my old neighbourhood. She said I could go alone because it was an awful place.

I drove my rented car down past the ice cream factory. They were not making ice cream any longer. It was now a street filled with flatbed trucks being loaded up with coils of steel wire. The white ice cream trucks with bungalows on the back were gone. The cardboard ocean was gone. On the corner where the boxes had been were two abandoned and stripped cars.

I parked and walked down 132nd Street. The kids on the block were mostly East Indian and Spanish, but they were like the gangs

The street where the ice cream trucks used to park and get loaded up looks different today. The Cardboard Ocean was against the building on the left. The rooftop was our beach.

of 1955. They were hanging out together and watching me. They knew I was an outsider.

I walked past Vinnie's house and past Vanessa's and Buster's and then I stopped and looked up.

"Oh, my God."

The kids stood safely across the street watching me. The delivery trucks kept passing and the trains passed behind them. An airplane was coming in overhead to land at JFK. The elevated train had been cut down. It only went as far as 130th Street where Rocky had lived. There it turned and went a different route.

I was looking up. On a wooden telephone pole about ten feet up was a shard of wood about a foot and a half long. It had a row of nail heads running up and down the centre.

The new kids on the block watched me staring up at a telephone pole and not moving. I was looking at Dorothy and Buster and Tommy and Joey bouncing a stolen ball and throwing it at a hoop of coat hangers. And I was looking at me looking at Dorothy.

The kids on the street were whispering and pointing at me. They had heard about crazy people, and now they had one right in front of them. They stayed back while I was looking at the remains of Johnny's hammering.

The kids kept looking while I stood there watching the greatest basketball game ever played. Then I turned around and walked away.

Battle Wounds

In the morning, I had peanut butter and toast for breakfast. For lunch I had peanut butter and jelly in school. When my mother came home at night, we would have our hot dogs and potato salad and a tomato. But one evening before she got home, I had a little accident. I heard her high heels on the front stoop.

"And why is your arm swollen?"

"I was playing king of the mountain around the corner and tripped on a weed."

"There aren't any weeds there."

"It was, and I tripped on it."

It was a hill almost half the height of the Bungalow Bar trucks that was covered with asphalt and it was right at the end of the street where the trucks parked. We figured it must have been a lot of left-over asphalt that the city workers had dumped a long time ago. And there was a little patch of weeds growing out of a crack at the top.

"I'm king of the hill," I yelled when I got to the top.

"Are not," said Joey as he ploughed into me from behind.

Hitting from behind was not illegal since there was only one way up the hill after someone else got to the top, and that was from behind.

I lost my balance and fell backwards and put my hands out and hit the hill halfway down and oww, that hurt.

"I got you," said Joey.

"Oww, my arm hurts," I said. "But you didn't get me. I tripped over that weed."

"Did not. I got you."

If I tripped over the weed, he wasn't king of the hill. It was a do over. But my arm was screaming like crazy and I didn't want to go up and do it again.

"Let's go read comics," I said.

We spent the afternoon sitting on Joey's front stoop reading Donald Duck and Spiderman and Plastic Man. I never understood how Plastic Man could stretch his arm around an entire city block. Flying and having a spiderweb come out of your wrist was okay to believe, but plastic was hard and it didn't stretch and Plastic Man was making it stretch. Some things you just couldn't believe.

I held my arm the whole time we were reading because it hurt so badly.

"I don't know how you tripped over a weed," said my mother, "but take some aspirin and get four hot dogs and a half pound of potato salad and a tomato for dinner. And make sure the tomato is good."

I walked up 132nd Street, past Dorothy's house and past Jimmy Lee's house and past Joey's house in the dark. It was always dark when my mother got home.

The houses were all stuck together. They were not really houses, not like you see in Dick and Jane books, they were rows of doors and a roof that went on from one street to the next. But I knew Dorothy was behind that door, and Joey was behind that one.

The train was passing overhead, over the deli.

"Four hotdogs, please," I said to the man behind the counter. He always smiled.

"Hav yov had a schlect day?" he asked.

I knew that was German, or Yiddish. They were the same.

"No, it's fine," I said. I said that every night after he asked me if I had a bad day.

"Yove want a tomato, too?" he said. He said that every night.

"Yes, and my mother said . . . "

"Don't worrvie, Mickey," he said. "I vill give you a gout tomato and remember, dings vill get better."

"And a half pound of potato salad," I said.

He spooned it into a container. His sleeve was rolled up, as it always was, and I could see the numbers tattooed on his forearm.

His wife, who always smiled and was as friendly as he was – no, she was more friendly because she would tell me she was glad to see me – she had numbers on her arm too.

I never asked about the numbers, because I knew what they were and when you are eleven you cannot ask a friendly adult what it was like to be in a death camp and starved while you are waiting for your hot dogs.

"Do yov vant a pickle?" the man would always ask.

His name was Herman, but I never called him that. When you are a kid, even eleven years old, you cannot call someone with numbers tattooed on their arm by their first name.

I could call Matty by his name. He ran the candy store across the street, just under the stairs of the El. His right arm was frozen stiff and bent at the elbow and stuck out like a spear in front of him with his fingers sticking straight out from his hand. It happened when he got a jolt of electricity while working as a lineman and he couldn't do that work anymore so he ran a candy store.

When he rang up something on the cash register he would put the tips of his right hand on the keys and lean forward. I always wondered what they would do when he died and put him in a coffin. His hand would stick up and they wouldn't be able to close it.

I could call him Matty. But I couldn't call Herman by his name. You couldn't do that to someone who had numbers on his arm.

"A pickle?" he asked again.

I nodded and he pulled a dill pickle out of a jar on the counter and wrapped it in a piece of waxed paper and gave it to me.

"Yov are a gentleman and a scholar," he would say. He said that every night, and I would walk out of his store while the train went overhead as I ate the pickle while walking home with dinner.

"This tomato is soft," my mother would say.

But we ate it with the hot dogs and potato salad and I was glad we did not live in Russia because they had meat only once a year.

And then I stopped thinking about that because I was thinking that Joey was two years older than me and Dorothy would never marry a guy a year younger than she was.

Someone was ringing the bell.

"Why don't you tell your friends not to ring the bell at dinner

Our shopping mall was made up of street shops. The store behind the dumpster on the left was the deli where I got pickles from a man with a number tattooed on his arm.

time?" my mother said. She always said that because they always did that.

I did not want to say it's because we eat later than everyone else so I just shrugged and said I would tell them.

Tommy and Joey and Dorothy were at the door.

"You want to go on night patrol? We're going to the cemetery."

"I gotta finish eating," I said.

"Why you eating so late?" Tommy said.

"Because my mother doesn't get home until late."

"You're lucky," said Tommy. "You don't got a father. You don't get beaten."

I ran back inside and sat down. My arm was not hurting as much anymore because of the aspirin.

"I'm going out with the guys."

"Where are you going?"

Her look of iron rules went through me. I wanted to tell Tommy that a mother was worse than a father, but he would not believe me.

"Nowhere, just up to the corner."

"Be back by nine or you won't go out again this week. And how is your arm?"

"Good, fine," I said, even though it still hurt like crazy.

I finished my hot dogs and put my plate in the sink.

"I'll do the dishes when I get back."

I ran down the hallway and outside and the air was cool and the night dark and this was heaven. The other kids were standing under the street light. They all had sticks.

"We're going after the enemy," said Buster.

He liked war games. We often played shoot 'em up on the street, crawling under parked cars and saying, "Got you. Got your dirty German machine gun nest."

"Don't say that," said Buster. "My father is German. He would have blasted you to kingdom come."

"Got you, you dirty Jap," I said.

We didn't have any Japanese kids around.

The fighting went on from after dinner until we had to go home, and we always won. John Wayne had taught us how to be casual and to kill without blinking.

But tonight we were going where no solider had gone before. We were going to the cemetery.

> Did you ever see a hearse go by
> and think that you were next to die?
> They wrap you up in a clean white sheet
> And bury you about six feet.

This was our favourite poem.

> All goes well for about a week.
> Then the coffin begins to leak.
> The worms crawl in,
> The worms crawl out,
> They eat your guts
> And spit them out.
> The wind blows in,
> The wind blows out,
> In your stomach
> And out your mouth.

"Line up," said Joey.

His father had been in the Army.

"Two by two, and hold your guns on your shoulders."

We did as he told us. We were in boot camp under the El and would be going into battle on our first night.

"Forward, march."

We stepped ahead and bumped into each other but kept going.

"You guys, do it right. We have a war to win," said Joey.

We marched around Barney's Pharmacy and up the dark street and then turned right on Hillside Avenue and were told by Joey to keep quiet.

"The enemy is out there."

We got to the cemetery. We had never been so far from home for a battle.

"Over the fence," said Joey.

"We can't go over the fence," said Buster. "That's private property, and it's a cemetery and it's a sin if you go in there."

Joey leaned down over Buster's face.

"It is hard to be a soldier, but the enemy is in there."

Joey was the first to climb the fence. It was chain-link, the same as around the cardboard ocean and we had no trouble going over it. That is, except for me. My arm was hurting so badly I had to climb the fence using just my right hand. I thought this is the way soldiers did it. When they were wounded they just went on.

We fell on the other side and hid behind the gravestones.

"Bang, gotcha," I said.

"Don't fire yet," said Joey. "They are further in."

We crawled from headstone to headstone, keeping our rifles up in case we were attacked. I dropped down on one side of a headstone and squeezed against it. The enemy might be right on the other side of it.

I moved my rifle around the corner of the stone. "Bang. Gotcha."

"Shhhh," said Joey. "They are further in."

My arm was hurting more but I tried to ignore it. Real soldiers didn't complain about little things.

We slipped from stone to stone, all of us on a mission to kill the enemy and save the world.

But really, I was scared. The moon was out and we could see the headstones and the monuments in the Jewish part of the cemetery, and then the giant crosses in the Catholic part. I figured the Protestants were the ones with the little headstones.

"If we get caught in here we'll go to jail," said Dorothy.

It was wonderful that she was with us, but it was strange. Girls were not soldiers. But Dorothy was in the lead and was heading the charge against the enemy.

I was looking at Joey. He was just in front of me, looking over a headstone. His mouth opened, but no words came out. He looked like he wanted to say something but couldn't. He was trembling. He was shaking. He dropped his gun.

I had only known Joey for a little while, but I had never seen him scared.

He grabbed the headstone in front of him and pointed.

"Look," he said.

I looked ahead. Oh my gosh. Oh my lord. Oh, please help me, Jesus. There in front of us were one, then two white ghosts moving between the headstones. They floated on air. They moved toward us, then away. They were not touching the ground. They were not walking. They were not real, but we could see them.

"I'm getting out of here," said Joey.

He started to run back to where we came from. He tore over the graves and I followed and Dorothy was behind but then ahead of us. Everyone was running. We dropped our rifles and ran and then bang! Vinnie ran into a headstone and got knocked backwards.

"Owwww!"

We stopped. Vinnie was behind us. But I could still see the ghosts moving toward us, and toward Vinnie. We did what we had to do. We ran back and grabbed Vinnie and started to drag him, knowing that if there were barbed wire we would throw ourselves on it for the rest of the Marines to run over our backs, or if there were a grenade, we would throw ourselves on it to save the others.

We picked up Vinnie and ran. He quickly started moving on his own and we were all running toward the fence. Everyone hit it on the fly and started over it. I tried to grab it with my hands, but my left arm was useless. It would not work, and it hurt, with shooting pains that went to my head.

I used just my right hand and when I looked up, Dorothy was at the top of the fence holding her hand down for me to grab. I reached up as I was falling back and she held me and pulled me up. I do not know how she knew I was in trouble.

We got over the fence and ran back to our street without stopping.

"We tell no one about this," said Joey. "They will think we're crazy. Just tell no one."

We went home. I got in the door with my key that I kept around my neck and my mother was putting cream on her face.

"Well, it's about time you got home. Where have you been?"

"Nowhere," I said.

"What have you done?"

"Nothing."

"Well, wash your face and go to bed. I have to be gone early in the morning."

She went into her room and I went to the bathroom. My arm was twice the size of the other one. I could not move it. I tried to wash, but it hurt too much.

I lay down in bed and held my arm. I had seen a real ghost. My arm was killing me, but the ghost was real. It was as real as my arm. Then I fell asleep.

Early in the morning, I was up before my mother woke. My arm hurt so badly I could not lay on it and I could not lay on the other side. I could not put it up or down. When her alarm clock rang, she came out into the kitchen.

"What's the matter?"

"My arm."

"Oh no," she said. "Get dressed. We'll go to the doctor."

I got dressed and she called work and said she would be late.

"I hope it's nothing serious," she said as we walked up the street.

The doctor's office was in an apartment just under the El at the end of the street. We were the first ones in the waiting room which was in the hallway outside the room that would be the kitchen in any other apartment.

"Broken," he said. "How'd you do that?"

"Tripped over a weed," I said.

"Amazing. How did you find a weed?"

He put a cast on my arm and my mother said she would pay him when she got paid and then she went straight to work without going home. I went to school and never mentioned the ghosts.

"How'd you break your arm?" some kids asked me.

"Tripped over a weed," I said.

"Could we see the weed?"

Ten years later, I was going to work at the *Daily News*. I was working nights and decided to take the subway from a different stop than usual. I walked past the cemetery. The gate was open and I was early. I went in, not thinking at all of the night of the army patrol. I just wanted to see the monuments.

I walked farther and farther past the rows of graves. I had never been there before, except when we saw the ghosts and that was a long time ago. It was nice and peaceful, far from the El and the factories. And there, in front of me was a pond. So pretty, I thought. Then, from nowhere, came two snow-white swans gliding over the water.

"I knew it was you," I said. "I wasn't scared. Not me. No sir."

I turned around and walked to the subway and went to work. I listened to the reporters and writers that night talking about murders and suicides and scary stories.

I could tell you a real scary story, I thought. But not now. Not tonight. First we have to write about the murders.

You Just Got to Help

One night, Rocky and his friends grabbed one of the little kids from our block when he was coming home late from school.

They pulled him into an alley and hit him a bit, but not too hard because he was little.

"The next time you walk by our street we're going to cut your fingers off, and tell your friends we'll do the same to them."

Then they let him go. The worst thing that happened was he wet his pants and he would have to tell his mother what happened and he would be too afraid to go to school.

I liked this little kid. His name was Patrick and he was born in 1950, which I thought made him very young and he and his mother lived in an apartment above the bar on the corner and their windows faced right into the El trains. It was very noisy.

I thought his mother was beautiful, so when I heard about what happened I said to Patrick that I would go back to 130th

Street and beat up Rocky so that he could go to school without a problem.

You can't say something like that and not do it. This was seven years before they cornered me and removed some of my dental work.

I walked alone under the El, and then under the LIRR trestle that went under the El and sometimes you could watch one train going over another train with traffic on Jamaica Avenue going by under both of them. I thought that must be one of the wonders of the world.

I was very worried what would happen if I saw Rocky. And there, in the no man's land between 132nd and 130th Street, under the LIRR trestle, which went under the El, was one of his guys.

"Where's Rocky?"

"What'd you want to know for?"

"I want him to stop hitting little kids."

My heart was pounding. I could feel it going real fast and I could feel my stomach trembling and my hands shaking. I did not want him to see that so I made two fists.

"I see your fists," he said. "I don't want to fight. I didn't have nothing to do with it."

I had never felt powerful before.

"Where's Rocky?"

"He's not here today."

"Well, you tell him to pick on people his own size."

Then I turned around and walked away.

"How did that happen?" I thought. I won a fight without fighting. That's impossible. It was the tactics the US and Russia were using in the Cold War but I did not figure that out for ten years. Right now I just knew that if you looked tough, you could win. I wanted to skip, but I thought if he saw me skipping that I wouldn't look tough and he would come after me and pound me in the back of the head.

The sun was setting because it was winter, and it was cold. I got back to 132nd Street and saw Patrick standing at the bottom of the stairs going up to the El station, which was just outside the door of the bar. He was waiting for his mother. I told Patrick that it would be okay for him to walk by that street anytime to get to school and he had nothing to worry about. And if anyone said anything to him just tell me and I would kill them.

He looked up at me with big, young, thankful eyes. This was better than being Superman.

Stumpy

It's not true that we didn't have any pets. I had a turtle once, and we all had Stumpy. The turtle was neat. I saw it in the pet department of Goertz's department store on Jamaica Avenue and 169th Street.

My mother loved Goertz's. We would walk from 132nd Street to 169th once or twice a week to go shopping. I hated shopping but the walk was fun and inside Goertz's was a wooden escalator that I rode up and down and down and up while my mother looked at blouses or whatever it was she was looking at.

But they also had a pet department in the store and one day I saw a bunch of turtles with pictures of palm trees painted on their shells. That was neat, a little thing that stuck its head out and looked at me and carried a picture around.

"Mom, can I have one? Just one. I'll take care of it. I promise."

The reason we walked was to save the forty cents round trip that it would cost if we rode the El that rolled by overhead as we walked down below. But I didn't know that. I thought we walked just because we walked everywhere.

"Can I, please? It's only fifty cents."

I had newts once when we lived with my cousin.

"What are you going to do with a newt?" my mother had asked.

"Have it," I said.

We bought one and I put it in a flower vase made of glass and it went up on a bookcase in my aunt's living room and I looked at it and it swam around and I fed it and I went to sleep.

The next morning it was gone. I don't think my aunt liked a newt swimming in her vase on top of her bookcase. I think it went down the toilet, but I never asked.

Maybe it was because the newt disappeared that my mother said I could have a turtle. Maybe it was my mother who made it disappear to keep my aunt happy while we moved into her apartment and moved her son out into the hallway. I didn't really care. I was a happy boy.

I carried the turtle home in a paper container that was also used for takeout Chinese food. I also had a jar of dried bugs to feed it. That was a total of a dollar, an hour's pay for my mother. I did not think about that. I only thought I had to walk home quickly so that my turtle would have a wonderful life with me.

I put the turtle in a bowl with some water and put the bugs in the water like my mother told me the instructions said on the back of the jar and I watched the turtle crawl up to them and snap, eat.

"Mom, it ate a bug."

I had never realized that things eat other things. I thought we just ate hot dogs and peanut butter and Twinkies and Wonder Bread that helped build bodies in eight ways.

I watched it eat and swim and hide in its shell all the next day. I hardly went outside. I took it out of the bowl and it crawled on the floor. I put it in the toilet and it swam.

"Look, Mom, it will drink milk," I said at dinner.

I tilted my three-quarters empty glass of milk almost sideways and put the turtle inside the glass. It crawled forward, down the gentle slope and there, right before our eyes, drank some milk.

"I trained it to do that," I said.

Then I reached in and took the turtle out and put it back into its turtle home that was on the table next to my hot dogs. And then I drank the rest of my milk. I was so happy.

The next night I had a better trick.

"Watch," I said.

I picked the turtle up out of its turtle home and put it into my mouth and closed my lips.

"Don't do that, it's dirty," said my mother.

I shook my head. Then I opened my mouth and the turtle sitting on my tongue stuck his head out. I knew he would because when I practised it in front of the mirror he always stuck his head out of his shell when I opened my mouth and the pitch black night suddenly had an opening and I had a friend.

I took him outside and showed him to everyone. I let him swim in a puddle in a pothole, except I had to sit in the middle of the street and grab him when a car came.

Two days later, the turtle was dead. Later I learned putting pictures over half of someone's body with lead-based paint does not make for a happy life.

When I grew up and moved to Vancouver I found turtles that have the best lives. There are turtles living happily in every pond in every park in the city. They hurt nothing and have no enemies. They crawl into the mud in the winter and in spring wake up and sit on the rocks under the warm sun.

I met a couple from Los Angeles who were taking pictures of the turtles in a small pond near the Granville Island public market.

"We just came back from a cruise to Alaska and saw nothing. The weather was so bad we could hardly go out on deck."

But the turtles were different. They were right here in front of them and the weather was beautiful and they were filling their camera with close-ups.

"We don't have wild turtles in LA," they said.

We don't have them in Vancouver either, I told them. At least we didn't before the Chinese moved in. Vancouver has more Chinese than nearly any other city in the world outside of cities in China.

From being used as cheap and expendable labourers a century ago, they now dominate most professions. They are the lawyers and doctors and bankers. University computer courses are basically filled with Chinese students.

And they are deep believers in anything that brings luck. And that faith has given turtles a good life, because the Chinese believe if you release a little turtle into a pond it will bring you luck. The result is Vancouver has many turtles now. And since the Chinese have done so well, it obviously works.

And none of the turtles have paint on them.

But our other pet, Stumpy, was different. Stumpy was a pigeon and we all had Stumpy.

Stumpy was like the man who loved worms.

This man might have been crazy. We weren't sure. But we sure learned a lot from Gus. He taught us how to hold a baseball bat and how to steal second. He used to play in the minors, on a double-A ball team, which means that if he made it to a triple-A team he would have been only one step below the majors.

Then he was hit in the head by a bad pitch, in the time before batters wore helmets. After that he just wandered about, unable to play and unable to hold a job for long. Sometimes he would get some work sweeping floors or unloading trucks, but he was never fast enough and he would eventually get fired.

"You do a hook slide by coming around," Gus was telling a bunch of us one afternoon. He sat on the front stoop of the house he shared with his sister and his mother. His sister was the only one of them who went to work. She left at night and there was a rumour that she did things most of us could not imagine.

The guys in the bar always stood by the window when she went by. That was Pat's Bar and Grill. It was a grill because they had one sandwich under a clear plastic cover on a plate on the bar. They had to offer food or they could not get a licence to serve beer and whisky. So they offered the sandwich. That fact that no one had a strong enough stomach to eat it did not stop them from getting a licence.

The men there watched Gus's sister walk to the train.

"You know where she's going," they would say with a smirk.

We kids would sit at the doorway of the bar and heard what was said when Gus's sister went to work and so we repeated it.

"You know where she's going."

Gus said she was a telephone operator.

"If you are going to do a hook slide, you have to bend your leg so you can steer yourself around the bag. But it can hurt."

We didn't care about Gus's sister and we didn't care what people said about her, or him. We cared about hook slides, until it rained. That's when Gus did the thing that made him odd, and we could only watch and feel sorry for him.

"There he goes again," our parents would say. "Crazy, crazy Gus."

In a downpour, he would walk the sidewalks picking up worms. They were crawling on the concrete. He would squat, slip a fingernail under a worm, scoop it up and carry it gently in the palm of his hand to a patch of dirt, dig a tiny hole with a finger, and place the worm in the hole and cover it up with dirt.

There was not much dirt, but here and over there next to the curb Gus would return a worm to its home.

People walking on the sidewalks, bent under their umbrellas, would leave a lot of space between themselves and Gus.

The worms came from tiny patches in front of some houses where there had once been attempts at miniature gardens. Now they were dirt covered with litter. When it rained hard, the ground filled with water and worms had to come out so they would not drown. They crawled onto the sidewalk and Gus said since they were blind there was no way they were going to figure out where they were.

We learned more than baseball from Gus. None of us had learned about worms, or blindness, in school.

"It's not their fault that we cover up their world with concrete," said Gus. "They're just lost."

"Man, you must be crazy," the men in the bar shouted through the open door. And then, safely inside away from the rain, they would add that worms are dirty and how could anyone touch them?

"Never shake hands with Gus," they said, "Ha, ha, ha. He's a goofball."

We got mad at the men in the bar but there was nothing we could do. I mean, those were big men with beer glasses in their hands standing in a group inside the door that we were not allowed to go through. In the summer we would sit on the ground just outside the door so we could see the baseball game on the ten-inch black and white television on a shelf on the wall at the far end of the bar.

We really could not see much, but it was real and a different world than radio.

"Hey, did you see that hit? That was a great hit."

We cheered. We really could not see the hit, but we heard it and we saw something moving on the screen before the men in the bar moved in front of the TV to watch the same hit and we had to move farther back on the sidewalk to see over their heads. But back here we could not see anything, or hear anything because of the traffic noise behind us and we were right under the El now and a train was coming in.

"That was a great hit," said Buster. "I saw the whole thing."

"Yeah, like you got to see Vanessa's bra," said Vinnie.

"No, I did, really. Just before they got in our way I saw it. Really."

But still, we could not tell the men in the bar to stop making fun of Gus because they might not let us sit in front of the door. It was a lesson in selling your soul, but we did not know that. We just knew we hated the men for making fun of Gus and there was nothing we could do about it.

"Don't worry about it," said Gus. "It doesn't bother me."

Our parents told us to stay away from him because he was strange. "And don't let him touch you. He's dirty."

But we knew he was almost a professional baseball player and he did not act like he was above us.

Then one day while it was raining, a guy from the bar stepped out on the sidewalk while Gus was walking up the street. The guy from the bar found a worm crawling on the concrete and pushed it around with the toe of his shoe. He waited until Gus was almost next to him.

"Hey, watch this," he said and slammed his heel down on the worm.

Gus did the only thing he could do. He punched the guy. We couldn't believe it. The men in the bar watching through the big picture window couldn't believe it. We had all seen fights in the bar before. The men in the bar had occasionally fought each other. And in their fights one guy would hit another and the other would hit back and there would be yells, but both men would be standing.

When Gus punched it was like a bullet, or a battering ram. The guy he hit went flying backwards and we all remember the shocked look on his face. He went back so fast he didn't have time to fall before he hit the stairs coming down from the elevated train station. He hit it so hard that his head snapped back and hit the steel bars that kept people from falling off the stairs. We heard the crack. It wasn't the steel that was making the sound, we knew. And then he fell.

The men in the bar ran outside and grabbed their friend, but he wasn't moving.

"He's dead," one of them shouted at Gus. "You killed him. You're gonna fry."

The sirens filled the canyon of Jamaica Avenue bouncing off the sides of the stores and echoing down from under the tracks and wooden ties above that let some of the wailing escape to the sky and sent some of it back to the street in a warble.

Gus was handcuffed and pushed in the back of a squad car. There were no Miranda rights back then.

"What happened?" the cops asked the guys in the bar.

"Sounds like second degree," said a cop. "Twenty to life."

They took notes while Gus sat in the back seat and we stood by the window of the cop car shouting through the glass to Gus that everything would be okay.

Then the cops left and the bartender came out and poured a pitcher of water over the spot where the guy's blood was and the men went back into the bar and got a round on the house, we heard.

We walked back down 132nd Street.

"He killed him, right there, just to protect a worm," said Joey. "John Wayne would've done the same thing."

"Yeah," I said. "I didn't know Gus was so strong."

"It came from baseball," said Joey, and we knew the secret. Gus didn't spend his time in the bar, he played ball so he was strong enough to kill someone.

We learned something that day. Baseball could make you strong, and we all wanted to be stronger than anyone else.

"See how crazy your friend is," said Tommy's father. "Stay away from crazy people."

But when we talked we all knew that Gus was not crazy. He was a strong man who defended something that was weak. Gus was our hero.

In court, we were told, the judge told him he could not protect a worm. "Worms have no rights."

He was convicted of second degree murder and just as the cop said, was sentenced to twenty years to life.

"Now he's going to meet a lot of worms," a guy at the bar told us as we stood around the open door.

We had no idea what he meant. We did not think there were worms in jail cells.

A few weeks later, we saw Gus's sister walking up the street to go to work. We asked if we could walk with her. She nodded.

"What kind of work do you do?" Vinnie asked.

"I'm a telephone operator," she said.

We could see the guys in the bar moving over to the window to watch her pass. They gave her the strangest faces, like stupid little boy smiles. Then they looked at us and frowned.

"I'm glad you talked to Gus," she said. "He used to tell me that you are the best friends he has in the world."

"How's he now?" we asked.

"He was allowed a phone call a few days ago," she said while standing on the bottom step of the El stairs, just outside the door of the bar.

"He said everything was fine. He always says that."

Then she turned around and ran up the stairs. We could see she was grabbing in her bag for a tissue. She was crying so loud by the time she got to the top we had to turn away.

"Oh, my poor Gus," was all we heard before she went

through the door into the station. Then a train came and drowned out all the sound, even though we couldn't hear her anymore anyway.

But I was telling you about Stumpy.

Stumpy was with us for more than a year. He taught us about relationships and obligations, although we didn't call them relationships and obligations. We just said we got to take care of Stumpy.

We didn't know he was a guy. We just called him "him," but from what I have seen of life, he was probably a she since she's are generally tougher than he's.

Stumpy was tough. Stumpy was a survivor. Stumpy was a pigeon with one foot.

"That's so sad," said Dorothy the first time we saw him. We were coming home from school and he or she was lurching around by the curb, trying to pick up a bit of invisible food. Every time he would limp toward one, some other pigeon would get it.

"We should feed him," said Vanessa. We still thought that all the world's unfairness could be fixed by us. And if unfairness could be fixed with some breadcrumbs, we would fix it immediately, or even quicker.

Someone had a cookie stuffed in his pocket.

"Do you think he likes cookies?"

"Try it," I said.

I don't remember who took the mushed up remains of a cookie out of his jacket pocket and threw it on the ground but suddenly between kids and handicapped bird there was a connection. We tried to shoo the other pigeons away, which was a battle. Pigeons who see cookie crumbs on the ground are not afraid of feet.

But we managed to give Stumpy a head start and he gobbled them up faster than we could believe. He was hungry.

Vanessa said she would go home for some bread. She lived closest. She came back with a couple of slices of Wonder Bread.

"You think it will build his body in eight ways?" Johnny asked. "That's what the advertisements say."

Johnny didn't often make jokes.

The bird ate all the bread, except for the bits that were grabbed by the other birds, but at least he got a good stomach full.

The next day he was in the same fix. He was getting out-manoeuvred by the other pigeons.

"He looks so strong," said Johnny. "If I only had one foot I couldn't walk at all."

"He's got a stump," said Joey.

"Well, Stumpy is a brave guy," said Dorothy.

We did not know his name was Stumpy until then, but from then on Stumpy was part of our gang. We saved cookies and bread for him and fed him every day after school. He was always in the same spot. We brought enough so that the other birds got some too.

We wondered how he lost his foot.

"It must have been awful," said Vanessa. "It looks like it rotted off."

"Probably froze off in the winter," said Johnny. "And then there was gangrene."

"Don't tell me," said Vanessa, who tried to put her hands over her ears.

We knew he didn't have any medicine or even aspirin. He didn't even have a way to complain. But we could give him cookies and in a few days he became our pet. As soon as we got home from school we would find out if anyone had fed Stumpy, and then someone would run home for bread or cookies and we stood around him dropping crumbs where he would get them before the other birds charged in.

No parent had to remind us to feed him. We wouldn't even tell our parents about him. The next thing they would be saying would be, "don't touch him, he's got germs."

We didn't want to hear that. We just wanted to take care of our pet. We even chipped in enough money to buy a box of canary seeds and fed him that for a few days. Dorothy kept them at home until a mouse got in the box and ate the whole thing one night.

But we talked about Stumpy so much at school that some other kids from other streets came to see him. Some of them were from Rocky's gang. We let them watch, but we wouldn't let them feed him. He was ours.

A summer and a winter passed and one day Stumpy was not there. Two days and then a week went by without Stumpy. We all stood on the corner, holding a few cookies just in case.

"He's dead," said Vinnie.

"I miss him," said Vanessa.

"He was my friend," said Johnny.

Thirty years later when I lived in Vancouver, I did a story for television about a man who drove twenty miles every morning. He carried a loaf of bread in his car. At the end of the trip was a seagull, waiting for him on the roof of a house. It was standing on just one foot, its only foot.

"That's Stumpy," he told me. He threw some bread on the ground and the bird flew down to get it.

The man had started feeding Stumpy when he lived in the house. He felt sorry for him because a seagull with just one foot cannot even swim straight, much less outrace other birds on land. When the man moved to a new house in a new city he did not break Stumpy's trust. Every morning for three years he drove back to feed him.

"It may sound stupid," he said, "but he needs me and I need him."

Stumpy is a name pets earn. And it is not forgotten.

Kick the Can

"I've got to bring Junior if we play," said Joey.

"Too bad he can't walk," said Dorothy.

"He can walk," said Joey, who defended his brother no matter what. "It's just that he doesn't walk really good."

Dorothy almost looked like she was going to hug him, but we didn't hug anyone on this street no matter what, not even a girl and boy. But it almost looked that way.

"But then you wouldn't have to carry him so much," she said.

Joey didn't say anything. The only time I remember him telling us something about Junior was after his mother and father put him in a home because it was too hard for them to care for him. Then they went to visit one day without telling the people who were supposed to be taking care of him.

"He was tied up and sitting on the floor like all the kids," said Joey. "My father just grabbed him and lifted him up and then I took him and we walked out. My father was looking for someone that he could kill, but there wasn't anyone there, so we left."

After that, Junior stayed with his mother and father and brother, sometimes laughing, sometimes screaming and almost always swinging his arms around. That's why Joey had to duck when he carried him around the street and that's why Joey was such a good fighter. No one could hit him after he learned how to duck away from Junior's flying fists.

"We're going to play kick the can," said Buster. "If you carry Junior, you can't run fast enough."

"Don't you worry about me," said Joey.

It was getting dark and it was cold because it was October but that was the best time to play on the street because you could hide in the dark. The best places to hide were behind cars and telephone poles and kids were skinny enough to stand behind a pole and disappear.

Dorothy brought out a can. Of course it was Dorothy who did that because she was always there with whatever we needed. She was wonderful.

"This had tomato juice," she said.

That was better than perfect because it was two quarts, bigger than the average can of beans and it would last longer.

But there was a problem. Stan was hanging around.

I don't talk much about Stan. He was the mean kid who lived at the end of the block. He didn't play with us very much, which made us happy because he liked to destroy things. It seemed to be his nature. Give him something and he would break it.

He was a lot older than us and he had been in the Army, but only for a short time. He didn't make it through basic training.

When Patrick, the little kid who lived with his mother next to the El, once got a new plastic six-shooter, which he wanted because he was still younger than the rest of us, Stan wanted to see it.

"No, you'll just break it," said Patrick.

"No, I won't. I just want to see it."

110

"Are you sure you won't break it?"

"Won't, I promise."

Patrick handed over his new pistol and Stan, who'd had a rifle in the Army, shouldn't have been playing with a little kid's plastic gun. He spun Patrick's six-shooter with his finger in the trigger loop.

"See, this is the way they did it in the old west."

He put it in his pocket.

"Watch this, quick draw."

He pulled it out.

"Bang, bang."

He spun it again.

"And you know what they did when they ran out of bullets?"

Patrick shook his head.

"They turned it around."

Stan grabbed it by the barrel.

"And they pistol whipped the guy they were fighting."

He smashed it into a telephone pole. The gun shattered.

"You broke my gun," yelled Patrick.

"That's because it's plastic. It's not my fault," said Stan.

"You broke it. You said you wouldn't." Patrick was crying. "I just got it. My mother just gave it to me."

"You'll get another one. I gotta go."

When we saw Stan hanging around where we wanted to play kick the can we felt rotten. We couldn't say "no, you can't play," because he knows there's no teams or rules in kick the can. Once you start, anyone who is nearby can play.

But we knew Stan would run as fast as he could to the can, not because he wanted to free anyone but because he wanted to kick it so hard that he would bend it in half. These were steel cans, and they took a lot of kicking, but once they were bent you couldn't straighten them out.

And if it was bent too badly it couldn't stand up anymore

and the game was over. Stan ruined almost every game he showed up at.

But this night we got together before we started to play. We had a plan.

Buster drew a large circle in the middle of the street. He used a piece of chalk he stole from school.

"Everyone who wants to play come in the circle. The last one in is it," he said.

We all ran and watched Stan run too. He was running hard. We ran harder. We wanted him to be it.

Vanessa was just coming out her front door.

"What are you doing?" she shouted.

"Kick the can. The last one in is it."

She ran down the street. Tommy grabbed her hand and pulled her. Vanessa didn't know the plan. We couldn't let her be it.

They got near the circle.

"Why are you helping me?" she said while she was being pulled.

"Stan," he said. "Stan has to be it."

"That's not fair," she said with the wind blowing in her face and Tommy still pulling.

Tommy yanked her into the circle.

"You always want to be fair and nice," said Tommy. "But sometimes you can't be. Stan is rotten."

We all made it just a second before Stan.

"You're it," we said to him.

No one had to explain what to do. He closed his eyes and started counting.

"One potato, two potato."

We ran in the darkness and hid.

"Nine potato, ten, freeze."

We stopped. No one cheated. You can't cheat and play, because then it was no fun.

"I see Johnny by the car, and Vinnie by the pole."

Johnny and Vinnie came back to the circle. Stan moved slowly further away from the circle looking for more kids. If he got too far someone could run up and kick the can and free anyone inside the circle.

The only time someone couldn't kick the can was if Stan was standing in the circle. It was exciting. You had to move away to find people, but you couldn't move too far away.

"I see Vanessa by the other pole and Dorothy by the car next to the other pole. And I see Mickey behind the fender."

We all came back. In a few minutes Stan had us all caught except Joey and Tommy. Then Stan moved far from the circle. We knew what would happen.

Out of the night Joey came ripping across the sidewalk, jumping off the curb and heading straight for us and the can. We moved aside so he wouldn't hit us. And then like a cannonball he almost put his shoe into the side of the can.

We took off running while Joey shouted, "I kicked the can! I freed you!"

Stan went running for the tomato juice can, but the rest of us didn't stop in the dark to hide. We all just kept going. And when we got about half a block away, far enough to hide where Stan couldn't see us, we started laughing at him.

"We taught him a lesson. Yeah, we showed him."

Now he had no one to play with.

Stan looked around for a few moments, a little confused, and then maybe he realized what was going on. The street was empty.

He put the can down and stomped it with his heel. Then he stomped it again. He sat down on the curb. We could see when he picked up the can.

"You think he's going to flatten it more?" I asked.

Then he kicked the can off the street and walked away. Usually kick the can was the best game, except for that night.

Fifty years later, the parents in a school in Vancouver formed a committee to draw up the rules for kick the can. They wanted to organize leagues so that all the kids in the school could play. They worried that their kids needed more physical activity.

They said that the old-fashioned games were loaded with activity which was good for cardiovascular health. However, they had some concerns that an actual can might be dangerous. They used a rubber cup instead.

They made the circle to be three metres in circumference, any less and some children might not be able to fit inside. They said the game would be played in the gym both to allow year-round participation in bad weather and to avoid the dangers of the schoolyard.

The term "It" was said to be derogatory. The designated one who would do the counting would be called the leader. And no child would be chosen as the leader until all other children had the opportunity.

Finally, kicking the can was thought to be aggressive. The can would have to be pushed out of the circle. The child freeing the others would have to stop, and then with a sideward motion of his or her foot move the cup until it was outside the line. Then the other children could run.

The parents put the game into their newsletter: "Kick The Can Returns To Southlands Junior Secondary." The story said that the old-fashioned street game had been revived. However, the kids found it boring and returned to their computer games.

A committee was formed to investigate what was wrong with the children.

Save the Celery

"Today we are going to learn how things live."

Miss Johnson stood in front of the classroom. She had a stick of celery in her hand. We were not allowed to bring food into the classroom.

"Celery is just like us. It gets thirsty and it eats. But it doesn't have teeth. It only drinks."

This was way too much information. We had just come from lunch. In the basement we heard the same announcement every day: "Free lunch kids line up over against the wall."

There was no worry we might feel bad. Half the school stood against the wall. The other kids sat on the long wooden benches and opened their Pinocchio lunch boxes and started to eat their peanut butter and jelly sandwiches.

The rest of us moved forward and the ladies with the white aprons handed us each a sandwich wrapped in waxed paper and a small container of milk. We sat and opened the milk. It was always room temperature and it always had pieces of wax floating around in it that was broken off from the containers.

We drank the milk and spit the wax at each other. The sandwiches were always the same, peanut butter and jelly, except we knew they were made the day before because the bread was stale and the jelly had soaked almost through one side of it.

In class we could not understand eating without chewing since most of us were still chewing on the sandwich which we had a hard time swallowing.

"It doesn't chew. It drinks," said Miss Johnson.

Impossible, we thought.

We watched her pour a half bottle of ink into a jar and then put the celery into the jar.

Ugh. Poor celery, we thought.

"Now you will see how the ink rises up in the veins of the celery," said Miss Johnson.

"You can't do that, Miss Johnson," said about twenty kids, and a bunch more wanted to say it.

Thirty-six kids all had the same thought of the horrible poison-ness of drinking ink. We knew you could get ink poison if you got stabbed by a pen, which was worse than lead poison if you got stabbed by a pencil, so we only used pens in fights when we really meant it.

"It will only take a short time," said Miss Johnson. "Celery is very thirsty."

Thirty-six kids curled up their tongues and pulled in their cheeks in sympathy and leaned over their desks. We were not allowed to leave our seats, except to go to the bathroom and then you had to raise your hand and tell everyone you had to go. Miss Johnson would stop her teaching and give you the bathroom pass out of the top drawer of her desk. It was a piece of old deep brown wood about the size of your hand with a chain through a hole in one end and a bell about the size of your fist attached to the chain.

"Hurry back," she would say.

But this time we didn't have to go. We were worried about the celery.

One hand went up. Usually there were no questions about anything. Three hands went up. Then ten.

Miss Johnson smiled. Her teaching was reaching us. She pointed at Richard French, who was sort of the teacher's pet since he couldn't walk because of polio. He had crutches.

Our mothers warned us not to touch the water in the gutters because we too would get polio. That would mean we might end up in an iron lung. We had all been shown pictures of that. They were big metal tubes lying on their sides. The kids inside had their heads sticking out one end. They were always lying on their backs and there was a mirror a few inches above their faces. The mirrors were tilted so they could look at the people who were standing behind their heads.

We were told the pressure was raised and lowered inside the metal tube which made them breathe. They could not move anything. They would spend their lives in there. What amazed me was the pictures always showed the kids smiling. I didn't believe them.

Some kids who got polio only got it a little, like Richard. So he could breathe but couldn't walk.

"Miss Johnson, that's mean and cruel making that celery drink ink," Richard said.

We could see she did not like that. Richard French was always the one who knew what she was talking about because he had looked it up in the encyclopedia. Most of us did not know what an encyclopedia was, or what looking up meant. But now Richard French was disagreeing with Miss Johnson. This was as good as a street fight.

"Don't worry, Richard," she said. "It's only celery. It doesn't know any difference."

Richard's mouth dropped open. I had heard mouths dropped open when they could not believe something, but I had never seen it. But Richard's mouth dropped open.

"But it does," he said. "You wouldn't like to drink ink, would you?"

Miss Johnson was losing. It was a fight without punches and she was losing and we could see it. First the open mouth of Richard French whose mouth never opened unless he was talking about things we knew nothing about. Then the disagreement. It was like he hit her.

"We will go on with the lesson," she said.

She lost. We knew that. It was like a technical knockout. We learned about those on the radio when some giant sweaty loser who couldn't hold his fists up anymore would be counted out by the ref even though he was still on his feet.

We tried that on the street. We would punch and hit each other until someone put down his fists.

"Technical knockout," the other kid would shout. "Technical knockout."

"Is not," said the guy with the dropped fists. "I was only resting."

Then he would hit the kid who was shouting "TKO" extra hard and knock him back onto the fender of a car and he would shout, "Real knockout, real knockout."

The kid who got belted would push himself up off the ground and say, "You can't have a real knockout after a technical knock-out. I TKO'ed you before you KO'ed me. So I won."

So when Richard French said "you wouldn't like to drink ink, would you?" to Miss Johnson we knew he had a TKO.

Miss Johnson ignored him and tried to tell us something about plants and oxygen and carbon dioxide, but we all sat in our seats looking at the poor celery.

Ten minutes later, Miss Johnson said we could come to the

front of the classroom one row at a time and observe the wonders of science. The celery was in the jar sitting on her desk.

There were ughs and yucks from the first kids who got up and looked. Then there were groans from the next row. The ink was rising in the body of the celery. By the time the fourth row was called, the class was in mourning for the green stalk that was turning black.

Miss Johnson was nice, I thought, even pretty. She was just doing what teachers do and we were doing what we did. The problem was we did not fit in with what teachers do.

Then while the fifth row was crowding around the celery, a kid raised his hand and said he had to go to the bathroom. Miss Johnson told him to get the pass and hurry back. He squeezed around the kids who were standing around her desk and got the pass and the kids kept saying, "Poor celery. We feel sorry for you."

"Celery doesn't feel anything," said Miss Johnson. "You don't have to feel sorry for it."

"But we do," said Richard French, who was back in his seat at the front of the classroom.

"You children are being silly," she said. "This is a lesson in biology and someday when you get to high school you will have to dissect a frog."

We said nothing.

"Do you know what 'dissect' means?"

Thirty-five kids had a blank stare. Richard French raised his hand. Miss Johnson nodded.

"It means cut up," he said.

"Oh, yuck," said thirty-five kids. "You mean we have to cut up a frog?"

Feet scraped under the desk and the noise rose with no real words being said.

"Ugh. Yuck. I don't want to cut up a frog," said Dorothy.

"What's a frog?" said Vinnie.

"It's an animal, you goof," said another kid.

Vinnie got out of his seat. "Don't call me that," he said.

"Well, you are if you don't know what a frog is. Everyone knows about frogs."

"I don't want to hurt one," said Dorothy.

Miss Johnson was having trouble. "They will be dead when you get them."

"Oh, no," said thirty-five kids including Vinnie. "We don't want to hold a dead frog."

"Quiet down," shouted Miss Johnson. "Quiet. That's not until high school and some of you won't get there. Right now we are just concerned with celery. So please, go back to your seats," she said to the kids standing around her desk.

"We want to look a little more," someone said.

"No, go back to your seats."

"Just a little."

"Do as you're told."

The kids started moving, but not to their seats. They shuffled around and changed places and said "poor celery."

Then the kid who went to the bathroom came back. He sort of slipped through the door and moved past the kids standing around the desk. He dropped the bathroom pass on Miss Johnson's desk and went back to his seat. The rest of the kids followed and went back to their seats.

"Very good," said Miss Johnson. "A quiet class is a good class. And now do we understand how celery drinks water?"

She walked back to her desk and looked down. If she was shocked or surprised she did not show it. She just looked and almost shook her head, then almost smiled. We were all good at seeing things that were almost. She said nothing about the water.

She looked up at us and said, "Tomorrow we will plant some seeds in a pot and see what happens."

We all looked at the jar on her desk. You could see it even from the back row. It still had the celery in it but it was filled with clean water.

I knew from that moment that Miss Johnson was a good teacher, even if she did not believe that we swam in the Mediterranean. I couldn't tell her she was a good teacher. I couldn't go up to her and say, "Miss Johnson, even though you kill celery and don't believe me, I think you're a good teacher," because if I did that, the other kids would beat me up. Being a kid in school is like being in a union. You don't say nice things to management, ever.

But later that day we were having our own graduation into growing up, and we didn't need school or teachers for it. We were going to shave.

The First Shave

At least Vinnie was going to shave. The rest of us said we would, but first Vinnie. If he lived, then we would too.

This was about six years before Jimmy Lee got married and we went to Augie for a shave. This we were doing on our own. Sort of.

Vinnie had watched his father for weeks, and now he was ready. He used his father's brush and swirled it around and around inside his father's shaving mug, then he rubbed the brush over his chin.

Holy mackerel. He was covered with soap. I was in awe. I had never seen this because of the lack of a father, but the other guys just said they could do the same thing with soap, except they didn't want to because they only put soap on their faces before bed.

"Let's see you shave," Buster said. "That's the hard part."

"I saved one of my father's old blades," Vinnie said. "Dull blades can't hurt as much."

He took it out of the thin blue paper envelope with the words,

Gillette Blue Blade. It was double edged and Vinnie ran his thumb across one edge to see how sharp it was.

"Owww," he said.

"What's wrong?"

"I cut myself. Can't you see I cut myself?"

He grabbed his wrist and held up his right thumb. Blood was oozing out of the open slit.

"I cut my stupid thumb."

"How'd you do that?" asked Buster. "I thought it was dull."

Vinnie squeezed his wrist tighter and leaned against the sink.

"It's still sharp," Vinnie yelled. "It's still a razor blade, you dummy. They're sharp even when they're not."

He held his thumb under the faucet and it looked like he was losing even more blood.

"I hope you don't bleed to death before you shave," I said.

A couple of us found a styptic pencil in the medicine cabinet. They are supposed to stop the bleeding. Vinnie moved his thumb away from the water, dried it with a piece of toilet paper, then we rubbed the pencil on it.

"Owww!" Vinnie shrieked and jumped and I wished that I wouldn't grow up too soon.

He stuck his hand back under the running water to wash away whatever was in the pencil then pulled it out and wrapped a giant wad of toilet paper around his finger.

"That hurts like crazy," said Vinnie. "It's like I got stabbed and you know how much that hurts."

"Come on, are you going to shave, or are you chicken?" asked Joey.

"No, I'm not chicken. I just have to stop bleeding in case I cut myself again because someone my fadder knows died when he lost too much blood."

"I think you're a chicken. I think you're using your finger as an excuse not to shave," said Tommy.

"Oh, yeah?" said Vinnie. "When my fadder was in the Army

he got shot in the arm once but he still kept on fighting. I'm just like him. I can shave with a bleeding finger."

"I thought your father was in the Navy," said Tommy. "You said he was on a battleship."

Vinnie looked in the mirror at Tommy's face.

"He was in the Army after he was in the Navy."

The truth is Vinnie's father had been in the Army, the Navy and the Marines. He had fought at D-Day and in the South Pacific. He had taken a hundred German prisoners and was one of the guys who raised the flag over Iwo Jima.

He was also in the merchant marine on a Liberty ship and his ship was blown up and he was one of only five guys who survived the sharks. That's the truth because Vinnie told us, and when he told us he said it right into our faces with our noses almost touching.

The fact that Vinnie's father looked like an ordinary guy going off to work in the morning with his lunch in his brown paper bag meant nothing. He was hiding his past because he was still on a secret mission, Vinnie said.

The fact that when he passed the bar some of the guys inside said, "Four-F" meant nothing. He did not go into the bar, which we knew meant he was better than the guys in the bar. And he wasn't Four-F, because Vinnie said he wasn't. He used that as part of his disguise.

He wasn't like the guy who lived below Johnny Martin. We knew he had been a frog man in the war because we had seen him once without his shirt on a summer day when he was cleaning the windows in his apartment. He had a row of holes across his back where machine gun bullets had got him.

Vinnie said his father had more bullet holes. He just didn't show them.

"But are you going to shave?" Tommy asked.

Vinnie put the razor to his face.

"Ouch!"

He cut himself on the first stroke. His shaving cream turned pink. He took more toilet paper off the roll and put it to his face, but the paper got soggy from the soap and messy and you can't stop bleeding with soggy paper.

He got more paper and held it against his cheek. When it stopped bleeding he picked up the razor again and took another stroke on his other cheek.

"Darn!" he said.

He cut himself again.

"Owww!"

This owww was louder than the first owww, and now his face looked like wet pink cotton candy.

I think the only reason he didn't stop was because we were there. He put more paper over the soap and blood and held it for a moment. Then with his left hand he held his outstretched index finger across his cheek and put the razor over his finger. Now when he pulled the razor down it didn't actually touch his face.

He rinsed off the soap and started to bleed again from all his cuts. He said it was stinging. He put more paper over his face and then put bandages on his face and thumb, and then he went outside.

"What happened to you?" Vanessa asked.

Vinnie tried to act surprised.

"Oh, you mean this?" He pointed to his face. "It's nothing."

"That must hurt," she said.

"Naah," said Vinnie. "I didn't even notice it. It's just a flesh wound. It's just like being in the Army."

Dying for a Smoke

*M*y mother was lying in bed reading. The smoke from her cigarette rose in a straight line, then about a foot up it broke into a twirl, then a circle, then it flattened out when it got to the ceiling.

She took another drag, held it in for a moment like she always did, then blew it out without taking her eyes off the page.

I knew it was bad to smoke in bed because you might fall asleep and set the bed on fire and burn to death as well as burning down the entire building and killing others and putting people out on the street. But it had not happened yet. Sometimes she put her cigarette in the ashtray that was sitting on the electric blanket next to her. She was always cold, so she used an electric blanket even though I thought it was weird to plug in a blanket.

But mostly I watched the smoke and thought when I started smoking I would pretend that my cigarette was a train with smoke pouring out.

It was better than the straw. We had been pretending to smoke since Miss Johnson read something called Dick and Jane to us. I had no idea of what the story was about, but we saw a drawing on the cover of Dick with a piece of straw in his mouth.

"What's that, Miss Johnson?"

"What's what?"

"That thing sticking out of Dick's mouth?"

Miss Johnson looked at the picture. "Is that the only thing you got out of this book?"

We nodded.

"Why do I bother?" she said.

"Well, what is that thing?"

"Straw," she said. "Just a piece of straw."

We screwed up our faces. "Where do you get straw from?"

She stood in front of the class and shook her head. "It's just straw. You are supposed to be learning about the relationship between friends and you care only about straw? Where did I go wrong?"

We stared back blankly. "You didn't go wrong, Miss Johnson," said Vinnie. "We were just wondering where you get straw, so we can be like him."

"But that's not the important thing," she said.

She put down the book and told us to take out our spelling books and learn the first column of words. Then she sat down behind her desk.

After school we gathered on the corner.

"Straw would be so neat," said Joey. "We could pretend we were smoking."

But we had no idea of how to get straw. We went to the variety store and asked the old man with the few strands of white hair hanging over his head if he had straw for sale.

"Are you kids nuts?" he said. "You don't buy straw. You pick it."

We had no idea where we would pick straw.

We had already been practising smoking with dry ice. In the

summer when we could find a few finger-sized slivers steaming on the ground by the ice cream trucks we would pop them into our mouths and blow out the steam, which looked like smoke.

If you kept your tongue wet the ice would usually not burn a hole through it. But if the piece was too large or you left it too long it would suddenly start burning through the soft flesh and leave you yelling, trying to spit it out and then getting it stuck on your lip which started burning like a hot iron and then it would swell up and you'd have a scar.

So straw would be better. But nowhere we went did they have straw for sale.

We were sitting on the bench at the bus stop on Jamaica Avenue looking at the steel pillars of the El. "Those are kind of like trees," said Jimmy Lee. "If we had straw, we could pretend we were in the woods and we would look like we were country kids."

"Wait," said Johnny. "Don't go away. I'll be right back." He jumped up from the bench and ran home.

We returned to thinking about the picture of Dick with his straw. I put my fingers up in front of my lips and pretended what it would be like to twirl the straw between them.

"What are you doing?" asked Joey.

"Pretending I have straw."

"How can you pretend when you've never had it?"

"I'm pretending I had it, and now I don't have it."

"Hey, don't pretend you're smoking," said Joey. "Tiny's coming."

We all looked down the street and saw Tiny, the huge cop who walked the beat on Jamaica Avenue. He was a giant and he walked from the station house on 117th Street to Van Wyck Expressway. That was about a mile, then he walked back. He was always whistling and swinging his night stick.

"You kids being good?" he said to us.

"Yes, sir," we said.

"No smoking, no drinking, no fighting, no cursing," he said. "You know the rules."

With each rule he pointed his night stick at one of us.

He had once let us feel the night stick – it was as hard as iron, and that was because it had lead in the middle. He gently hit each of us on the rear that night and told us if we ever did anything wrong he would not be so gentle.

"I'm proud of you kids."

Then he went on with his beat.

Johnny was back half a minute later.

"I have straw," he said.

He held out his hand as he got closer and there, for sure, was a bunch of straw. He handed us each one.

"Be careful. One end is dirty," he said.

We looked, and sure enough, one end was dirty, so we put the other end in our mouths. It was wonderful. We already figured out that just by moving our teeth we could make the straw flip up and down. This was just like being in the country.

"Where'd you get the straw?" asked Tommy.

"From my mother's broom," said Johnny. "I heard her say it's a straw broom so I got some scissors and cut off a hunk. I hope she doesn't notice."

We hoped so too because all of a sudden the concrete wall we were leaning against was a tree and the street was a stream and Jane was going to come and sit alongside us and admire our straws.

We all went home that afternoon carefully carrying our straw, and I put mine on the windowsill. The next morning when I got up after my mother had gone to work it was gone. It either fell off and went behind the radiator, or she threw it out.

A week later Tommy opened a pack of Camels.

"How'd you get that?" I asked.

"I told Matty they were for my father. That's why I had to get

Camels, cause that's what my father gets. I really wanted Luckies because LSMFT."

"Lucky Strike Means Fine Tobacco," we both said because the commercials on the radio said that.

We knew our butts. We knew women smoked Chesterfields, like my mother. And we knew the men in the bar usually smoked Pell Mells because they were longer. I remember standing at the door once and seeing a guy while he was still sitting on a stool fall asleep with a Pell Mell between his fingers. I knew it was a Pell Mell because it was long and I watched while it burned closer and closer to his fingers.

I wondered what it would be like when I got into the bar and could only have beer. I felt sorry for those guys because it was more fun to choose among Coke and Pepsi and orange soda and cream soda and Yoo-hoo. Sometimes we would get a Cherry Coke, but you couldn't do that with beer.

And the cigarette burned closer to the guy's hand.

If we were really broke, we could get just a seltzer water for two cents. It was still good. We could sit on the stool and pretend we were in the bar next door and watch Matty stack the packs of cigarettes against the wall in slots. He sold a lot of cigarettes. He would pile them up with his left hand and then poke them into the slots in the wall with the stretched-out fingers of his stiff right hand. He didn't smoke. That was odd. But we could buy a pretend cigarette which was made of white, hard candy with a red tip at one end and then sit with our Coke and make believe we were smoking.

Now I was watching the burning end of the cigarette reach the guy's fingers but he just sat there, slumped over, sound asleep on the stool leaning against the bar with his cigarette hand hanging down. That's impossible, I thought. It must hurt.

Suddenly it was impossible. He jerked awake with a loud, hard-to-imitate sound followed by yelling profanity. Then he swung his hand in the air and grabbed it with his teeth and bit his hand. The other guys just laughed.

"Wow, did you see that?" I asked Tommy. We were standing by the open door of the bar. "That was fun."

Then Tommy opened the Camels and I smelled the sweet smell of tobacco, the same odor that would come from thousands of other packs when they were first opened.

We each took a cigarette and put them between our lips and Tommy lit a match. He cupped it in his hand for me. I felt special because he gave it to me first. I sucked in as the match touched the end and oh my God: the burning, the poisoned gas that came across the ground and fell into the trenches, the ripping of my throat and lungs.

"Cough, cough."

Gag. Yell. "Oww. My chest."

The pain.

"How's that?" asked Tommy.

"Good," I choked. Then I coughed and tried to suck in air. "Good," I repeated.

He lit his own just before the flame on the match reached his fingers. He drew in the smoke and blew it out.

"That was your first, wasn't it?" he said to me.

I nodded. My chest and throat hurt too badly to talk.

"Do it again, and it won't be so bad," he said.

I took another drag and sucked it in and blew it out. He was right. It didn't hurt as bad. It only hurt like a hundred knives instead of a thousand.

Another drag and I was feeling dizzy.

"Keep doing it," said Tommy. "You'll get used to it. Remember, doctors recommend Camels."

He was right. Nine out of ten doctors said Camels were less irritating. In the magazines there was always a picture of a doctor in a white coat smoking Camels.

I took another drag and did not feel as bad. At least I could stand. We finished and flipped the burning butt ends out into the street. I felt like a man.

When I got home, the light in my mother's bedroom was out and I went into the bathroom and brushed my teeth. My mouth was stinking. We had tooth powder which I didn't like using because I thought it was sissy. So I always just brushed my teeth with water, but not tonight. Tonight, powder piled thick on my brush.

Then I went to bed and felt sick.

Forty years later, I took my mother to the hospital to have one of her lungs cut out. After we signed her in, she said she had to go outside to have a cigarette. A few years later I was back at a different hospital, but the same patient.

She was on life-support: a breathing machine, wires, tubes, inserted into her limp body, and each time the machine forced air into what remained of her one remaining lung, her body jerked on the bed.

She was unconscious. They told me she was brain dead. I whispered into her ear and a tear came out of her eye. One of the machines said that her heart rate went up, if only for a moment.

She had left instructions for me and everyone that she was not to be kept alive by machines. I signed the papers and they unplugged her. But she did not die right away. It is something in nature, I suppose, that makes a living creature try to hold on, no matter what. The doctor said it was her brain stem automatically keeping her diaphragm going, but every breath was a gargantuan struggle to pull air into a lung that was useless. She was breathing like a person with acute asthma climbing a mountain. We wished she would die.

She had started smoking when she was a teenager. No one told her it was bad for her health, and even if they had, she would not have listened. Smoking was glamorous. It was beautiful. Exciting men and women did it.

We sat by her bed for four days, four eternally long days after the life-support machine was turned off. Four days of watching every breath sweated and strained over before it was let go, and then the struggle began again.

After that we went though boxes of her old photographs. She was young and happy. She was a person I didn't know because you don't know your mother when she is young. She was smiling and laughing and she had a cigarette in her hand in almost every photo. At the beach she was smoking. At family gatherings she was smoking. Everyone was smoking. She had a cigarette while she was holding her baby.

Everyone was smoking. The few who didn't were oddities. "He probably doesn't drink either." The implication was that he was a wimp.

My mother's burial was beautiful. She wasn't religious and she wanted no service or memorial, but she loved shopping. She did not own much, but she loved going through high-end department stores, looking, touching, comparing. When she found something she deeply wanted, a blouse usually, she would wait and wait until it went on sale. If she missed the sale or if the remaining blouse was the wrong size, she would shrug and let it go. It was a small gamble, and it put some excitement in her life. Before long she would set her eyes on some other potential Kentucky Derby winner on a wire hanger.

After we picked up her ashes my daughter came up with a list of the best department stores in New York. Then her brother and she and I took Grandma to Bonwit Teller and Saks Fifth Avenue and Lord and Taylor. We spread Grandma where she most loved to be. She was secretly put to rest in front of the counters where the blouses were sold. She was spread in the shoe department. Then her grandson went into Tiffany's and while the security guards were looking at him because he is not the type to shop there, his hands were by his sides spreading his grandmother in front of the diamonds.

We took a subway downtown to get something to eat, and when we came up the stairs to the sidewalk we saw a bus passing by. On the side was a big ad with a picture of a glamorous young woman with a cigarette in her hand. The woman looked a lot like my mother when she was younger: same smile, same joy of living, same cigarette, and possibly, same future.

I didn't know any of that when I was buying a pack of Luckies a week after the Camels.

"Who are these for?" Matty asked.

"My mother," I said.

"She smokes Chesterfields."

I held out my quarter. "She wants to switch because LSMFT," I said.

He gave me the cigarettes, took my quarter and gave me my two cents change.

"Make sure you don't smoke them," he said. "They'll kill you."

I left the store, went around the corner and lit a Lucky. Now I was grown up. I no longer needed straw or dry ice, or even someone else to smoke with. I was eleven.

Milk is Good for You, If You Don't Get Caught

"Wanna get some milk?" Buster asked.

Good idea. We had nothing else to do for a half an hour. To get milk we went to the end of our street where the dead end was and the factory that made instruments.

"What kind of instruments do you think they make?" we would ask when we passed by. We always asked that.

"Secret war stuff," someone would say. Someone would always say that. It was a good answer.

Then we climbed the chain-link fence at the end of the dead end. Someone long ago had taken off the barbed wire from one section that was at the top. We jumped down from the top of the fence and climbed up the steep bank that was covered with asphalt, and had some weeds growing out of cracks. I wished that I could show my mother and the doctor that there were weeds here, but I could never let them know what we were doing.

At the top of the hill was a wide flat surface that went on

forever. On it were four train tracks, two going to the city and two away. In the middle, between the tracks was a path wide enough to stand or walk on even if two trains were passing each other at the same time.

Everything was covered with railroad rocks, so thick on the ground and under the wooden ties that you could not get your fingers through them, or even poke a stick very deeply. And every one of the rocks was shaped sort of like a pyramid but with only three sides and about the size of a golf ball which I had never seen back then, and every one of them was dirty and brown, which is the colour they were, dirt brown.

It was just yesterday that a little kid named Lester had one of the railroad rocks. Lester was only about eight so he didn't hang around with us much. We almost never saw him. We knew there was a lot of yelling from his apartment and we felt sorry for the people next door, who happened to be Dorothy and her mother and father and grandfather, because you can't listen to the radio if the people on the other side of the wall are making too much noise.

Sometimes Dorothy's grandfather would pound on the wall, but then there would be louder pounding back from Lester's side. Still, it always quieted down shortly after that, Dorothy said, because she figured the people next door were afraid of her grandfather. He was very tall, with white hair and an accent that made him impossible to understand. But he always got his way, and the wall went quiet after he pounded.

That was when we saw Lester sitting on his front stoop looking at a railroad rock that he was holding.

"What are you looking at?" Tommy asked.

"Nothing," said Lester as he kept on looking.

"Must be something."

"Nope, nothing."

But he kept his eyes on the rock, hardly blinking and then Vinnie came over. Vinnie always seemed friendlier than everyone else. We thought it was because he was Italian and his mother hugged him all the time. His mother hugged everyone. It was nice to ring Vinnie's doorbell to ask if he could come out because if his mother opened the door she would hug you.

"What are you doing with the rock?" asked Vinnie.

"Just pretending," Lester said.

And maybe because we didn't laugh, he quietly told Vinnie and Tommy and me that there were some people, some farmers, living on the side of the mountain.

"You see where those little holes are in the rock?" He was barely whispering. "They live in there."

Then he put the rock in the palm of his hand and said, "The evil king lives at the top and he's taking away all their food."

Vinnie tried hard to see the people. "You're making that up," he said.

"No," Lester looked up in defiance, but he didn't want to sound stupid. "They're really small. And the good guys are down at the bottom of the mountain."

He started talking faster because we guessed he didn't want to sound like he was making it up.

"And they can't climb up the hill fast enough because they haven't eaten for a long time and they're weak."

All three of us were listening and staring at the rock.

"And the bad king's army is just about to take over the farmers' land and throw the good guys out when one of the good guys says he'll save them because he's in love with a girl who lives on the farm," said Lester.

"Then what happened?" asked Tommy.

"The good guy sneaked up the back side of the mountain."

Lester turned the rock around and we all watched as he moved his fingernail slowly up a crevice. "And then he fought off the king's guards and captured the king."

This was like the movies. We just kept looking at the rock.

"Then the king's army had to go back and try to free the king," said Lester. He was talking even faster now. "And that gave the good guys at the bottom time to get to the farms and get some food, and then they attacked the bad guys and threw them off the mountain."

Vinnie's mouth was open. Lester had a big smile.

"And the good guy and the girl got married."

"Did all that really happen?" asked Vinnie.

"Yeah," said Lester, "and then they all went back down to right here." He pointed at the middle of the rock where the holes were, "and had a feast."

A few days later some kids from Rocky's gang came by and saw Lester playing with his rock. We don't know why they walked down our street. Lester couldn't tell us much, but he said they were from Rocky's gang. They surrounded Lester and took his rock away from him and threw it back on the tracks with a million other rocks. Then they went away laughing.

When we heard about it we went to Lester's apartment to make him feel better, but he was outside, sitting on the front stoop. We knew he had been crying, because we could see the stains down through the dirt on his cheeks. We didn't know if that was from losing the rock or from something that just happened inside his apartment.

But he wasn't crying now, and there was a smile on his face when he saw us.

"Those big boys are rotten," we said.

"Doesn't matter," said Lester. "The farmers and the good guys escaped just in time."

He turned over his hand and in it was another rock. It was a railroad rock, just like the first one, but it was no ordinary rock. It had cracks and chips and holes in it, Lester showed us, and he told us if we looked close enough we could see the people living deep in the shadows of the valleys.

"I helped them get out just before those big boys took the other rock. Then I got a new home for them. This one's better."

But that was yesterday. Today we were walking over the rocks going for the milk.

"Whoooo," the trains were big. And fast.

"I hope we don't get killed," said Buster.

I agreed with him, but I didn't want to say anything because I didn't want to sound like I was scared just because we were standing between two passenger trains going in opposite directions each about fifty miles an hour and we didn't have enough room to stretch out our arms.

"They're big," said Tommy.

No kidding. We were shorter than the wheels because we were in a kind of sunken hollow and the trains were giants flying by and there was so much wind we could hardly breathe. I think the breathing problems came not because of the wind but because we were scared silly.

Woosh. Then they were gone. Both at the same time. Suddenly we were standing on an open field that stretched forever this way and that way but not sideways and we were watching the trains going away and we could see over the rooftops of the houses and factories.

"Don't touch the third rail," Joey said. "Mrs. Arnold said she saw a kid get electrocuted when he peed on the third rail. She saw it right from her back window."

Mrs. Arnold lived in one of the apartments facing the tracks. She lived alone and went shopping and talked to everyone and then went inside and came out the next day and went shopping again. But there was something about Mrs. Arnold that you did not argue with. If she said she saw something, she saw it.

The third rail ran alongside the track on the left and was about six or seven inches higher than the rails that the wheels went on. It had a wooden cover over it. Two flaps of steel stuck out from each car on each train and they rubbed along the third rail and the train got its power from it.

But we knew that the electricity only came along about a minute ahead of the train. We knew because we could touch the third rail and nothing happened if no train was coming.

"Go on, try it," said Joey.

I bent over and held my finger over the flat polished metal. It could kill me. But on the other hand I didn't want to be a chicken.

"Go on, chicken."

"I'm not chicken," I said.

"Well then, touch it."

I breathed in and slam. I hit the rail and pulled my fingers away before I could blink.

Ha, ha. They all laughed. If there had been electricity I would not have had a chance to get away.

"I can do it too," said Vinnie.

He put his hand on the rail and held it there. Then Buster did the same.

"That's only because I tried first," I said.

"So?" they said.

Then the pack of Joey, Vinnie, Buster, Johnny and I went off together, walking between the tracks to get milk. Another train went by on an outside track. That was a local and we waved to the people sitting inside. They just stared back.

Other times we put pennies on the tracks and watched them get flattened, but not today. Today was milk.

When we got close to the Sealtest Milk sign with the clock, we left the middle of the high-rise walkway and jumped across the other two tracks and then scrambled down the hill and climbed the fence that went along the hill forever. The barbed wire was gone from this spot too.

The problem now was that we were on 130th Street, Rocky's

Street. But it would be okay, we hoped, because Rocky's usual hangout was up at the other end of the street, near the El. We were two blocks away and were as safe as two blocks of open street could make anyone.

At the end of the street was a tunnel that went under the railroad yard. If it wasn't in Rocky's neighbourhood, we could play there all day. The tunnel was a fantasy land. It was long and dark and when you got inside you could yell and your voice echoed.

Cars came flying through it and there really wasn't any sidewalk, just a little edge, and the cars sometimes went over that and drove on the only place there was to walk. That was scary and exciting. When they came too close we flattened against the wall although that would not really help. It would only mean we would be crushed quicker.

But that never happened and at the other end we came out and walked up to Atlantic Avenue. What a wonderful street. There was nothing on it but factories. And the first factory made Ex-Lax. And it was painted brown.

Tommy pushed Vinnie against the wall.

"Got you, yuck," said Tommy.

"You bum," said Vinnie.

It was the Ex-Lax game. Push someone against the brown wall because you knew what Ex-Lax did to you and the wall looked like what it did.

Then we went on to the milk factory. It was huge. There were tanker trucks moving in and out and steam coming up from the smoke stacks. We had no idea what they used steam for since milk was always cold, but our object was to slip inside and get to the lunch room.

We went in a back door and walked along a catwalk that went between giant shining stainless steel tanks that we knew were filled with milk. We had done this dozens of times and had never been caught. Down below we could see men and women working. They all were wearing white. We were the only dirty ones in the place.

At the end of the catwalk was a metal stairway that we climbed. It ended at the lunch room, a sealed space with windows overlooking the work area. We never got there at lunch so it was always empty. And just inside it was a water fountain, like any water fountain, a faucet sticking out of a stainless steel sink.

But when you turned the spigot, milk came out. There were paper cups in a dispenser on the side, and we each took one and turned the spigot and filled our cups.

"It tastes so good. It tastes better than at home," said Vinnie.

And it did. It wasn't just because we were stealing it that it tasted so good. It did taste better than at home. It was rich and cold and amazing.

We drank five or six or seven cups each, pushing each other away from the fountain and spilling some and then Joey said, "We better go."

That was all the warning we needed. We better go. We crushed the cups and threw them into the garbage can and went down the stairs and along the catwalk and moved quickly because we did not want to get caught with our stomachs full because if they punched us in the gut, they would get the evidence they needed to lock us up.

We got outside and were free. We felt great. We were on a milk high. We had energy and were laughing and pushing each other against the Ex-Lax wall and feeling high.

Then Vinnie saw one of Rocky's gang.

"Look, he's by the tunnel."

We saw a kid we knew even though we didn't know his name. But we did know he was one of Rocky's. He was watching us and then he climbed over the fence around the rail yards that went over the tunnel and disappeared.

"They know we're here," said Vinnie.

We moved together as fast as we could. We went back into the tunnel, but this time there was no shouting to make echoes. We ran through it, rubbing against the wall to avoid the cars and staying together. No one would be left behind.

At the other end we climbed the fence and ran up the hill to the tracks. Once we were there we would be safe. Even if they came after us with bigger numbers than we had, we could outrun them to our street.

We made it and the sense of relief was so good we picked up rocks and threw them back at where we had left. It was like firing rifles into the air, but it felt good.

I found an iron bar and swung it like a baseball bat. The others laughed and I stuck the bar down on the third rail and walked along dragging it.

I didn't know why they did it. Why did my friends take a baseball bat and hit me across the back of my head? Why did these guys who I liked try to kill me? It hurt like nothing had ever hurt in my life. It was not a hurt. It was a brain-crushing bang and I saw blackness and bright lights and then nothing.

"Man, are you still alive?"

I heard that, but I could not answer. I didn't know the answer. I moved my hands and felt the sharp points of the railroad rocks and tried to push myself up but I fell down again. My face hit the rocks, but they didn't hurt this time. Everything else hurt more. My head was still exploding and there were bright lights even though my eyes were open.

"What happened?"

I heard them asking me that, but I did not know what happened.

"You almost killed yourself."

I heard that.

"You okay?"

I nodded, I think, but the rocks rubbed against my face.

"Good, because we can't stay here. If you die, we'd get in trouble."

I knew that. So I couldn't die.

I pushed down with my hands and got up on my feet. I was dizzy. I put my hands to my face and felt the wetness.

"You're bleeding."

I took my hands away and saw they were covered with muddy blood.

"It was that iron bar, you idiot."

Now I remembered. The iron bar. Wow. That was some belt.

"I read in a comic that's how some superheroes get to be strong. Are you strong now?" asked Vinnie.

I had no idea who was talking, but I could barely stand.

"Let me see if you're strong," said Joey.

He grabbed me in a headlock. I was limp.

"You're not super strong," he said. "Those comics lied."

We walked back between the tracks and a train came and I felt the wind on my face. I was so cold and weak I could barely keep up.

We got back to our street and went down the hill and climbed the fence and were standing at the edge of the dead end. Jimmy Lee was with Dorothy and Vanessa. I wished I had been with them.

"Where were you guys?" Jimmy Lee shouted. "I looked everywhere for you."

"We got milk."

Johnny Ride a Pony

"Aww, I was taking care of my brother," said Jimmy Lee. He couldn't get milk with us.

He came out two minutes ago and we weren't there on the street where he thought we would be and instead he had to talk to the girls, which I know he didn't like because he wasn't in love with either of them.

Jimmy Lee didn't get much chance to just go off with us without asking his mother because a lot of the time he had to stay in the house to take care of his brother. His brother could never be alone.

"Want to play Johnny Ride a Pony?" asked Dorothy. She was chewing bubble gum and blowing bubbles.

"What happened to you?" she asked me.

"Nothing. I fell."

How could I tell her that I put an iron bar on the third rail and dragged it until I almost got killed? I wanted to impress her and that was not the way.

"And yeah, I want to play."

If Dorothy wanted to do something, I wanted to do it. And in Johnny Ride a Pony you got to wrap your arms around someone. Maybe, just maybe. You never know.

It was getting dark but I wasn't tired. No sir, not me. If I just used my handkerchief to clean my face I could go on all night if the game lasted that long. My handkerchief was stiff with dried snot and it scraped my face when I used it, but it was working. I could see the blood on the cloth which meant I had less of it on my face.

"You look terrible," said Dorothy. "Let me help you."

She took the hanky and spit on it then rubbed my face. I never wanted to wash again. I was being cleaned by the girl I loved. I had never been so lovingly rubbed before, even if some of her rubbing hurt like crazy.

"Okay, you're clean enough to play," she said.

We chose sides with odds and evens. That was the greatest game, after Rock Paper Scissors, which really was the greatest game, but that took too long. So Tommy and Joey did odd and even.

"Evens," said Joey.

They faced each other, "one, two, three," and each threw out their hands. Joey had two fingers out, Tommy, one.

"I pick Dorothy," said Tommy.

I knew why he did that. He would figure out a way to be in front or behind her, it didn't matter which. Behind and he would hold her, in front, she would hold him. But maybe if Tommy picked me I would end up in front or behind Dorothy, depending on how the lineup was decided.

"I pick Mickey," said Joey.

Darn. The best I could hope for was she would jump on my back and dig her fingers into my armpits and that would probably hurt.

When we finished picking, Joey and Tommy did odd and even again for who would be first. You wanted to be first to jump because the other team might get hurt and not want to play anymore and then your side would win. We had one less player, but they had Vinnie and he was as big as two so it was even.

Tommy won the evens and odds. We would bend over.

We lined up at the corner of the factory and Joey bent over and put his shoulder into the edge of the brick wall. Then he put his hands on the walls and held on.

"You go next, Mickey," he said.

I put my head down along his hip and grabbed him around the waist.

"Then Jimmy Lee," said Joey.

Jimmy Lee latched onto my bent over rear end.

"Don't fart," he said.

"Then Buster."

He got behind Jimmy Lee.

"Your pants stink," I heard him say.

The head guy was the coach. He has to put the weakest player somewhere because they would try to jump hardest on him and break your team and they would win. Buster was smallest, even smaller than Johnny.

"Hey, you want to trade," said Tommy. "We've got two girls. We'll take Buster and you can have Vanessa."

Joey stood up, which knocked me backwards and I knocked Jimmy Lee backwards. "Why'd you do that?" I asked Joey.

"Cause I can't take Vanessa for Buster," he whispered to me. "She's not as strong as Buster, but if I don't take her she'll be sad and I don't want Vanessa to be sad."

I knew what he was thinking. He was thinking that if she was happy she might someday undress again, but if she was sad she might go home and hide under the bed.

"So take both Dorothy and Vanessa and trade Jimmy Lee

and Buster," I said. I said that before I realized how dumb it was because then we would have two girls. But I said it because Dorothy would be on our side and I was dreaming of her wrapping her arms around me instead of Jimmy Lee.

"That's dumb," said Joey.

He looked at Vanessa. He stopped breathing. Something was happening to Joey.

"I'll take Vanessa for Buster."

"Awww, gee," said Buster. "I'm only as good as a girl."

"Okay, get down again," said Joey. "Vanessa, you get in the back where Buster was."

At least he didn't put her second. He was not so dumb as me wanting to get two girls on our team just so one of them would be Dorothy.

"Here I come," said Dorothy. She was the smallest on the other side. She ran up behind us and jumped over Vanessa and put her hands down on Jimmy Lee's back and kept going right over me and wound up on Joey's back.

"Oww," he shouted.

She was a good jumper. Then she wiggled and moved backwards while getting a better grip and her bottom ended up on the back of my head. She wrapped her arms around Joey's body and her legs around mine with her heels digging into my chest. I didn't mind. She blew a big bubble and I heard it pop.

Tommy shouted that he was coming and he was a good jumper too. He wound up flattening himself behind Dorothy, sitting on my backbone.

"Ugh," I muttered.

Dorothy's rear end was still sitting on the back of my head and when she moved she scraped the seam of her dungarees on my ear which was still raw and sore from the rocks by the tracks. Being in love was hard.

Then Johnny who could jump really well flew up and landed on Tommy's back.

"Ugh." Again. That knocked my breath out. My legs sagged.

"Sorry," Johnny said.

"It's okay," said Dorothy.

Why is he saying sorry to her? She's got Tommy between her and him.

Then I knew why. He had landed on Tommy's back and Tommy was on top of Dorothy and Vinnie was coming. And they were all on top of my head but Johnny was worried that Vinnie would hurt Dorothy.

"Here I come," shouted Vinnie.

I braced my legs. Vinnie was big. It was because he ate spaghetti, he said.

He jumped. He landed.

"Owww." "Ugh." "Ahhhh, damn."

"Hey, watch your language," Dorothy shouted to me.

Darn, I thought. I don't want her to get mad at me, but Vinnie was killing me. I had to keep sliding my right foot to keep my balance and once you start doing that you don't have much time left. I could move my head enough to see Jimmy Lee trying to keep his balance too.

Buster shouted that he was coming. There was still a lot of room for him to land. He had all of Vanessa's back, but I didn't think I could last ten more seconds and we had to wait for him to land and then try to knock them off before they said "Johnny Ride a Pony" three times.

Buster jumped and held on at the top. I was biting my lip trying to hold on at the bottom.

"Johnny Ride a Pony, Johnny Ride a Pony, Johnny Ride a Pony," they shouted. We fell.

"We won," they said and we all wound up in a pile.

That game hurt, but it was fun.

Then we switched places.

Me and Jimmy Lee and Vanessa jumped on their backs.

Then we heard Junior shrieking. He had gotten up from the curb where he was watching us and was doing his kind of running across the street toward us.

"No, you're not really going to let Junior play?" Tommy asked.

"Why not?" said Joey. "You have one more than us."

"But we have girls," said Tommy.

"I don't care. I want him to play," said Joey.

That was enough to shut up Tommy. You don't argue with Joey when it comes to Junior. Joey took care of him. But Junior was heavy. He was heavier than everyone else, except Vinnie. And he was solid. He didn't do push-ups or anything but he was all muscle.

But worse than his pounds was that when he grabbed on, he kept grabbing. He swung his legs and his feet and he kept on swinging and grabbing and swinging like he was riding on a bronco in the rodeo, which I had heard of but never saw. And his heels kept banging into whoever was below him and his elbows into whoever was in front of him.

Tommy looked back and gave the warning.

"Junior's coming."

Joey was holding his hand and leading his brother to the butt end of Tommy's pony.

"Fair is fair. You can't help him jump up," said Tommy.

Joey and Junior stopped behind Buster who was at the end of Tommy's team. We all knew Tommy was right. He could not help Junior.

But when it came to Junior, Joey didn't care about right and besides, Junior had no idea of how to jump.

"Now, Junior, jump up."

Junior just stared at the row of butts and sort of laughed and grunted and swung his arms around.

"You gotta jump, Junior," said Joey. "I'm going to help him just a little."

"No," shouted both Johnny and Vanessa. "And hurry up too. This is not fair."

I was on top but I could only hold on for another minute because Vinnie kept moving below me trying to make me fall, and I know Vanessa could only last a minute because I felt her slipping off while she was on top of Johnny who was behind me.

Fifty years later, I remember that moment.

"I'll just hold his hand," said Joey.

And before anyone could complain anymore he took Junior's hand, moved him back two steps and then pulled him toward the pile of bodies – just before Johnny's rear end, he lifted his hand toward the sky and Junior got the idea and jumped, sort of, up and "uffph," he landed on my back and immediately hit me in the head.

They were groaning beneath us, but mostly I could hear Junior's shrieking laugh. He was having so much fun that he swung his hands and feet and punched me in the ribs.

"I quit," said Vanessa.

She fell and their whole side collapsed even before Joey jumped on.

"Oww," said Buster. "My neck."

"What are you complaining about?" asked Joey. "You won."

Then Junior swung out his fist and came back and slugged me in the left cheek. That hurt. But I saw Dorothy on the ground looking at me and I didn't say anything.

"Hey you, you dirty, stinking schweinhunds."

That was the only German word we knew, but none of us were saying it.

"We've come to settle the score."

We knew the voice. It was Rocky's.

I turned around and saw him and more than a dozen of his

gang. They were standing on the other side of the fence down from the railroad tracks.

"What'd you want?" asked Joey. He sounded very much like he wasn't scared at all.

I was.

"You were on our street today. We want to settle scores."

"So what? It's a free country," said Joey.

"You were in our milk factory. You don't want us in your boxes and we don't want you taking our milk."

"It's not your milk."

"It's not your boxes."

We both knew the difference. There was plenty of milk, but only one pile of boxes.

They started climbing the fence. I tried counting. I got to twelve and there were still a few more. I knew there were only ten of us, including Vanessa and Dorothy and Junior, so that was not really ten.

Then we saw them taking things out of their pockets and slipping them over their hands. They were the steel handles they pried off garbage cans that became brass knuckles when you wrapped your fist around them.

"Don't touch my brother," was all Joey said as he walked straight toward them.

"Don't tell us what to do," said Rocky as he jumped down from the fence and went straight at Joey.

The two of them grabbed each other, and Joey pushed Rocky down and the brass knuckles weren't much good as they rolled on the street. Then the others attacked the rest of us. I got hit in the side of my face with a piece of steel and just like I had always heard, I saw stars.

But I got up and grabbed one kid around the neck and kicked him in the shin. I didn't feel any pain in my face.

I saw Vanessa kicking a guy and screaming at him, and Dorothy had one guy backing up as she kept kicking and kicking him. Then some other kid tried to hit her. I saw him winding up behind her.

I stomped on the foot of the guy I had around the neck and I think I broke some bones because I felt something go crunch under my heel. Then I ran over and tried to grab the kid who was going after Dorothy.

I was going to grab him around the neck but suddenly there was another bang in my back and it knocked me to the ground. I rolled over and started kicking at the kid who just punched me into the ground. Kicking while on your back was good. He couldn't get to me. But I saw Dorothy get hit.

"Junior!" yelled Joey. "Leave Junior alone! I told you that."

I heard him yell and looked over. I saw the kid who was trying to hit Junior, who was swinging his arms at the kid.

"He tried to hit me," the kid shouted.

"I said leave him alone."

Joey kneed Rocky in the face as he got up and ran across the street to Junior. He grabbed the kid who was fighting with his brother and slammed him down to the ground. Then he kicked the kid in the ribs.

Two other kids jumped Joey from the back but he grabbed one of them and threw him down and put his knee into the guy's stomach and he screamed. Then Joey spun around and punched the other guy so hard in the chest that he backed up three steps and went down on his bottom.

The sirens were at the far end of the block. Joey grabbed one more kid and pow, punched him square in the nose. He screamed.

I had never seen anyone so strong.

The sirens were halfway down the block and Rocky got up and ran to the fence. He was up and over it before the first police car stopped. His gang was following him, including three who were limping to the fence just as the doors of the police cars were opening. One of the limping kids was the one I had stomped on.

"You kids, stop, or I'll shoot."

Two of them stopped, one pulled himself up to the top of the fence and fell over and he must have got cut by the edges of the top of the wires because he was screaming in pain. He ran to the top of the hill with the tracks and I was surprised, the police never did shoot.

"Alright, what's going on?" said Tiny.

He had gotten out of one of the cars. They must have picked him up on the way to our street.

"Tell me what happened or I'll wallop each of you in the ass."

He pounded his night stick into his hand.

"Tell me, Johnny."

He liked Johnny best because sometimes he would help Johnny's father get home from the bar.

"Don't grow up like your father," he would tell Johnny. "You can do anything you want if you don't spend your time in the bar."

Tiny was our guardian. He even once took us down to the 102nd Precinct and locked us in a cell. It was so scary we all promised him we would never rob a bank or a store or a car or anything. I thought it was strange that he warned us not to rob a car since none of us had ever really been in a car and we had no idea of how to start the motor.

"Those are the kids from 130th Street," Johnny told him. "They didn't like us drinking their milk."

"Whose milk was it?" asked Tiny.

One of the other cops was bringing back the two who did not make it over the fence.

"It was the Sealtest milk," said Johnny. "We went inside and drank it out of their fountain."

"So you were stealing their milk," said Tiny.

"No, we were just drinking it," said Johnny.

The other cop was holding onto both boys with one hand. They looked petrified.

"I found these on the ground," the other cop said, showing Tiny the garbage can handles.

"Whose are those? Those are lethal weapons. You could be charged with attempted murder."

The other two boys pointed at us.

"It was theirs," they said.

"Was not," said Vanessa. "We were playing Johnny Ride a Pony when they came, and me and Dorothy didn't even drink their milk."

"I know," said Tiny. "Put these two punks in the car and we'll deal with them later. You guys go home and get washed up and don't steal any more milk, you hear me, or I'll lock you up along with those two punks."

"Thank you," said Joey.

Junior waved his arms wildly and let out a scream.

"You take good care of him, Joey," said Tiny.

It didn't sound like he was telling him to do that. It sounded like Tiny was telling Joey that he knew he was already doing it.

Then the three cars left and we all sat down on the curb. My head was hurting badly. Can you imagine the police now dealing with that scene? Interrogation, reports, more reports, press releases, enquirers, charges, bans on publication then charges dropped. Tiny knew how to handle kids.

"Maybe we could finish the game now," said Vinnie and we all started laughing.

Real Make-Believe Sex

"I got a French book," said Tommy.

My head jerked. My breathing stopped. You don't have to breathe when you hear someone has a French book. You can breathe later. First you have to find out if it's true.

"Where'd you get it?"

"Found it in my father's fishing box."

I took a breath. It might be true.

"I didn't know your father went fishing."

"He did a long time ago. He even has a picture of a fish taped to the top of the box."

I had no thoughts of fish in my mind.

"Can I see the book?"

Tommy's head nodded like the needle on a sewing machine.

"But it has no pictures," he said.

Suddenly the fish I wasn't thinking about got away.

"What good is it?"

"It has things written in it, like real dirty stuff, like it has the F word and they do it right in the back of a carriage while a horse is pulling them."

I thought that would be bumpy, but I didn't say anything.

"Wanna see it?"

Of course I wanted to see it, but I hated to admit to him that reading was really hard for me. When we were sitting around reading comics I would mostly look at the pictures. I knew "POW" in Superman and Batman, and I knew "WOW" in Donald Duck. But the rest of the words were too hard to read and the pictures told the story so I didn't need to know what they meant.

"Show me and you can read it," I said.

He opened the fishing box and took out a tray with rusty hooks and tangled fishing line made of plastic. Then he lifted some sinkers off a piece of sheet metal that made a false bottom and there, plain as can be, was a thin paperback book with a drawing of a woman with a huge pile of hair curled on her head and a dress pulled down in front so you could see almost her whole bumps.

"They're called tits," whispered Tommy.

"I knew that," I said.

"Shhh, if they catch us down here we're dead."

He sat down on the concrete floor and leaned against the wall.

"How'd you ever find that?" I asked.

"I can smell a naked woman."

"Can not," I said. "How'd you?"

"I wanted to know what my father was doing spending so much time down here, so I hid behind the furnace in the dark and waited for him."

"Weren't you scared?"

"Only when I saw the rat," he said. "But then the light went on and I had to freeze."

I thought Tommy was like a secret agent in the war, hiding in the dark and watching the Nazis make their plans.

"What'd you see?"

"I saw him go to the fishing box and take stuff out and then he got out this book and he stood under the light of the work bench and he read it and then I can't tell you what I saw."

"What'd you see?"

"Can't tell."

"Come on, tell me."

"Can't."

"Can."

Tommy looked away, then said, "I saw him rub himself."

"I thought just kids rubbed themselves," I said.

"No, big people do too. I think because their wives are cooking," said Tommy.

"What'd you do then?"

"Nothin', I didn't do nothin'. If he saw me he would've killed me. Then he finished and put the book back and he went upstairs."

I was jealous. I didn't have a father to learn this from.

"Read the book," I said.

He began: "'I was in need of some extra finances and thought I could supplement my meager purse by engaging in a bit of highway sport.' Madam Toufant was pondering the only solution to her woeful state."

"This is boring. When's the sex stuff come?" I asked.

"I'll skip ahead," said Tommy. "It's got a lot of stuff that comes before the good stuff."

"Did you already read all this?"

"Twice," he said.

He moved ahead half a dozen pages and then read: "We were in the coach moving at a steady trot. I suspected by his glances that my travelling companion would be interested in a transaction, in brief, his gold coins for my pleasure."

"What does all that mean?" I asked.

"It means she's getting ready."

"How do you know that?" I asked.

Tommy looked annoyed. "Just listen."

He read: "We engaged in a brief conversation and then settled on a going rate. I took his coins and put them in my purse and then elevated my dress and he proceeded to plough me. Just at the last moment I told him to remove his manhood and deposit his seeds on my stomach because I did not wish to be inconvenienced by a child."

"That's mean," I said.

"What's mean?"

I knew Tommy was angry because I interrupted him and said something bad about what he was reading. I knew that was wrong because you do not ever say something bad about something that someone is doing for you, like reading, or anything. I learned that from my Uncle John who said to me when someone does something good for you, don't ever say anything bad about it or you will hurt him and he might kill you.

"It's mean that she didn't want a baby. Babies are nice," I said.

"Babies are not nice if you have to have sex for a living because the lady's stomach will get in the way."

He had a point. Tommy was much smarter than me. Mostly he learned this because he could watch his father rub himself and all I could do was watch my mother smoke.

I wanted to ask him a question, but I felt stupid so I didn't. But I thought seeds were little hard things that grew into plants, like Miss Johnson showed us. I knew what came out of my penis, because I had seen it when I rubbed myself, but it was all milky and there were no seeds in it.

I thought I would check again the next time. I usually rubbed myself while my penis was in a sock so my mother wouldn't find any of the stuff. Next time I would look inside the sock before I washed it.

Then we heard walking around above our heads. I could

almost see Tommy's hair stand up on his head. You could really see that if someone was scared more than they've ever been scared.

That was like the time when Johnny had to hide his Party Doll record.

That was a sin, a real sin. It was not like reading Tommy's father's book which you could just get killed for doing. But Party Doll was different. You could go to hell for that.

Buddy Knox had just recorded "Party Doll." It was a cool song. It was number one on the hit parade, but the pope said anyone who listened to it would burn through eternity.

That was because there was one line in it that was sinful, and if we listened to that line it would corrupt us. So we all wanted to hear it.

But every mother said if the pope said it was a sin you can't listen. That applied to the Jewish mothers also who did not want their children going to hell with the Christian kids.

And we were told we could not listen to just part of the song because we might slip and hear the whole thing.

Buddy Knox had come from a town in Texas called Happy. It had only 690 people.

How could anything sinful come from there?

And he formed a band with two other guys and they paid $60 to record the song he wrote. They had no drums so the drummer used a cardboard box which they stuffed some cotton inside to make it sound like a drum.

How could anything sinful come from that?

And they had to record the music at midnight because the traffic in the street outside the recording studio was too noisy to do it in the daytime.

How could anything sinful come from so much dedication?

Buddy's sister sent the record to a music producer in New York who put it on the air and it sold a million copies.

But we couldn't hear it.

So we chipped in together and bought a record. A 45 rpm, which had a fat hole in the middle and one song on each side. And we sneaked into Johnny's basement and put it on a record player and listened. Then came the sinful line right out there in the open where innocent ears could hear them, the unthinkable words about making L-O-V-E.

Holy mackerel, we couldn't believe it. We had sinned, and we were still alive.

"What are you kids listening to?" Johnny's mother asked from the top of the stairs.

"Nothing, nothing, just some cowboy music," we lied. Now we were in deep trouble, lying about sinning.

We ripped the record off the player and Johnny stood on it. By the time his mother got to the bottom of the stairs, Party Doll was grinding into the concrete floor.

"Just make sure you don't do anything bad," said his mother. "Don't turn out like your fathers. And that goes for you too, Mickey, even if you don't have one."

She went back upstairs and Johnny moved. We carefully wiped the cement chips off the vinyl but when we put it back on the record player the needle jumped from the front to the middle then slid off making a terrible unmusical sound.

The pope was right. Sin had cost us the price of a record. And we weren't sure about our future. But we all left that basement feeling very grown up. We had learned the line and knew sin could indeed come from a place called Happy.

Back in Tommy's basement with the dirty book we jumped up and he put the book back and put the sheet metal on top of it and grabbed the sinkers and put those into the box so fast I was afraid he would drop them and his father would hear what we were doing and then kill both of us. As you can see, there was a lot of killing going on. And that would happen before I got the chance to rub myself again while thinking about ploughing, whatever that meant.

Tommy put the top tray in just as we heard the door at the top of the stairs open. He closed the box and slid it back to where it was under a shelf on the work bench and I could see Tommy's father's legs coming down the stairs.

"What are you doing down here?" he asked. His voice was not friendly.

"Just playing," said Tommy.

"What are you playing?"

"Nothing," said Tommy.

"Well, you two get out of here and don't go snooping around. I've got rat traps set everywhere and if you stick your finger in one, it will break your finger right off."

"Yes, sir," I said, and we ran up the stairs and out into the dark early evening.

"See, that's sex," said Tommy. "You got to be careful about it."

"I know about sex," I said. "I saw Vanessa naked that night."

"You did not."

"Did so."

"Not."

"What'd you want to do?"

"Don't know. Want to get a comic and a Coke?"

We came up with fifteen cents and went to Matty's and got a Superman comic and one small Coke. If we had a penny more it could have been a Cherry Coke, but plain was okay. Tommy drank first because he had put in a dime. Then I drank from the other side of the glass. If we both drank from the same side it would be like you were out with a girl. The comic was between us on the counter and this, we both said, was a better story than the woman in the carriage, even if it didn't have sex.

Rock Paper Scissors. Slap

"That hurts."

"It's supposed to hurt."

"Ready?"

I nodded.

"One, two, three."

I threw out rock. Jimmy Lee threw out scissors.

"Ha," I said.

He held out his right hand. The top of his wrist was almost bleeding. The rules were you could not switch hands. He made a fist. I licked the underside of my index finger and middle finger, took his fist in my hand and smacked down as hard as I could on the tender skin with my wet fingers.

"Owww."

You could yell as loud as you wanted, but no flinching. If you flinched you got hit again.

"Ready?"

He nodded.

Rock Paper Scissors was not just a way of deciding who went first, it was the game that kept us going when we needed an instant game because there was no one else around or no balls to throw or no comics to read.

"One, two, three."

He threw out scissors again and I was standing there with paper, a flat hand and a stupid move. I should have known he was going to repeat what he did last. He always repeated it, but I forgot.

He laughed. I held out my wrist. It was in worse shape than his. The blood was running over my wrist bone and dripping on the street.

"You want to quit?" he asked.

"Not until you do."

He licked his fingers and smack. The pain went up to my eyebrows. I almost felt myself flinch, but not quite. I looked at him and my breath was short. Would he call me for that or not?

He looked into my eyes.

"Ready?"

He didn't call me. Sometimes you can tell a real friend.

"Wanna quit?" he asked.

That was not the question of do you want to quit because you've had enough but do you want to call it a night. We had our fun. Let's do something else.

"Yeah, I guess so," I said.

"Tommy said you have some gin."

I had found a bottle in the bottom of the closet, behind the broom.

"So?"

"Tommy said maybe we could have some."

I was angry.

"Tommy's not going to tell me who I am going to give gin to."

Jimmy Lee stepped back. "I wasn't saying he was saying you

would give it away. I was just saying maybe sometime Tommy says we could see what it tastes like."

"Maybe, I'll let you know. I'm going home now."

I ate my hot dogs and watched my mother drink her tea and I had my milk and she went to bed with her cigarette and her book and I went to the closet and pulled back the broom.

It looked like water and it was three quarters full. I had told Tommy I knew about gin because he said his father drank it every night and I didn't want to sound like I didn't know what gin was, so I told him my mother has gin too, and then I said it tastes pretty good.

That was when he said he knew how it tasted and maybe we could taste some of my mother's, and I said maybe. But that was all I said. Now Jimmy Lee thinks that he can have some.

I went to bed thinking about the gin. It looks like water, I was thinking, when I fell asleep. At least I know I fell asleep because I saw the train going by and everyone in the windows of every car was drinking gin in glasses that I could see and I watched them and I thought it looked like water.

The next day after school I saw Tommy and told him he shouldn't say I was giving away gin.

"Didn't say that. I didn't say it," he said.

"Jimmy Lee said you did. And you said he could have some."

"Didn't," he said.

"But if you have some, could we taste it so I can tell you if it is different than what my father drinks?" said Tommy.

I don't know how I let him talk me into it. I knew it was wrong. But I hated to say no to Tommy because he was what I wanted to be. He had a father who did not go to the bar.

"Alright, you can have some, but just a little because my mother knows how much is in the bottle."

I was just saying that when Jimmy Lee and Johnny and Vinnie and Buster were coming down the street.

"Want some gin?" asked Tommy.

"Don't," I said, but it was too late.

"My fadder drinks gin," said Vinnie.

"I thought your father drinks wine," said Johnny.

"He does, but he also drinks gin. He loves gin."

We came to a stop in front of my place, and I let them in the door.

"Shhhh, Mrs. Kreuscher is upstairs."

Mrs. Kreuscher was the landlady and sometimes I could hear her at the top of the stairs and sometimes she would call down to me not to smoke because I might burn down the building.

I almost never saw Mr. Kreuscher, but one time when I was hunting around the cellar I found that typewriter of Mr. Kreuscher's that I knew was old. I could see the letter J was yellow. I knew that was from the nicotine on his finger. But what I found in a box under the typewriter was a lot more impressive.

I opened the lid and there was nothing in it. So I started to close it but then I thought it was strange that there was nothing in the box because there is always something in a box, otherwise why did you have a box?

So I opened it again and put my hand in. There, I knew there was something in there. It was hard and cold under my fingers and almost round but I could not see it. I slid my hand down to the bottom.

I know what this is, I thought.

I put my fingertips under the edge at the bottom and lifted out a very heavy steel Army helmet. It was so heavy. How could they wear this on their heads?

It was from World War I. I knew that because of the shape and the rim around the edge at the bottom.

Then I saw a gouge along the side. I put my finger in it. That was a bullet that did that. I put the helmet on my head and it was even heavier than when I was holding it. I put my finger in the gouge. If the strap went down here under my chin then the gouge would have started right in the front of the helmet. That means it probably would have gone right past the front of his head and when it hit the helmet it would have smashed the steel into his skull.

I was scared just pretending it happened to me, and I was in the cellar all alone with no one shooting at me.

But now I wasn't alone. And now we didn't have the enemy, we had the landlady.

"Shhh," I said again. "Mr. Kreuscher may be sleeping."

They tiptoed to the end of the hallway and I opened our door with another key. Once we were inside, Tommy took out a pack of Camels.

"Anyone want a smoke?"

We all lit up. It was so grown up. We puffed and inhaled and blew smoke rings.

"Where's the gin?" asked Tommy.

I opened the closet door and reached behind the broom and took out the bottle.

"I drink mine with water," said Tommy.

"Me too," said Vinnie.

I opened the bottle and poured a little into a couple of glasses.

"I could drink some more," said Tommy.

"No way, my mother would notice it gone."

I put some water from the tap into the glasses and handed them to Tommy and Vinnie.

"Got some ice?" asked Tommy.

"Sure, of course, I always use ice," I said.

I opened the refrigerator and pulled open the freezer

compartment door, taking out an ice tray. It was frozen over the top. I pulled a handle and the ice cracked and I took out a few cubes and put them into the glasses. They clanked.

"I like that sound," said Tommy.

He took a glass and sipped it then handed it to me. I took a sip. Ugh. It was awful and I felt a tingle in my lips and a burning in my throat.

"That's good," I said, but I wasn't able to say it clearly. I was trying to cover up the bad taste that was holding my tongue.

"Give me some," said Vinnie.

I handed him the other glass. He drank and spit it back into the glass.

"Yuck," said Vinnie.

"Come on, that's gross. Now you have to drink it all," said Tommy.

Vinnie looked terrified. "I can't drink that. It tastes like poison. It tastes like the time you pissed in my orange soda."

"We didn't piss in your orange soda," said Johnny.

But Johnny didn't know that we did. We were playing cards in Johnny's cellar and peed in Vinnie's soda when he was outside in the lane to do the same. Johnny was upstairs checking on his father. When Vinnie came back and took a drink, he spit it out all over the cards.

"I'm going to kill you guys," he said.

But we laughed and after Vinnie washed his mouth out with some Coke he laughed too, but I remember that he didn't really look like he was laughing. He looked more like he wanted to kill someone.

Then Johnny came back down and wanted to know how the cards got so wet and we told him we peed in Vinnie's soda and he drank it. But Vinnie said that was not so, that he just spilled the soda.

We dried off the cards next to the furnace and tried to play again, but this time the cards all stuck to each other so we went outside and sat on the stoop and talked about what we would do if there was another war.

"If I get drafted I'm never taking off my helmet," I said.

"You can't sleep in your helmet," said Buster.

"Yes I can, because a helmet can save your life."

"Can not, a bullet will go right through it," said Vinnie.

"How do you know?" asked Tommy.

"Cause my father was at D-Day. He drove a landing craft and he said he saw hundreds of guys get killed as soon as they ran off his boat. And some of them got shot right through the helmet."

"He didn't say that," said Tommy.

"Did so. I know what my father said."

"You're making that up just to make us scared," said Tommy.

"I don't care what you say, I'm still going to sleep in my helmet," I said. "I saw Mr. Kreuscher's helmet and it saved his life."

"Kreuscher's a German name," said Tommy. "Maybe he's a Krout who stole the helmet."

That's when I got mad. Mr. Kreuscher was a nice man with no accent and he sometimes told my mother that it was okay for her to wait another week to pay the rent.

"Don't say that or I'll punch you."

That was the end of the talk about war for that night. Now we were in my kitchen telling Vinnie he had to drink his gin.

"Can't do it," he said.

"Okay, I'll drink it," I said.

I took a swallow and almost gagged. Then I forced another gulp down because I didn't want anyone to think I couldn't.

I watched Tommy take another drink and I had another one. And I started to feel funny.

"Who else wants a drink?" I asked.

I poured some more gin into my glass and put some water and

ice in and Jimmy Lee took a sip, but it was only a small one. Then I took another. Tommy finished his glass and wanted another. I poured some more in.

I started laughing and Tommy was laughing and I think everyone was laughing and we lit up more Camels and I held the smoke in my chest for a long time. I had never done that before. Then we finished the cigarettes and the bottle was half empty.

"I know how to fix that," said Tommy. "Put water in it. It looks the same."

So I held the top of the bottle under the tap and that was hard because I couldn't hold the bottle still. But I got some water into it and screwed the cap back on and put it back behind the broom, but I had a hard time getting it down on the floor without knocking it over and then I couldn't get the broom to stay in front of it. I kept laughing when the broom fell over.

Finally the bottle was behind the broom and that was funny. And we all went outside and I heard Mrs. Kreuscher close her door as we staggered through the hallway. Tommy kept banging into the walls. I wanted to tell him to be quiet, but I kept laughing.

A few hours later when my mother came home from work she said, "I'm having your aunt and uncle for dinner Saturday." Then she looked at my face. "Are you sick? You look sick. You should go to bed."

I thought I was going to die.

Christmas Eve

Miss Flag made us sing "Rudolph." We had stopped singing "Old Black Joe" in the fall and now it was winter and we were singing about a reindeer. She played the piano in the auditorium and we sang, "You'll go down in hist-or-ree."

"It's almost Christmas, children, and you know what that means."

It was the only time she was not scolding us.

I knew what Christmas meant – time to make Manhattans. I was getting good at it. Three parts rye and one part sweet vermouth, with a dash of bitters.

Christmas was a happy time. Everywhere there were pictures of Santa going down the chimney with a carton of Camels sticking out of his pack. And the night before, my mother and I picked out a tree from the man who had them leaning up against the wall of the bar under the El. There were only five trees left and none of them came up to my shoulder.

"Are they on sale yet?" my mother shouted.

It was dark. It was cold. A train was going overhead. The bar was crowded, because it was Christmas Eve and that was a good place to celebrate, and the man with the trees was shivering. He had been there all day. He pulled his knitted Navy surplus hat down over his ears and blew out steam.

"A dollar fifty," he said. He didn't shout. The train had passed.

"Are they going to go any cheaper later?" my mother asked.

He shook his head. "Then I might as well throw them out," he said.

"But you can't sell them tomorrow."

I knew my mother made fifty dollars a week. I had once seen her paycheque.

"It's Christmas Eve, you have to put them on sale," she said.

"You want it, you buy it," the man said. "The sale comes tomorrow."

"But no one will buy them tomorrow."

He dropped a scrawny tree on the ground. "You think I care? I got my own problems."

I wanted to say something but that would have gotten them both mad at me, and besides, this was just the way Christmas trees were sold. You get mad.

"Okay, a dollar," he said and smiled. "Now pick one and get out of here."

I took the biggest one and my mother dug through her pocketbook for the money.

"Is that the one you want?" my mother asked me.

I nodded. "It's the best one."

"We can carry it together," she said.

She took the heavy end, which wasn't very heavy, and I held the other as we walked down the block with her in front. I looked back, and under the street light, I saw the steam coming out of the Christmas tree man's mouth.

"I bet we could get it cheaper later," I said to the back of my mother's head, but she shook her head and when the street got quiet between the trains I could hear her sniffling, which meant she was crying.

We passed the other homes and I could see trees with lights in most of them. There were no other decorations.

When we got inside our apartment my mother said she wasn't feeling well and had to lie down. I got out the tree stand from the corner of the cellar where we could store some of our stuff, and got the lights from the shoebox that was next to the stand and put the tree up and the lights on and plugged them in.

Nothing. There were two extra bulbs in the box. If one bulb was out they all would be out. So I unscrewed the first bulb and replaced it with one of the extras. Nothing. Then I unscrewed the replacement and put the original back. Then unscrewed the second and replaced it with the replacement. Nothing.

I could see the lights on the tree across the street. And then it was snowing. Christmas Eve and snow and we had a tree which really smelled like a tree and tomorrow Manhattans.

"Come on, bulb. Be the right one."

I wanted to get this done so I could put the red glass balls on the branches and then the tinsel and then wrap my mother's present and get to bed so Christmas would come and the family would come and I could go out in the street and find out what everyone got and then mix drinks.

Woops, I forgot Jesus. There was the crèche and the baby and Mary and Joseph. I had to put those under the tree. I felt bad for Joseph. He never got sex.

The next light lit and bingo, instantly the whole string lit up and I was so happy I dropped the bad bulb back into the box with the other spare. Darn. I'll wait 'til next time to figure out which one it is.

I put the tree in the stand. It weighed almost nothing. My mother did not have to help carry it. Then I screwed in the screws and it was straight enough to stand by itself. I wrapped the lights around it and it looked so good.

The red balls were in another box, but when I opened them half of them were broken. They were just thin glass and sometime during the year someone must have moved something. But I still had four good ones. And there was leftover tinsel from last year which I took off the tree before we threw it out.

And finally, the manger with Jesus and Mary and Joseph. They were wrapped in toilet paper and put in a tiny box all by themselves. They were made of plaster and painted and sold by the tens of thousands in the five and ten cent store, but once you got them home they were sacred. I saved the toilet paper. Once something touches something that is close to God you can't throw it out.

There was also some shredded plastic that looked like straw which the baby Jesus was supposed to lay in because that's the way it happened in the first Christmas. I put them out under the tree and I could feel the meaning of Christmas. It was almost like being in church, except this was better because I didn't have to pray and drink the grape juice that was supposed to be wine that they gave us during communion.

I liked going to the Catholic church with Vinnie and his family because then you would go to the altar and kneel down and get real wine. It was just a sip, but it wasn't bad. It didn't taste like blood to me and I liked the tingle on my tongue.

But in the Protestant church you stayed in your seat and they passed around trays with little shot glasses filled with grape juice. I figured they must really worry that we would get tipsy on one sip, and if they thought that, then they didn't know anything about anything, not God and not people.

Anyway, I put out Jesus and his mom and pop. When I was smaller I couldn't figure out why Joseph was there at all because God had snuggled up with his wife. But now that I knew about sex I just felt sorry for old Joe.

Now a present. What can I get for my mother?

I looked through the drawer in my dresser where I kept my good stuff: a rubber snake, an ashtray that I stole from the variety store on the corner. That was from a bet that we could steal something and I ran by and grabbed it. Fifty years later I would remember that and feel bad because the poor guy selling it got hurt.

I thought of giving it to my mother for Christmas, but no. You can't put something you stole under the tree. That must be a sin.

And then I found a scarf that Dorothy had given me when it was cold and she took it off her neck and said it would keep me warm. I didn't want to give it away, but it was a girl's scarf because it was from a girl and ladies liked girl things. It was made of wool and it was green and red and I guess I should have given it back to Dorothy but I forgot.

I got some Christmas paper from the closet and folded the scarf and wrapped the paper around it. I taped it closed, tore off a piece of paper and wrote, "To Mom, Love, Santa," on it and put it under the tree and then I looked in the refrigerator.

There was peanut butter and Wonder Bread, which helped build bodies eight ways. I didn't understand that, but I smeared a glob of Skippy on the bread and had a glass of milk and went to bed.

I forgot to brush my teeth. I tried to scrape the peanut butter off with my tongue but I didn't get very far before I fell asleep with visions of Manhattans dancing in my head. Of course they weren't dancing. I was just thinking of how to make the best Manhattan ever.

Then I thought of Rudolph and wondered why the other reindeer didn't like him.

In the morning it was Christmas.

The Day After Christmas Eve

"Wake up, Mickey, it's Christmas morning."

My mother was standing at the door of my room wearing a bathrobe and holding a cup of coffee and smoking a cigarette. I didn't often see her in the morning because she was gone to work before I got up.

"Let's see if Santa brought anything." She seemed excited.

I followed her to the living room and she had plugged in the tree and the lights were on.

"Look, Santa must have come. And the tree looks very nice."

There was a small pile of presents on one side and my one little package on the other.

"Well, open one," she said.

I was dying to pee, but I didn't want to disappoint her. I sat down on the floor and opened the first package. I knew it was a book; I hoped it would have pictures.

"Gee, thanks," I said.

It was a birdwatching book, filled with pictures. I skimmed through it. Lots of birds. Later I would look for pigeons.

"And I see Santa left something for me," she said.

She opened the package.

"Oh, how nice, a scarf. But you know I don't like green."

I wanted to ask for it back, but I thought you can't do that with a Christmas present. Then I thought I might swipe it from my mother's dresser in a week or so, and give it back to Dorothy, but my mother might see her wearing it and think she broke into our home. Christmas was a difficult time.

"I have to go to the bathroom," I said. "Then I'll open the other one."

"Hurry," she said and she took a long drag on her cigarette, blowing the smoke up to the ceiling.

I could just smell it as I hit the bathroom. I went. I flushed. I waited for the toilet tank to fill up. It didn't. It kept running. I took the top off the tank and saw the chain was wrapped around the stopper that went into the hole that the water went out of.

I unwrapped the chain, put the tank top back and listened for the hissing of the filling to get lower. It did.

I went back to the tree and Santa and the cigarette, which by now I was wishing I had one because every time I saw Santa with the Camels, I wanted a smoke.

"See what else Santa left for you," said my mother.

I saw one box, wrapped in Christmas paper. I picked it up.

"What the heck is this?" I asked. "It's heavy."

"I'll tell you it's heavy. I had to carry it home on the subway and it almost pulled my arm out of its socket. But I did it for you."

I opened it. That is what you do with a Christmas box that almost pulls the arm out of the socket of Mrs. Claus. You unwrap it. It had pictures of a man with muscles and dumbbells on the box.

"Well?"

My mother was excited.

"What is it?" I asked.

"What do you think?" she said. "It's heavy and it's small, so what do you think it is?"

I was looking at a picture on the box of a man flexing his biceps. He had no shirt. Above it were the words: Weider's Barbells, with the word "Barbells" slashed out with a broad black line of ink and below it "Dumbbells" was written in.

"Gee, thanks," I said.

But inside myself I was the most excited guy in the world. I was looking at a picture of Joe Weider who I had seen on the back of comics with his shirt off, flexing his arms and chest and saying, "You too could have arms of steel in only six weeks."

Joe had arms of steel. They looked greasy, but I thought that was the way you looked when you had arms of steel. He had biceps that looked like boulders under his skin. That's what I wanted. In six weeks I could have that.

"Thank you."

The words came out extra strong, I thought.

"I hope you like them. I had to carry them home myself with no help," said my mother. "They were very heavy. I didn't think I would make it."

"Thank you."

"I had to put the box down several times. Some man asked me if I needed help. I wish I could have said yes. He looked big and strong."

"Thank you."

"I thought of all the things you wanted and I thought you would like this but I didn't think it would be so heavy to carry."

"Thank you."

I opened the box and put my fingers around one beautiful

piece of iron with bulges at each end. It was cold and smooth. I lifted it up and held it over my head.

"Do you like it?"

"Thank you. Thank you. It's what I always wanted."

"But do you really like it?"

I took the other one out of the box and lifted it and held both of them up.

"Thank you."

"Don't drop them."

I lowered them and looked at them. Each had a number 5 engraved in one end. Five pounds. That's ten pounds together which means I would have arms like ten pounds of steel in six weeks.

"Thank you."

"Do you really like them?"

I had a dumbbell in each hand.

"Yes, and can I go out now? I want to show the other kids."

She took another drag and blew the smoke into the tree. I thought it looked like a real forest with mist rising through the branches, except I had never seen mist rising in braches. But I figured that was what it looked like and so the tree in the living room looked real, and I wanted to take a drag so I could blow smoke and make it look more real. That was a good reason for smoking.

Then she smiled. Good, she wants me to go out.

"I'm glad you like them. They were very heavy to carry."

I looked down at the box with Joe Weider on the front flexing muscles bigger than I could hope for, but they would be mine in six short weeks.

"Don't you want breakfast?" she asked.

"No, later," I shouted as I ran to the door. I tried to grab the doorknob, but my hand was around the bar between the bulges and the five pounds of steel slammed into the wood, bang.

"Careful," she shouted. "If you break something with them, I'll take them back and they are very heavy for me to carry. So be careful."

"I will."

But I still could not get my outstretched fingers around the knob and I was turning my hand and arm and the steel was scraping over the door.

"What's going on down there?"

I could hear Mrs. Kreuscher shouting from upstairs.

"Nothing," I shouted back through the door. "I'm just trying to open the door."

"Is it stuck?"

"No," I shouted louder. "I'll get it."

"I'll send Mr. Kreuscher down to help."

"Noooo."

I didn't want an old man to help me open a door when I was about to have arms of steel that could break anything I wanted.

"Noooooo."

I heard him coming down the stairs. I put one dumbbell down on the floor and opened the door, bent down and picked the dumbbell up, grabbed the door with my foot and tried to close it as I stepped out of the doorway. But I wasn't quick enough – the door hit me in my arm and hit the steel again. Bang.

"Careful there, son," said Mr. Kreuscher.

He looked at the dumbbells, and started to say, "You will get mighty strong with . . . "

But then my mother shouted again.

"One more time and I'm taking them back, and I'll just have to carry them all by myself."

I put one down again and closed the door.

"Can I feel that?" Mr. Kreuscher asked.

Give up my dumbbell before I even had a chance to get

strong? My lifeline to my future and he wanted to try it before I had a chance to lift it and flex my muscles?

"Okay," I said.

He cradled it in his yellow-stained fingers, then raised it up to his shoulder.

"This is called 'curling,' you know. It makes your biceps strong."

I nodded in total amazement. He knows? He knows the secrets of getting strong?

"I used to use these every morning. I had arms of steel," he said.

I just stared at this skinny old man with sunken cheeks. He knows.

"And you can also put them behind your head and lift them backwards. That builds the triceps."

He put his fingers around the back of my arm searching for muscle. He found only bone.

"Good luck with them, Mickey," he said as he handed my future back to me.

I walked quickly down the hallway, but this time I put one of the weights down before I opened the door, then I picked it up and stepped outside and put it down again and grabbed the handle. I stuck my head inside the door. Mr. Kreuscher was watching me.

"Thanks," I said. He was better than Joe Weider. I didn't have to send him ten cents for the secret.

Outside the kids were already gathering. I saw Dorothy talking to Tommy. Someday, I thought, I will hammer Tommy right across the street and she will be in love with me. And there was Joey coming out of the house with Junior following behind him.

"Whatjuget? Whatjuget?"

"I got a basketball," said Joey.

"What are we going to do with the old one?" Tommy asked.

"This is a good one. This one is rubber so you can grab it."

"I got jacks and a book of romance stories," said Dorothy.

"What's jacks?" I asked.

"Don't you know nothing?" she asked, and suddenly I wished more than anything in the world, including more than having arms of steel, that I had not opened my mouth.

She held out a small rubber ball and some little pieces of metal things.

"You drop those on the ground," she said as she bent over and dropped half a dozen of them, "and then you bounce the ball and try to grab as many of them as you can before you catch the ball."

"Oh, yeah, I knew that," I said. "I just forgot."

"It's a girl's game," said Dorothy. "It's because we're very quick."

"What's those?" asked Tommy.

"My dumbbells. That's for guys," I said, then I saw Dorothy's face with a look that was not loving and sweet and I wished more than arms of steel I had kept my mouth closed again.

"Let me try," said Joey.

This time I did not mind. This time I wanted them to try because they would know that in six weeks I would have arms of steel and then they would know who would back down to no one.

Joey took them both.

"They're not so heavy, I can lift them."

"They're not supposed to be so heavy. They're supposed to be just this size and when you use them, when you curl with them, your arms will get stronger than steel."

"Let me try," said Tommy.

He took them and started lifting them over his head. "I could do this a hundred times," he said.

"Yeah, but do you know how to curl?" I asked. I was getting angry. They were taking away my strength.

"Yeah, I know how to curl," said Tommy. "But I don't want to do it right now."

"Give me them," I said. "I'll show you how to curl. That makes your biceps big." I saw that Dorothy was watching.

I started to move them like Mr. Kreuscher had done.

"Feel my muscle in the front."

I wanted Dorothy to do it but Tommy felt it.

"Mine's bigger," he said. "Feel this," he said to Dorothy.

She put her hand over his arm and even with a coat keeping them apart I was dying.

"Feel mine," I said.

She looked at me then, and I could see that it was almost out of pity that she touched me.

"Whose is bigger?" asked Tommy.

Dorothy looked at me, then him. "Tommy's is bigger."

I died.

"But Mickey's is harder."

Heaven and earth opened up. The angels sang. I heard them. I really heard them. I know it says in comic books that the angels sing when something good happens or when someone dies and no one can see them, unless you were reading the comic, but I saw them. Dorothy said I was harder. I moved those dumbbells up and down and up and down until it felt like my biceps were going to snap. In six weeks, six short weeks, I would pick her up in my arms of steel.

"I gotta go back," said Joey. "My mother's making breakfast and Junior and me gotta eat."

Junior was skipping around on the other side of the street.

"He got a teddy bear," said Joey. "Let's see your teddy bear, Junior," he shouted.

Junior kept jumping around. He was not going to show off his present.

I went back in after watching Dorothy walk down the street to her front door.

"We'll let Mickey make the drinks," my mother said.

My mother bought a canned ham. My uncle brought the rye and the vermouth. Family gatherings happened once or twice a year, and the only difference was each time I made better Manhattans.

"You make them very good," said my Aunt Betty, who was old and who lived with her father who was also my mother's father. It seemed always one sister in each family would have to take care of the very old mother or father and never get married.

But she did like my Manhattans.

"I need some cloves for the ham," said my mother.

I knew cloves were some tiny, dirty sticks that you stuck in the ham after you got the can open and the gelatin washed off. The can opening part was the hardest because the key that was attached to the bottom of the can would break by the second turn as you tried to unwind a metal strip around the can.

"Darn," said my uncle when the key broke. He was a Mason and never used profanity.

He took his cigarette out of his mouth and put it in an ashtray next to the sink.

"Where are your pliers?" he asked my mother.

She looked at him like he was using profanity. "Pliers?"

He did not bother saying they were the pliers he had left last Christmas after he brought them in case the key broke. He went through the kitchen drawers until he found them and then slowly peeled back the metal until my mother could squeeze a fork in between the edge of the meat and pry out the ham.

"Is it time for a drink?" he asked.

Except for me, my mother was alone with my uncle. She looked at him with eyes that said something. I knew what they said, but he was my uncle so I could not say it.

"Let Mickey make the drinks," said my mother.

I was as happy as a pigeon who had just found someone giving away a loaf of Wonder Bread.

My uncle took two bottles out of a brown paper bag. One, Canadian Club rye, the other Rossini's sweet vermouth.

I could barely read the labels, but I knew what to do. I got the large cocktail mixer out of the closet and poured half the bottle of Canadian Club into it, then I opened the vermouth and poured a quarter of the bottle into the mixer container.

I added some bitters from the small bottle with a dried, crinkled label wrapped around it, stirred the mixture with the cocktail stirring spoon my mother kept with the shaker and lifted out a spoonful.

"First today," said my uncle as he watched me.

I smiled at him. It was like I was a real man. Into my mouth went the liquid.

"Tell me when you have it ready," he said and went into the other room.

Oh, it burned, oh, it was good. It was cold and it burned. It was good when it got past my throat.

"How is it?" my mother asked.

I tried to talk, but choked. My mother and aunt laughed.

"Needs more bitters," I said.

I opened the bottle again and shook out a few more drops. I could not count them, they came out too fast.

Then I tilted the container and tasted it right from the cocktail shaker.

It burned even better.

"I'm getting there," I said.

I put in two more drops and tasted it again. So smooth, so rich.

"Needs more rye," I said.

I tilted the bottle and poured in a couple of swigs and tasted it again. I was starting to feel very happy.

"A little more rye," I added.

Another taste.

"Better get out the ice before Mickey finishes it," said my mother.

"One more taste," I said.

I took three.

"I think it's ready," I think I said.

The rest of the night went by slowly and fast. I remember sneaking a few more Manhattans into my glass when I finished my Coke. Then I think I had a few more. I tried to lift the weights to show my uncle but they were hard to hold straight over my head and I remember him taking them from my hands.

Then came morning.

The Strongest Men on Earth

I loved the mornings after my mother had company. The ashtrays were full and many of the butts were long enough to light again, plus I had my pick of five brands. I didn't like the ones with lipstick. I sat by the tree smoking and not feeling well. I blew smoke up into the tree but it did not have the same look as the morning before.

Then I looked at the dumbbells and almost got excited. I picked up the box and looked at Joe. In six weeks I would be like him, and Tommy better look out. Rocky too.

The doorbell rang and I stuffed out the cigarette into the overflowing ashtray. I didn't want to get caught smoking in case it was some grown-up at the door. They might tell my mother and she would be mad and then I would have to listen to her tell me how bad smoking is and promise not to do what she did but to do what she said. And my head was hurting.

I opened the door and Vinnie and Tommy and Joey and Jimmy Lee were there.

"You've been smoking in the house?" said Joey.

"How'd you know?"

"Because it's still coming out of your mouth."

I shut my lips.

"Gee, you're lucky," said Tommy. "You don't have a father. I have a father and I can't smoke in the house. If he caught me he'd kill me. But you only have a mother. I bet she doesn't even hit you."

Then a voice came from the top of the stairs.

"Would you please close the door? The heat is going out."

Mrs. Kreuscher.

But I could not let it look like I was being told what to do by a woman, especially one who was the landlord.

"I'll close it in a minute," I shouted.

"Please," she shouted.

"In a minute."

"I'm sending Mr. Kreuscher down."

I pushed the boys back and stepped outside.

"You don't want to fight with him," I said. "He used to be a weightlifter."

I closed the door behind me and felt the cold air go through my shirt.

"Darn, it's cold out here," I said.

"We know how to get strong," said Joey. "We figured out who the strongest men are around here."

I was thinking of Joe Weider.

"The garbage men," said Vinnie. "They can lift hundred-pound cans with one hand. If we were garbage men we could do the same."

I knew the cans weren't a hundred pounds because my mother had weighed herself at the drugstore with one of those scales that you stand on and put a penny in.

"This can't be right," she said. "I'm not 110," she said. "I was never more than a hundred pounds."

I could not imagine the garbage men picking her up over their heads with one hand even if she left ten pounds on the ground. But still, they were strong.

We were off from school for the rest of the week for Christmas vacation and we worked out a plan. We would have the strength of garbage men, then no one could touch us.

The next morning we waited. The truck came around the corner. We stood by the first can at the end of the street.

"We wanna be garbage men, like you," we said. But a train was going by overhead.

"Wad you say?" said the first guy who had a big coat over his vest. But they were all open. Underneath was a huge body that did not jiggle when he moved.

"We wanna be garbage men," shouted Vinnie, but by then the train had passed.

"Why you shouting?" said the man with the open coat.

"We wanna be garbage men," said Joey, who always looked like he was the one people would listen to.

"We want to do your job so we can be as strong as you," said Joey.

"You gotta be kiddin," said the other man who had a cigar squeezed between his teeth. "Youse couldn't lift dese cans."

"And besides," said the one with the open coat, "you don't got no Teamsters' cards."

They were proud members of the union. The Teamsters controlled the waterfront, the airport, the garbage trucks and the pizza industry, which is the reason New York pizza tasted so good. The quality was controlled by Two-Finger Louie who wanted his profits good and his pizza perfect.

"My fadda's a Teamster," said Vinnie.

We knew that wasn't true. But anytime anyone said they were

anything, anything at all – Swedish, albino, Catholic, Jew, Army hero, Teamster – Vinnie would say his father was the same thing.

"So your fadda's a Teamster," said the guy with the cigar. This made all the difference. This was the son of a union brother. This was someone who could walk in his footsteps.

"Come on, grab a pail."

Vinnie looked so proud. He put his hands around the handles on a forty-gallon steel pail and lifted.

"Uhg."

"You gotta take the top off first," said open-jacket man.

Vinnie knocked the top off and put it down on the ground.

"Naaah," said jacket man. "You gotta toss it over there."

Vinnie watched as jacket man sailed the top like a Frisbee over to the front of the house next door. That was the first time we learned that it was not an accident that the lids got mixed up.

Vinnie struggled to lift the can to the back of the truck. He laid it on the edge of the giant, open mouth waiting to be fed.

"Naaaah," said jacket man. "You gotta bang it, or you don't get the garbage out."

He took the can from Vinnie, lifted it and power slammed it into the heavy steel jaw at the back of the truck. The can dented.

"You do it dat way."

Joey tried to pick up the next can but it had no handles.

"Dose rotten SOBs," said jacket man. "Dey steal da handles and we gotta work harder."

He made a fist with his work glove.

"If I catch one of dem I'll show them what real knuckles are."

Joey threw the top off the can, tilted it to put one hand under and the other on the top and almost lifted it. He got the can six inches off the ground then it hammered back down onto the side-walk. I thought Joey could lift anything.

"Some people trow out a lot of bones," said cigar man. "Try again."

The driver blew the horn.

"Hurry up, we don't got all day," said cigar man.

Joey took a breath and wrapped his left arm around the can, tilted it and put his right hand under the can and groaned. I thought his cheeks would burst but he got it up and took a step then some glop inside splashed up and hit him in the face.

"Yuck." He staggered toward the truck.

The men laughed.

"Need some help, kid?"

"I can do it," said Joey with the slime running off his face.

We stared. We could not help. We could do nothing but watch and think about what was in the next can.

Joey made it to the back of the truck and dropped the side of the can on the lip of the truck and pushed up the back. Out came a garbage-can-sized avalanche of slop and fat and bones.

"Some people butcher a side of pig in their kitchens," said cigar man. "They make sausages. Tastes good, but you gotta be careful of those pails."

He whistled and the truck pulled forward ten feet to the next set of steel-wrapped surprises. I picked one that had handles, but I could not get it off the ground. I threw off the cover like he had said and dragged it off the curb and to the truck.

"Can't lift it," I said.

Jimmy Lee gave me a hand and the two of us got the household slop and unspeakable goop into the truck.

"Don't forget to bang the cans," said the open-coat man.

He picked up one as though it was empty.

"Gotta put a dent in it. It's like your mark."

He slammed it onto the steel lip and presto, he had made his mark.

More than anything I wanted to make my mark.

He whistled and the truck moved. Cigar man pointed at Vinnie and then at a can. He said nothing. Vinnie picked it up and got it into the truck.

"Four hundred a day. Can you do that? A Teamster can."

He whistled again. The truck moved. Tommy grabbed a can and was struggling to get it up to the truck. I didn't want him to be able to do it, so I helped him. Even with the two of us it was heavy. It was filled with bones. Who cuts meat at home?

By the time we were at the end of the block, the garbage men were whistling and we were picking up the cans. Some were light, some had garbage neatly wrapped inside the cans and some smelled so bad I gagged.

The men told Vinnie he would make a good Teamster. The truck turned around. We still had the other side of the street to do.

"I think youse guys are okay," said cigar man. "But yzs needs more practice, and we gotta get going. If we get done early we get to drink beer on company time."

He picked up a can again and made it look light. Bam, slam, onto the lip and he tossed the can back onto the sidewalk. It stayed upright. That was as amazing as picking it up.

He whistled and the truck pulled ahead. The two of them were moving faster than the five of us. We sat on the curb. No, we collapsed on the curb with our arms quivering and our jackets and pants soaked with stuff we didn't want to touch.

"I don't want to be a garbage man," said Vinnie.

It is good to get some of life's lessons early. Vinnie was one of the few kids in that neighbourhood who stayed in school and eventually got a job where he wore a clean shirt. And he was one of the even fewer people who, when the janitor came around to empty his wastebasket, he said thanks.

"Duck and cover!"

Miss Johnson shouted it. She didn't say, "Duck and cover,"

she shouted, "Duck and cover!" louder than anything else she ever said in the classroom. She did not yell it. She demanded that we do it in a way that made us afraid not to duck and cover. It almost sounded like she was afraid.

She was talking about George Washington when she stopped in the middle of a word and shouted, "Duck and cover!"

It was the best time in school. I forgot what I was thinking about and fell off my seat and my knees hit the wooden floor and I pulled myself under my desk, which was bolted to the floor and the front of which was the back of the seat of the kid in front of me.

I put my head down and grabbed the back of my neck with my hands and closed my eyes.

"Duck and cover," Miss Johnson yelled again, but I knew if it was for real that second time would have been too late for anyone who did not get down and duck and cover the first time.

"You did well," said Miss Johnson. "You can get up now."

We did not get many compliments. We climbed out from under our desks, all of us awake now, and sat with folded hands. We would hear the same lesson, but it was good because we would not get a test on it and it would take up the next ten minutes.

"If that had been a real atomic attack," said Miss Johnson, "there would have been a bright flash out there."

She pointed to the windows on the left. We figured the atomic attack would come at 168th Street where Goertz's department store was.

"The windows would be blown in and if you did not have your hands over the backs of your necks, your heads might be cut off. So make sure your hands are there."

I was thinking that if Tommy did not get his hands up in time I could see his head rolling down the aisle.

"Those Communists want to kill us," said Miss Johnson. "If they get their way they will drop an atom bomb out there and take over our country. So we must always be ready to duck and cover and remember, the American way of life is good. The Communists are bad. Don't let anyone tell you any different."

She had told us that Air Force bombers were taking off from bases from across the top of America heading toward Russia, "just in case they decided to do something." They were taking off every day and night without stopping, even on Christmas.

There were some things she taught that did stick with us, but mostly those things were real and did not come from books.

"Those bombers are flown by brave men who know they will not come back if a war starts," she said.

I thought that they were the same as the kamikaze pilots who we were told were crazy, but I didn't say anything because she said the American pilots were brave and you would be unpatriotic if you argued with that.

Richard French raised his hand. Oh, no. We knew he would ask something we had not thought of and we would look dumb and he would look smart, even if he couldn't walk.

"What's it like to live in the Communist world?" he asked.

Miss Johnson smiled. Someone did have a real question.

"In Communism they work all day but they get nothing for what they do. If you were a farmer you could not own your farm. If you were a tailor you could not own your tailor shop."

We looked at her with interest. This was better than George Washington.

"In Communism they have only potatoes and bread to eat. Would you like to eat only potatoes and bread?"

Thirty-four kids shook their heads.

"They get meat only once or twice a year. We eat it three times a day. That's why we are better."

I was wondering when I ate meat except for the hot dogs at night. But I was glad I did not live under Communism because I would get hot dogs only once or twice a year.

"And in Communism everyone is poor," said Miss Johnson. "We have a great deal of wealth and none of us are poor like they are in Russia. Russia is bad."

I was thinking that at lunch time I was told to line up with the other poor kids against the wall. We would get our peanut butter and jelly sandwich and container of milk. I did not think that was rich.

But luckily we didn't live in China where kids were starving and because of them we should eat the crust on our bread. "How can you leave that behind when you think about all those kids starving to death?"

So I wasn't poor, but I was told to line up because my name was on a list and I got the sandwich, wrapped in waxed paper and the milk that had pieces of wax floating inside the container. Plus the milk was warm, or room temperature since it was kept in stacks of crates in the basement from morning when it was delivered until noon when we got it.

But heck, I wasn't going to complain because of those kids in China and because I was glad I was not living under Communism.

I once asked Miss Johnson why the starving Chinese kids didn't eat peanut butter, but she said peanut butter was an American food, and we were lucky to have it.

On my way to school a week later I went into Matty's to check out the candy bars. I had gotten a dollar from my aunt for Christmas and I still had not spent any of it. Matty was in front of the candy counter putting candy bars in and it was hard to squeeze by him. I looked at the comics, but right next to it was a wire rack with paperback books. I never bothered looking at them before because there were no pictures inside.

But there, right in front of my face, was a picture of a boxer in a ring with his arm being held up as the winner. He looked bloodied and sweating, but he was the champion. The title was Somebody Up There Likes Me.

I could read that, and it sounded religious, and the boxer looked strong. I bought the book, twenty-five cents, and a bottle of cream soda and a Three Musketeers.

"Great boxer," Matty said.

"Yeah?" Then I added, "Yeah!" as I meant to say.

"I liked him better than those fancy fighters. He came from the streets."

"Pretty strong, right?"

"Very, and you want all this stuff in a bag?"

I nodded. A bag meant you weren't a kid. I stepped out of the store and started off for school, but then turned around and walked home with the rumble of the elevated train behind my head and the thought of iron arms in the paper bag in my hand.

The trouble was, I could barely read. I got through the first few sentences, then opened the soda and the candy and ate and drank and got through the next few sentences. Then I fanned the rest of the book. There were a lot of pages.

For the rest of that week I left for school but stopped at Matty's for a cream soda and a Three Musketeers, then turned around and went home. I read all day long, sometimes only getting a few pages done.

What I learned was Rocky Graziano was a street punk whose father made him box his older brother to entertain his father's friends. Rocky always got beaten until he pretended he got knocked out. It was the only way out of the fight.

He was not Rocky Marciano who was a heavyweight and was fighting around the same time. Marciano was famous. Graziano was called a bum.

At the end of the first week the mailman brought a postcard from the Board of Education to my mother saying that I had not been in school for five days. It said she should write a reason for my absence on the back and sign it.

I wrote, "Michael is sick," and signed it as best I could in my

This is the candy store where we got our pretend cigarettes and Cokes, and I bought a book with a picture of a boxer on the cover and stayed home from school for two weeks to read it.

mother's handwriting. I wrote "Michael" because that is who it said was absent.

By the middle of the second week of cream sodas and Three Musketeers I learned Rocky made up his last name from the Italian wine his father drank. His real name was Barbella. But what I really liked was that he got in the best shape of his life when he was shadow boxing while in jail.

I started shadow boxing. And I got another postcard.

"Michael has been absent eight days. Please explain his absence."

"Michael is still sick."

And I signed it in my mother's handwriting.

By the end of the second week I had learned that Rocky's secret punch was just to hit the other guy so hard he knocked him out.

And I got another postcard.

"Michael has been absent for two weeks. Please explain why."

"Michael is very sick."

I was getting good at signing my mother's name.

By the end of the second week I had bought ten cream sodas and ten Three Musketeers and I was starting to love reading. I learned that Rocky's favourite saying was, "Ahhh, don't worry about it." He said that every time something bad happened.

While we were having dinner one night, the doorbell rang. I ran to get it. A man in a dark suit was standing there.

"Are you Michael?"

I nodded.

"I would like to speak to your mother."

"She's not home."

I could hear her moving behind me.

"Who is it?"

"I am the truant officer," said the man in the suit.

"What do you want?"

The two of them were face to face. I moved back down the hallway trying to find a shadow.

"Your son has not been in school for two weeks."

There was a very loud sound. It came from my mother. It sounded something like "WHAT???!!!!" followed by "MIKE!!! COME HERE!!!"

I stepped out of the shadow.

"What have you done?"

She was holding several postcards.

"This is terrible. It doesn't even look like my writing."

I tried, "Ahhhh, don't worry about it."

That was when I learned that Tommy had no idea what he was talking about. I went to my bed with my cheeks stinging from my mother's hand slapping across them.

The next morning the man in the suit was standing outside my door.

"You don't have to be here," I said.

He folded his arms across his chest.

"I have a knockout punch," I said.

He shook his head with a look of pity.

I held up my fists like Rocky did.

"I don't need anyone to take me to school."

He grabbed the front of my jacket and lifted me off the ground.

"Don't try to be tough with me," he said.

"You don't scare me," I said.

He slammed my back into the wall behind me. My feet were still off the ground.

"US Marine Corp," he said. "You want to be tough, be a Marine. Now we will go to school."

When he put me down, I went on my way to Miss Johnson's class.

"Where have you been?" she asked.

"Reading," I said.

"That's good because we are going to spend today reading," she said. "Who wants to take over with the sheet called 'Country Life'?"

She handed out mimeographed papers. You could hear the mimeograph machine cranking out one page at a time when you passed the principal's office. Usually some kid who had done something bad had the job of turning the handle that turned the wheel that produced the papers from one stencil page. The only trouble with that was the pages were so blurry you could hardly tell what was on them.

"We will start with the first person in row one reading the first paragraph," said Miss Johnson.

"Country Life" did not have any boxing in it. What's the point of reading, I thought?

The Party

"We're going to have a party in Johnny's cellar."

"How?" asked Vinnie.

"Because no one's going to be home," I told him. "Johnny told me. Friday night."

Vinnie was gleaming. He had never been to a real party before. Not one where we could have a party because no one was home. Neither had I but I wasn't going to tell him that.

"Parties are fun," I said. "That's the time when you get to be real close to girls and maybe even dance with them. Slow."

Vinnie's eyes went down.

"I don't know how to dance."

"You don't have to know," I said. "You just dance, like they do on *American Bandstand.*"

We had seen it at Dorothy's house. Her parents had a television, ten inches, black and white, in a dark wooden box on its own special table.

"Look, that's the way they dance in Philadelphia," she said.

"I can't see anything," said Johnny.

"Move the antenna around," said Dorothy. "When a train passes, sometimes it slides off."

Johnny moved the rabbit ears back and forth and the picture got clearer, then it filled with television snow, then he moved it and it was clear, like magic.

"Stop. Stop moving it," said Joey. "You got it."

Then a train went by and the antenna moved and the picture went fuzzy again.

Johnny asked Dorothy for some tape and fixed the antenna and sealed it down and we watched the girls in wide skirts and the boys in neat shirts and ironed pants. They were amazing. They all knew how to do it. None of us had ever stood next to a girl before and moved in anything except our dreams.

But a party it would be like *American Bandstand*. We would dance. We would hold girls close. We would swing them around and they would come back to us like they did on television.

We did have a party once before. Judy had it. We almost never saw Judy because she lived on the corner near the bar and her mother kept her home most of the time. But she invited us to a party and we went.

When we told our mothers that we were going to a party each mother told us we had to have a clean shirt. That was step one on how to ruin a good night. A clean shirt felt so stiff. That was because our mothers put starch in the wash and the shirts did not bend and how could you have fun in a straightjacket?

When we got to the party there was Judy and Eileen, who was a year younger than most of us, and Dorothy and Vanessa and a couple of other girls from school who were in Judy's class.

Standing behind them was Judy's mother, and coming into the room was Judy's father who drove a moving truck. We said, "Hello, Mrs. Tracy," because we were all polite. But we were thinking, "Would you please go into the next room for a while, Mrs.

Tracy?" But she never did. She disappeared only for a minute at a time to get more soda and potato chips and what can you do in a minute?

We also wished for slow dances so we could snuggle and breathe deeply, but Mrs. Tracy seemed to have organized the records so that only fast music came out of the record player, and the girls were the only ones who could dance to that. So the boys just stood around talking about baseball and the cars we hoped to own.

But Friday night at Johnny's would be different. No parents. The cellar with the old coal bins that had never been cleaned out would be the party room of our dreams. It had a bare concrete floor, and bare light bulbs and an overflow sewer drain that had overflowed several times and then dried. But it didn't matter. Girls would be there without any parents.

We got a six-pack of Rheingold.

"How'd you do that?" Tommy asked me.

"My mother always drinks Rheingold. They let me have it at the deli."

The girls started arriving shortly after dinner. They had told their parents that they were going out for Cokes with their friends and six of them showed up. We had been waiting like hungry puppies, wrestling and falling over each other and talking about what we hoped would happen.

"Are you sure your mother's not home?" Vanessa asked.

"We could run around naked and no one would know," said Johnny.

"Who would do that?" asked Vanessa, in a tone that left Johnny wishing he had just said "no, my mother's not home." But he had said something that would probably make Vanessa not talk to him for the rest of the night.

The girls brought a stack of records and we had a 45 rpm player with a three-inch speaker on the side. It would make music we could squeeze by. We were aching, then the girls put on Bo Diddley.

"Hey, we can't dance to that," Tommy tried to shout over the music, but the girls were already dancing, ignoring us.

We stood by the coal bins with our hands in our pockets.

"The next one will be slow," said Vinnie. "They're just burning off their excitement."

But the next record was "Maybellene." "Why can't you be true?" Chuck Berry shouted across the cellar.

"Can't you put on a slow one?" Vinnie yelled, but the girls didn't listen and didn't stop dancing. Vinnie and Tommy looked through the records, flipping them down like a deck of cards. "Fast, fast, fast, fast."

Then Tommy's hands stopped. He pulled out a record and held it in the air like a trophy. "Hey There," by Rosemary Clooney.

When "Maybellene" finished he quickly put on Rosemary. "Hey there, you with the stars in your eyes."

It was music to hug and grope and get excited by until there was a scratch in the record and the words repeated over and over. You hugged, groped, hugged, groped, hugged. Am I hugging or groping? I am still not excited. Music is hard to understand. Then Tommy pushed the needle forward but you forgot if you were groping, or hugging, or just wishing.

"I think I hear your mother upstairs," said Jimmy Lee.

"No, that's the mice. When I'm up there they run around down here, when I come down here they run around up there," said Johnny.

Then came the beer. It was warm. We had to carry it one can at a time inside our shirts in case someone spotted us, so when we opened the first can it had already travelled a block squeezed between a belly and a belt and got shaken with every step.

When the can opener went in, the beer came out, up to the ceiling and down over Judy's hair.

"Aaahhhgh!" Judy did not like beer on her head. "Oh God, I can't go home like this."

The other girls stopped dancing and huddled around her as if she were a wounded ally. They got paper towels from the roll we had next to the chips and tried to dry her hair, then they got water and tried to wet it. They scrubbed and combed and circled her, comforting her and talking about whatever it is that girls talk about.

I could not hear what they said because I was on the other side of the room with the boys, talking about baseball and the cars we hoped to own someday.

The next day when we sat on the curb watching the traffic, things were different. A failure? A bomb? No way.

"What a party. Wow," said Vinnie.

"Wild," said Tommy.

"You know, when Judy had that paper towel on her head, she looked pretty," said Johnny, "just like she was getting out of the shower."

And the best part was we could have another party soon because we still had five beers stashed behind the furnace. All we had to do was wait for Johnny's parents to visit his mother's sister again. The only potential problem was that Johnny overheard his father saying he couldn't stand his sister-in-law. But if he changed his mind and the girls were willing and we could find a slow record and find a way to chill the beer, we would have a time that you couldn't believe.

Something else happened that night. We saw a picture of Elvis on one of the record labels. Over his pouting face was a magnificent pomp of hair. It hung almost to his eyebrows like a dark cloud.

"Looks like poop," Vinnie said. He told us he saw the girls aahing over it and decided he hated that kind of hair.

But on this day after the night before while we were sitting on the curb watching the trucks go by, Vinnie stuck his fingers into the front of his hair and pulled it down.

"Whatcha doing?" asked Johnny.

"Nothing."

"You're trying to look like Elvis," said Tommy.

"Am not."

"Are so."

"Not."

"You are," said Tommy. "I want to look like that too."

"Me too," said Vinnie.

We chipped in to buy a tube of Brylcreem, which we squeezed out onto our fingers. It was thick and hard. Then each of us rubbed a blob into our hair, which made us look like ball joints ready to be slid into sockets. When we shook our heads our hair stayed glued. We all pulled plops down over our foreheads and asked each other if we looked like Elvis.

No, we did not look like him. No sideburns. So we went to the barber, who told us we that we would not have sideburns until we had whiskers. "And you won't have those until you start liking girls," he said.

"I like girls," said Vinnie.

"I mean really like girls," said the barber.

"What do you mean 'really' like girls?" asked Vinnie who had images of Vanessa almost naked in his mind.

"If you have to ask what I mean, you're not old enough to know what I mean and you're not old enough to have sideburns."

This was one of the mysteries of life. We found a cork and burned it and the next day we all had sideburns. We spent the rest of the winter rubbing tubes of Brylcreem into our hair and running Ace combs through it with globs of cream packing up on one side of the comb like a snow plough and rubbing burned cork over our cheeks to make us look like we had sideburns even if Augie the barber said we couldn't have them.

"You look cool." We kept saying that to each other to prove we did.

Months had gone by and I noticed Vinnie and Joey were using less and less cork and both were spending more time talking to Vanessa. Joey and Vinnie were almost a year older than me.

We never had that second party, and worse than that, when we went to look for the beer a few months later, it was gone. Johnny hadn't taken it and no one else could get into his cellar. Except he remembered that when his furnace broke down his Uncle Ted came to fix it. His uncle could fix anything and he was usually very fast at fixing things.

But this time he spent a long time in the cellar and when he came upstairs he said he had to use the bathroom badly.

"I like root beer better anyway," said Johnny. So Jimmy Lee and Johnny and I got a can of root beer from Matty's and sat on the curb under the El and talked about Elvis and girls and parties and we passed the can around, and none of us ever wiped off the mouth of the can before we drank. We didn't have to. We were buddies who partied together.

The Queen of Marbles

Elvis came on big. He came on like we had never known anyone to come on like him. We had bubble gum cards with Elvis.

"Do you think Elvis or Frankie will last longer?" Tommy asked but Vinnie was sitting next to him with a stack of comics. We were on the stoop of Johnny's place waiting for Johnny to come out.

Dorothy walked by.

"Who do you think is going to last longer? Frankie or Elvis?"

"I love Elvis. He sings great, and I love the way he . . ."

She stopped talking. She wiggled her bottom. I had never seen a girl wiggle her bottom. I thought I was going to explode. I thought that was the most wonderful sight I had ever seen. I was in love with Dorothy, and her bottom.

"I love the way Elvis wiggles his bottom," she said.

"But will he beat out Sinatra?" asked Vinnie.

Dorothy walked up the steps and stood in front of us. She was blowing bubbles with bubble gum. She had one leg on a high step and the other on a lower one. Her jeans were tight. I was going to die.

"Frankie is old," she said. "My mother listens to him. But I love Elvis. And I am going to listen to Elvis as long as I live so he will beat out Frankie."

I wanted to have a long life with her. I slid my fingers into the front of my hair and tried to pull it down lower over my forehead.

"You think I look like Elvis?" I asked.

Dorothy looked at me and laughed. "You look like Mickey with greasy hair."

My long and happy life was over.

"I'm playing marbles tomorrow. Wanna come?" she asked me.

It was not like she asked everyone, she asked me. You could see that. She was looking right at me when she asked.

I nodded and felt the pomp in my hair hitting my head.

Dorothy was the world's champion marble player. It probably was the way she hooked her thumb into her index finger that gave her incredible aim, or maybe it was the way she put her head down so close to the ground that she could see a straight line from anywhere. Or maybe she was just good.

Her reputation had spread way past our neighbourhood and even past our school. Kids from South Jamaica or Hollis would take a bus to our street just to compete with her. Once in a while she lost, but I think that was only because she felt sorry for someone if they were small and were losing all their marbles.

"A kid from 102nd Street told his friends to tell their friends to tell me that he was coming on Friday after lunch. That's tomorrow," she said.

"I'll be there," I said and I think I could feel the heat from my head rising into the grease in my hair and melting it because I felt all wet.

I could hardly sleep. I got up early, and school went by and then I was watching for the bus.

Dorothy and I and Vanessa and Vinnie waited on the corner at the bus stop under the El. Dorothy had been in so many games that not that many of our gang came out to watch anymore. We knew she would win. She never needed help. She had her bag of marbles. It was not very big.

A bus pulled up and a kid got off gripping a heavy cloth bag. The challenger. He had a mean look on his face. Four kids got off behind him. The bus doors closed and it pulled away with a loud diesel groan just as a train was going overhead. We all stared at each other in the noise.

Finally, almost a minute later, "You Dorothy?" said the mean-looking kid.

"You want to take me on?" she said.

He held up his bag. The kids with him laughed.

"Where?" he asked.

She looked around. "How about there?" She pointed to an empty space between two parked cars. It was half a car length and big enough to get a circle in and kneel down, so long as you didn't kneel on the street side because then your legs would get run over.

"Good," said the mean kid.

Dorothy took a piece of chalk out of her pocket, blew a bubble and made a circle.

"Gonna play no rules?" asked the kid.

"No rules," agreed Dorothy.

No rules was simple, you followed only the rules that everyone followed and beyond that there were no rules. The rules were you each put a marble in the middle and then you stayed outside the circle and tried to knock that marble out of the circle. Then that marble was yours. If there were four or five marbles in the circle when you knocked out the other person's first marble then you got them all. There were seldom more than a handful of marbles that you could win or lose because most kids who played marbles were good. Some later went into pool halls and bowling leagues. They did not go into golf, but they would have been great at it.

The kid laughed. His friends laughed. The kid put his hand in his bag and pulled out the biggest marble we had ever seen. It was three times bigger than the marbles we got from the variety store where I stole the ashtray. We almost gasped, except we would never do that and show that we were impressed.

The kid put it down in the middle of the circle and laughed again. No way could Dorothy's little marbles move that big marble. It was like a bully in the ring. The kid laughed again. A train passed by overhead. A delivery truck went past us. A police car went down Jamaica Avenue with its siren on. Dorothy blew a bubble.

"No rules," she said.

"No rules," said the kid, knowing that he could use any size marble he wanted.

Dorothy blew another bubble and took a marble out of her bag. It was less than a third the size of the kid's marble. The kid laughed. His friends laughed.

Dorothy took the gum out of her mouth and wrapped it around the marble. No one said anything. Then she rolled her gum-covered marble along the edge of the gutter at the bottom of the curb. It was a place you didn't want to go. It was filled with mud and gravel and broken glass and cigarette butts and pigeon goo. We didn't know it but it was filled with the heavy metals from the outflow of some of the factories and shavings from the asbestos brake linings of passing cars and trucks and sediment from other things we still don't know about.

She rolled it that way, then this way, then back again. The marble grew.

"You can't do that," said the kid.

"No rules," said Dorothy.

"But I mean that's not allowed. You can't put stuff on your marble." He looked mean.

"No rules," said Dorothy. She looked him in the eye.

He said nothing.

She kneeled down on the ground, put her head down on the asphalt and looked, then she fired her pebble-studded musket ball with a rubber bumper, and it slammed into his oversized attempt at fame, and one giant marble from another neighbourhood wound up outside the ring.

The kid knew what he was up against. He cut his losses, picked up his bag minus the giant marble, and followed at a distance by his friends, crossed the street and stood at the bus stop going the other way. He said nothing.

I don't know who it was but one of us started to sing, "You Ain't Nothin' But a Hound Dog."

We laughed. We hit each other. We sang. I pulled down the pomp on my hair. I looked at Dorothy. My hero.

White Christmas, Don't Be Silly

A few months later, it began to snow. It snowed all night. It always snowed a couple of times in the winter. That's what winter was for.

And in the morning the snow was white.

"Hurry up," said Jimmy Lee. "It won't last."

I knew what he meant. The snow would be around for a week, but white snow would last only a few hours, sometimes even less.

In Manhattan and Brooklyn and Queens and the Bronx, coal was being poured into furnaces by Con Edison to make electricity. Mountains of coal were being eaten by fires and the colder it was, the more coal that went into the stomach of the flames, and the more coal that was turned into flames, the more soot went into the air. Sometimes the air was grey, but around the furnaces it was black.

In the summer when the furnaces were only simmering there was still enough soot falling that the shoulders on a white shirt would have a coating of black specks before you got to school. In the winter, black specks turned into dark downpour.

"It's turning black," said Jimmy Lee.

"No it's not, we have all afternoon," said Vinnie. Vinnie always looked on the bright side.

He was wrong.

"Turning," said Jimmy Lee.

Trucks passed by grinding through the white and with each one there seemed to be a trail of grey behind it. The exhausts were all black. The dripping oil was black. The snow was white, but just for a short time.

Jimmy Lee picked up a handful of snow and made a ball then started picking out the black specks. Then he threw it at Vinnie.

"Black ball coming your way," said Jimmy Lee.

It hit Vinnie in the face.

"Uhh. You bum."

Vinnie grabbed snow and all in one motion made a ball and threw it. His aim was as good as Jimmy Lee's. Every one of us could split a thread at thirty feet, even though no one would ever be so silly as to hold up a thread for us to hit.

Jimmy Lee put up his hands and blocked the ball.

"That's cold."

"You need gloves," said Vinnie.

"If I put on gloves I can't hit you," said Jimmy Lee.

That was the problem with having a snowball fight and trying to keep your hands warm at the same time. If we tried for the warmth we lost the aim and without the aim it was not worth having a snowball fight.

But it was cold so Jimmy Lee and Vinnie said they would go home and get gloves and meet back at this same spot in five minutes. Both ran home, but it was hard running since both had the same Army and Navy surplus shoes they wore all year. Every mother on the block bought their kids shoes in the military surplus store and everyone's shoes looked the same. They were round in the front and highly polished when they were new. They also cost a dollar which was cheaper than going to a shoe store.

Later when each and every one of us wound up in the Army or Navy or Air Force, except for Buster who went into the Marines, we all had the same thought when we were issued our first dress shoes along with our boots. They were the same shoes we wore on 132nd Street. They also were useless in the snow.

Both Jimmy Lee and Vinnie came out of their front doors the same time with their hands covered and grabbed handfuls of snow and made them into balls on the run and then threw them almost at point blank range. Both missed. Both fell down because their shoes had no grip on anything except a parade ground.

"I'll get you," said Jimmy Lee. But he didn't. He threw another snowball, and missed.

Vinnie came running at him with a snowball in his right hand, hauled back his arm like he had done a thousand times playing stickball and handball and catch. He used all the aim he had in his life and missed.

"Can't get me," said Jimmy Lee.

"You can't neither," said Vinnie.

Both of them threw again and missed.

"You can't throw with gloves on," said Jimmy Lee. "And besides, my hands are cold again."

They both peeled off the socks they had on their hands.

"You can't get your thumb around the ball," said Vinnie.

He picked up a handful of snow, packed it into a ball, and threw across the street. It hit a telephone pole smack in the middle.

"It's getting dirty, look," said Jimmy Lee.

He was right. Only a couple of hours after it stopped falling, it was turning grey. At night we couldn't see what was happening, but by morning the white snow would be grey, which we called black, which is not the colour snow is supposed to be.

"Let's go inside and read comics," said Vinnie.

"You know that song 'White Christmas'?" said Jimmy Lee. "I think they made that up."

Urban Farmer

*I*t was still snowing, but I said to myself, "I'm going to have a garden."

That was impossible of course, but I said out on the street, "I'm going to have grass and we all can play on it and I'm going to ask Dorothy and Vanessa if they want to lay down on the grass like the kids did in one of those books that Miss Johnson read us."

Tommy looked like he didn't believe me. But he wasn't paying any attention to me anyway.

"I'm going to have a garden, even have to cut the grass," I said.

"Yeah, sure, and I'm going to have a '49 Ford V8 with four on the floor and four spinners and fuzzy dice," said Tommy.

"But you don't know how to drive," I said.

"Well, you don't know how to cut grass."

But I knew I was going to have a garden. I taped two quarters to a piece of paper and wrote my name and address on a coupon I had cut out of a comic book. There was a picture of a backyard with a dog playing on the grass and a man with a lawn mower cutting the grass and a mother with a large skirt holding a pitcher of lemonade and watching her two kids playing on the grass.

"Grow your own mini-backyard right in your kitchen or bedroom," the ad said. "For only fifty cents you can bring the outdoors indoors."

That's what I wanted – the outdoors indoors. I pictured my mother and me having hot dogs on the lawn. It would feel cool below our feet and we would pass the mustard without worrying about dropping it and if some potato salad slipped off our plates it would not matter. The grass would cover it up.

The ad said the home garden would be 12" x 15" and would grow in just a few weeks. I got out a tape measure. Twelve feet was how long our kitchen was. But it was only seven feet wide. The garden could not go there.

I measured the living room. Twelve by fifteen. We would have the outdoors indoors if I could just move the chairs and the coffee table and the record player out of the room. No problem. My mother would be happy. We could take off our shoes and walk through the grass. We could not take off our shoes any other time because the floor was so chewed up that if you walked barefoot or in your socks you were sure to get a splinter driven right up between your toes and that hurt.

"I'm going to invite everyone for a day in the country," I told Joey. "Even Junior. He can play on the grass and not get hurt."

I waited every day for the UPS man because I knew that a garden that size would take a delivery truck. Then came the snow. I saw Vinnie and Jimmy Lee having a snowball fight, but I did not have the time to join them. I was getting ready for my garden.

Then there was a pounding on my door.

"A UPS truck is stuck."

It was Vinnie. I looked out onto the street and there was a big brown truck with its wheels spinning.

UPS, my garden, needing help. I did not put on a jacket. In two steps I was outside in the snow, slipping on my Navy surplus shoes running to the truck.

"Can you push?" the driver asked.

"I can push," I said. "Do you have a garden in there?"

He was a big guy. "I don't know what you're talking about, but can you push?"

"Of course I can push." I felt my shadow boxing muscles flex.

He looked down at me from behind his steering wheel. He was large.

"You get in here," he said to me. "I'll push."

He got out of his seat. He was almost a giant. I got up in his seat. I put my hands around the wheel. I was driving. Me. I was driving. It was snowing and I was driving. And there was Tommy coming. I could see him through the side window and I was driving. And there was Dorothy coming. And I was driving.

"Just hold the wheel straight," said the driver.

"Okay," I said. I was driving. Do you out there on the street in the snow know that I am driving? I am behind the wheel of this truck and I am driving? Me? Driving? Me?

"Put it in first," said the man.

I wasn't driving.

"What?"

"First, put it in first. You know how to drive?"

"Of course I do. But where's first?"

He jumped up on the running board and sighed. I know he did. I saw him. I wasn't driving.

"We'll try once. The worst you'll do is stall it. Push that pedal down with your left foot and hold it."

I pushed, and he moved the gears and put it in first.

"Don't lift your foot up until I tell you. And then lift it just a little and slowly. And at the same time just lightly push on that one with your right. If I tell you to stop, slam down on your left foot and hold it."

He got outside and told everyone to push.

"Lift your left and push on your right," said the big guy.

I did. I was trembling. I was staring at my feet.

"Not so hard," he said.

I froze.

"Easy."

I lifted my right.

"Easy!" he shouted.

I trembled more and lifted the left.

"Nooooo!" he shouted louder. "Down on the left."

"I can do it," I heard Tommy say.

"Just push," the driver said to Tommy. "Now ease up the left."

I eased, they pushed and the truck moved.

"Steer," he shouted.

Oh, God. The wheel. Steer at what?

"Hold it straight."

I can do that. The truck moved and there was a cheer from behind me.

I got it right. Me. I got it right. Me. I am driving a truck. And Dorothy is out there. And Tommy. And I am driving.

"Down on the left."

I went down and held it like I was pushing it through the floor.

The truck stopped. I held on to the wheel. I could have driven away, because I could do it, I knew that. But I didn't want to because Dorothy would not have seen me get out of the truck.

"Stop."

Stop? Is he crazy? Stop? How do you stop? I picked up my left foot and the truck started going.

"Stop," he yelled. "Hit the brake."

Brake? Middle one?

I pushed down. The truck jumped and stopped. The motor jerked, and stopped. Not good, I thought.

"Great. Thanks," said the big guy. "I'll take over."

He was standing on the platform next to me. No, you won't, I thought. But I said, "Okay, hope this helped."

Why did I say that? I wanted to say "I could take over from here," but I didn't. I got out of the seat and jumped down to the snowy street and he slid in and started the motor and waved and was gone.

I drove a truck. Me. I drove it.

"We did all the work," said Tommy. "You had it easy."

"But I drove it," I said.

"Awww, come on. You just steered it."

"No, I drove it."

"Steered it," said Tommy.

"Drove it."

"You did really good," said Dorothy.

I love you. I'm not saying that out loud. But I love you. Have I ever told you that I love you? No. Well, I'm telling you now, except not out loud. I love you more than I have ever loved anyone, even more than Babe Ruth.

"Thanks," I said to her.

"I thought he was bringing me my garden."

"You don't got no garden," said Tommy. "It's winter. Nobody got no garden, whatever a garden is."

We all went home. The snow was falling. No, the soot was falling. It did not matter. Dorothy said I did well. She said it. She really said it and I heard it. And Tommy heard it. And Dorothy said it. Did I say Dorothy said it? She did.

Back in my apartment I thought of grass. No, I thought I had driven a truck. No, I thought of Dorothy.

The next day the mailman came with a brown envelope. My name was on the front. It was not from the school board.

I ripped it open. There was a flattened piece of aluminum foil and a packet of dirt and another smaller packet of seeds.

"Fold the edges of the foil up into a receptacle, then fill it with the soil and place the seeds on top. Water and wait for your mini-backyard garden." The instructions I could read, but did not believe.

It was the size of my forearm. It was not a backyard. I measured it. It was 12 x 15 inches. I thought two marks after the 12 in the ad meant feet, since feet were bigger than inches and I thought one mark meant inches, since inches were smaller than feet.

We could not eat hot dogs on this. I could not invite Junior to play on grass that was the size of one of his hands with the fingers stretched out.

I went outside and made a snowball. No, I made a grey ball. The soot had stopped falling but the snow was still turning. I threw it at the telephone pole and hit it smack in the middle. I was not the first to nail that target; it was covered with stuck lumps of greying snow. I threw another, then another.

"Are you okay?"

Dorothy's voice.

"Yeah, sure."

"I saw you out here alone and wondered how you were."

"You did?"

She smiled.

Who cares about a garden? Something was growing in me.

The Forest

"It's coming. The leaves are coming out."

It was a couple of months later and the life in the tree was returning. It was impossible, but it was true and it was happening right there in front of us, sort of. This truly was a miracle of nature.

My little garden of grass had not grown and my mother threw it out one day when I was not home.

"It was just a tray full of dirt and it was going to draw bugs," she said.

What's the point in arguing? It was just a tray full of dirt sitting on the radiator in my room. It got hot when the days were cold, but I was thinking that would keep the seeds warm, like an egg with a chicken.

"No kiddin', it's blooming."

To say we lived in a neighbourhood of no grass or trees is not true. The grass part was true, but not the trees. At least not one tree. We had a tree.

We noticed it the first time only the year before and it was amazing. You did not have to tell us this is not the way life is supposed to be. If you stood near the corner, next to the bar, and looked down through the metal grating that covered a hole in the sidewalk there was the top of the tree reaching up.

The hole was supposed to let light into a window in the basement, but it was so filled with litter and cigarette butts and empty paper coffee cups and newspapers that the window was half covered. But somehow the seed of that tree had come to life down there and it had grown a stubby trunk and had branches that were reaching up toward the grating. Last summer it had leaves that we could see and almost touch.

"That's a miracle," said Joey. We knew that a tree had grown in Brooklyn once upon a time because some of our parents had talked about a book that was written about it. But this was a tree in Queens on 132nd Street and that was better.

On sunny days we watched to see if the sun would get to it, but the sun never did. The only light it got was a reflection off the window of the bar and that was only for an hour or so around lunchtime.

"It's a sumac," said a guy who came out of the bar. "They're weed trees. They grow anywhere." Then he poured half a glass of beer down through the grating.

"That should kill it."

"What'd you do that for," said Joey. "That's not nice."

The guy went back into the bar and Joey and Vinnie and Jimmy Lee and Vanessa and I said we would not let it die.

"We got to get rid of the beer," said Vanessa. "Let's pour water down there."

She lived the closest to the bar and we all ran back to her apartment. She let us inside. We had never been in there before. It was dark and quiet. There was a crucifix over the kitchen door. Her mother was sitting alone at the kitchen table staring at a wall.

"Mother. These are my friends. We are just getting some water to help a tree."

Her mother said nothing. Vanessa got out a brown plastic bucket from under the sink and put it under the tap and half filled it. It was too heavy for her to lift so Joey helped her.

"I'll be back soon," she said to her mother, who still said nothing.

I felt very creepy. It was like her mother was dead, but she was still breathing.

We all went out and Vanessa closed the door quietly behind her.

"What's wrong with your mother?" asked Joey.

"After my father died, she just sits. She doesn't say much. My sister and I cook and watch her, but there's nothing we can do. A doctor said she's depressed, but we knew that."

I felt bad about trying to see Vanessa naked. You are not supposed to see someone naked when they are taking care of their mother. But then I looked at her again with her long, dark hair and her bumps that were bigger now than last fall when we were up on the roof and I wondered if I climbed up there again if I might see her. That would be wrong, but I still wanted to.

We carried the bucket to the corner and poured it down over the tree.

"That should wash away the beer," said Vanessa.

By May the leaves were almost up to the iron bars. Sometimes people would walk over the grating and we would have to tell them to be careful.

"Don't kill the tree," we shouted.

But they mostly looked at us like we were crazy. We noticed that most people did not even notice it. That was almost as amazing as the tree being there. How could they not see it? It was true that if the light wasn't on it you could pass overhead and not see it, but still, it was a tree growing in prison and you should see things like that.

When we told some people to look down, a few said, "Yeah, so what?"

It was hard when you give someone something that was the most incredible thing in the world and they didn't care.

By June some of the leaves were sticking up past the bars. That was not good. People were stepping on them.

We got some plastic milk crates from the grocery store across Jamaica Avenue and put them on each side of the grating. That worked for about an hour until the man who ran the store came across the street and took them back.

Then we got some garbage cans and put them on the sides of the grating, but the bartender came out almost immediately.

"Are you kids dumb or something?" he shouted. "Get those cans away from my window."

We carried the cans back to the sides of the houses where we had taken them from. The owners would probably miss them anyway.

"Why don't we just play here?" asked Buster. He was hanging out with us again. You had friends for a reason or a season someone had said. Buster was last season and he had come back this season. No one asked why. He didn't move away. Nothing had happened that we knew of, he just moved back into the gang like he had never left.

"We could toss baseball cards here, or pennies," he said.

That is brilliance. That's not the kind of thing you learn in school. That's how to fix a problem with just a little tweaking instead of replacing. But we didn't know that. We just took out some pennies and began tossing them.

"Buster wins."

His penny was closest to the wall. The wall was next to the window of the bar. He picked up all four pennies and we started again back at the line.

"Hey, Vinnie, don't lean over the line," said Tommy.

"I can lean if I don't step over it."

"Can not."

"Can so," said Vinnie.

"What do you think, Vanessa? Can he lean over the line?" asked Joey.

The line was the edge of the sidewalk. It was about five feet to the wall. The game is simple; anyone, any number can play at any time. Everyone throws a penny and the closest to the wall wins.

"He can't lean over the line. He's got to hold his hand behind it," said Tommy.

"I just have to keep my feet behind it," said Vinnie.

Vanessa looked at the two of them and I swear she smiled like she wanted to laugh at them but wouldn't do that because it would make them feel bad. I was glad they didn't ask me what they should do because no way could anyone say the right thing.

"Why don't you flip a coin? Heads, Vinnie wins, tails, Tommy." Vanessa was smart.

Even Vinnie and Tommy looked surprised.

"Okay," said Vinnie.

"Yeah, okay," said Tommy.

Vinnie flipped, caught it, turned it over on the back of his wrist and held his hand over it.

"Call it," he said.

"Heads," said Tommy.

Vinnie took away his hand.

"You win."

They went back to flipping with their hands behind the line. It was like they always played this way.

The next few tosses Buster lost.

"I can't play anymore," he said.

"Why not?" asked Vinnie, who was winning almost every toss.

"I don't have any more money."

"Wanna flip cards?" asked Vinnie.

Buster brightened up. "Yeah, sure. I'll be right back."

Baseball cards were poker chips, money, tools of street gambling. Only if you had a Joe DiMaggio or Pee Wee Reese or Jackie Robinson did you save it. And you only saved it until you ran out of your other cards and needed to flip that to win back some of your cards that you lost. And sometimes if Jackie Robinson wasn't bent or creased too badly you would save it so that someday you could say you had a Jackie Robinson card instead of saying you had one but you lost it, because everyone could say that.

"You want to flip against the wall or matches?" asked Joey, who was very good with matches.

Buster came back with his cards. "I want matches, too." Tommy and Vinnie and I went home and came back with handfuls of battered, bent and folded cards.

You got a card with a flat piece of bubble gum for a penny, but the bubble gum mostly cracked and didn't make good bubbles even when you got it chewed. Double Bubble was good for bubbles even though you didn't get a card with that and it still cost a penny. There was a cartoon wrapped around the Double Bubble but mostly the jokes were so dumb and the writing so small that we hardly looked at it.

Double Bubble was the big wad of gum that you put between your teeth and squeezed. It gave way slowly and felt good with the sweetness running out on your tongue and your jaw muscles tightening. You could feel the strain at the back of your teeth.

"What do you do, chew bubble gum all day?" the dentist would ask. "You have nine cavities. Your mouth is already full of silver."

I sat up straight and he bent over and drilled. I watched the thick string turning the pulleys that turned the drill. He operated it with his foot pushing a pedal and I could smell the burning of my tooth and I knew the pain was going to hit any second.

"Owwww," I tried to yell but his hands were in my mouth along with his drill.

"It won't be much longer, at least not on this hole," he said. "Eight more to go."

Three quarters of an hour later – I knew because I was watching his big clock – he was done. My teeth were killing me. He rolled some filling stuff, mostly mercury and silver, in the palm of his hand, then squeezed it into a little instrument that looked like a Tiny Tim tin can on the end of a metal rod and then forced it into the last hole in my last tooth.

"Try to brush them occasionally," he said as I was leaving. I did not feel well.

On the way home I stopped at Matty's and got some Double Bubble. I needed something to bite into. I bit and screamed. The sugar squeezed into the new fillings.

"I wish my teeth wouldn't hurt," I thought. I chewed some more to get rid of the sugar and walked home blowing bubbles.

Outside the bar, Buster said, "I'll go first."

He held a card at the tips of his fingers and flipped it. It somersaulted to the ground and landed flat with the face side up.

Tommy took one of his cards, stood over Buster's and flipped it. It missed Buster's card and landed tail side up.

"Ha," said Vinnie, which was like saying that was the worst throw he had ever seen.

Vinnie flipped his and it landed face side up, but missed touching Buster's.

Joey flipped and it hammered onto Buster's landing flat on top, but tails up.

You had to get your card the same side up as the first card and touching it. You have to have some rules.

I flipped and also got it tails up, but I hit Buster's card, which then disappeared under mine and Joey's, which now meant that the next person would have to match my card. More rules . . . .

"Can I try?" asked Vanessa.

Buster, Joey and I all handed her cards. She took Buster's.

"Hey, please be careful of the tree down there," said Joey to a couple of men who were walking home from one of the factories. They both carried lunch boxes.

"You're blocking our way," they said.

"We're just playing," said Vinnie. "And we don't want our tree stepped on."

"You can't block the sidewalk, that's public property," said one of the men.

Vinnie took a deep breath. He always did that before something bad was going to happen.

"We just don't want you to hurt this tree," he said.

The same man who spoke was angry. "Don't tell me where to walk, kid."

"I'm not telling you, we just want you not to hurt the tree."

"You mean that stupid little thing?" he said, pointing at the bars on the sidewalk and the few leaves sticking up past them.

"Please, mister," said Vanessa. "This tree is going to get hurt if you step on it."

Then she moved over to the grating and stood in front of it.

"I can't hit a girl, you know. But if you kids block this way tomorrow, I'm going to call the cops," said the first man.

"Come on, let's go," said the other man. "It's not worth it."

They left and we looked at Vanessa with wonder. She had done what we didn't do.

"That was really brave," said Joey.

Vanessa almost blushed. "I can't let it get hurt," she said.

We left the cards on the ground and stood around our new hero.

"They'll be back tomorrow and stomp it," said Buster.

"Whose turn is it?" asked Vinnie.

"Vanessa's," said Buster.

Vanessa moved away from the grating, stood over the pile of

cards and flipped one of hers. It landed face side up right over top of my card.

"Hey, Vanessa wins," said Joey.

She picked up all the cards and then gave back the ones she had borrowed.

"You don't have to," said Buster.

Vanessa looked like she was far away. Then she said she had an idea.

"They won't push us aside if we are playing handball here," she said.

More brilliance. We all knew that handball games had invisible no trespassing signs around them. People could walk right through your penny or card game. But in handball you were moving and jumping and swatting and ducking so no one could walk through a game. Hands were flying. The ball was flying. If anyone tried to stop that, they would be nailed and besides, you don't break up a handball game. You just don't. That was a New York rule. Handball was the city's game, even more than stickball because everyone played it.

Every park in the city had concrete walls for playing and every wall in the city outside the parks had handball games going on so long as the weather wasn't freezing or raining. Adults played. Kids played. It was played in schoolyards. It was played against walls next to bars. It was played because there are a lot of walls in New York.

The next day we were playing, two games going on at once. One two-man game with Vinnie and Jimmy Lee, and a four-man game a few feet away, with Vanessa and Dorothy playing Buster and me.

We saw the two guys from the factory coming up the street. We kept playing. They got closer. We kept playing, hitting the ball against the wall, then whack, someone else slammed it back. It was fast. It was furious. It was racquetball without the racquets, but we didn't know that.

"You're blocking the sidewalk," said the mean man.

We kept playing. He started moving toward us.

Jimmy Lee hit the ball and drove it right next to the man into the wall and it shot back to Vinnie.

"You trying to hit me?"

"You can't break up the game," said Jimmy Lee.

Vinnie hit the ball even harder. Wap. It bounced off the wall. The mean man whipped his head to watch it then turned around and walked out into the street to get past us. He said nothing else.

We won. We knew it. We kept playing but none of us could stop smiling. We hit the ball and grinned and hit the ball again and tried to watch them climb the stairs to the El, but you really can't take your eyes off the ball for even a blink or you'll miss it. But we all knew it didn't matter who won the game, we all won.

We would be back the next day, just in case. There was not much else in life better than winning at handball, and we could do it every day before a good game of stickball.

The next day we were walking up to the corner to play when we saw a truck backed onto the sidewalk and a couple of men standing around the grating.

We ran. The grating was open and the tree was being pulled out by the men who had a rope around it.

"What are you doing? Why are you doing this? This is our tree."

One of the men laughed.

"You kids crazy? This is just a big weed."

"No, it's a tree. Look, it has branches and leaves," said Vanessa.

The man broke off one of the branches. "Okay, it's a weed that looks like a tree. Anyway, doesn't matter, the roots might go through the wall and cause flooding in their basement."

"It wouldn't hurt anyone," said Vanessa.

The man shook his head. "Little lady, we're getting paid to take this tree, or whatever it is, out. That's our job, so don't make it hard."

Then they all pulled and the tree came up with its roots holding on to rotting newspapers. It was like they said in the newspapers when they wrote about a body that was being dragged out of the East River after they got the grappling hooks on it.

"That's terrible," said Dorothy. "You guys are mean."

"Girly, watch your mouth," said the man. "Now all of you, just get out of here and let us do our work."

We looked at the tree lying on its side. Its branches were now reaching for a tire on the truck. One of the men took a saw and cut the trunk in half, then threw the severed parts of our forest into the back of the truck.

We stood still, saying nothing. They put back the grating and drove away. We looked down in the hole. There were still piles of newspapers and cigarette packs and soda bottles, but no tree.

"That's what happened to my father," said Buster. "The police came in the middle of the night and took him away. He did some crime or something, I don't know what. My mother told me not to tell anyone, but it's like that tree. It didn't do nothing. I never saw it do nothing, and then they took it."

"Sorry, Buster," said Vanessa. "Maybe someday your father will come back and you can tell him how you tried to protect the tree."

We walked down to the other end of the block. We did not want to flip cards or toss pennies, or anything. We just sat on the curb and talked about the tree.

"It was a real beauty," said Buster. "When I grow up, I'm going to plant a whole lot of sumacs and nobody is going to touch them."

Missing the Train

The weather was getting warm and Tommy was playing box ball with Johnny. It was a close game. The ball was flying back and forth and they were hopping and hitting fast.

They stood way back behind two squares on the sidewalk. It wasn't gentle hitting. They were about ten feet apart slamming the ball into their opponent's square.

"Over the line," shouted Tommy.

"Did not," said Johnny.

"Did."

"Did not."

"Do over," said Tommy.

They started again. If you were feeling lazy you could have a gentle game of hitting the ball back and forth and back and forth, sort of like passing time by kicking a can down the street, but that would be a stupid thing to do because playing box ball was neat. Half an hour could go by and you were still concentrating on hitting the ball into the other guy's box. Years later we would see tennis.

"Hey, that's box ball." They stole it from us.

"You want to see the new bowling alley?" asked Buster.

He was hanging around with us more now and he was fun because he had new ideas, like hang your legs over the edge of the station on the elevated train line and see if you could pull them back before the train came.

"I'm not scared," I would say. "If you do it, I'll do it."

I was scared like crazy, but you can't say that. And besides, I was sure I had gotten too big to crawl under the turnstile so I couldn't get up to the station to play. Buster was much smaller than all of us and he squirmed on the concrete floor of the station and easily slid under the big steel revolving gate. It looked more like a drum with indentations to fit into as you pushed your way around to the other side after you put your dime in the slot.

We waited until no one was around and slid flat as you could. When you got older, or bigger, like me, you had to turn your head sideways and lay your cheek on the ground and then breathe out and pull hard because you were really wedged under the revolving entrance.

That's where I was when the train came in, except I wasn't moving. Darn. I tried to go forward, but when you get scared you have to breathe and when I started breathing I got stuck tighter. I tried not to breathe, but the train's brakes were screeching which they did when it was stopping. I had to take a little breath. The station rocked. The train had stopped. I could hear the doors opening. I could hear the shoes on the metal steps.

I was going to be caught and someone would call the police from the emergency phone right there, right where I could see it if I moved my head even slightly, but I didn't want to move because my head would get jammed under the steel door the same as my bottom was jammed.

The police would come and arrest me and my mother would be really mad and yell at me. She was still mad at me for missing school and told me not to do anything bad again. "Nothing, do you hear me, nothing."

Then she added, if I did do something to get her mad again, "I would never know what hit me."

I didn't know. But that was a heavy duty threat, and now the thing I didn't know was going to hit me was actually going to hit me because I was doing something bad again.

"What are you doing there, kid? Get out of the way."

I couldn't see him, but I could hear him. He was behind me on the other side of the turnstile.

"I got to make that train."

"I can't move," I said.

"That's your problem," he said.

I heard the dime fall into the slot and then the turnstile started moving. He was going to push me right around and I would be a pretzel bent on the bottom. On top of that my mother would still hit me.

I felt his shoes inching ahead alongside my legs and the turnstile moving above me. I was trying to pull with my fingernails and he kept pushing and I was being pushed out like something coming back up your throat when you didn't chew it enough.

I popped out and he stepped over me just as the doors burst open and a crowd of people who had come off the train were rushing home. They always rushed. Every day they rushed even though they got the same train every day. Sometimes we would sit on the bottom steps and talk and read comics and the people would yell at us for blocking their way. They always said they were in a hurry, even though they came home at the same time every day.

They rushed in as I was getting up on my knees.

"You okay, kid?"

"Nah, I was just tying my shoelaces."

"You better not be trying to sneak onto the train," said one man. "The police will get you."

"I'm not," I said. "I'm just tying my laces."

"Just warning you, kid."

Then he was gone. Buster was waiting for me on the platform at the top of the second set of stairs.

"What took you so long? We already missed a train."

"I got stuck."

"That means you're going to have to start paying."

It was one of those shocks of reality, something you didn't think about each time you slipped under the turnstile. Growing up comes with a price.

"So what do we do?" I asked.

He sat down on the concrete platform and hung his legs over the edge.

"You sit like this and see how close the train can get before you pull them back."

"What happens if you miss?"

"Ahhh, don't worry. You won't. It's just a game."

So we sat a few feet apart and waited. A couple of people walked by behind us and looked at us, but said nothing.

Buster was sitting to my left, which meant the train would get to him first. That was okay with me because he would be hit first and I would have time to get away. It would only be half a second, but it would be time.

Then Buster got up and walked around behind me and sat down to my right.

"Why you going there?" I asked.

"Because I want to. I like this better."

We sat for a minute saying nothing when I got up and walked around behind him and sat down.

"Why'd you move?"

"Cause."

"Why?"

"Cause I want to."

Then we could hear the train. It always started as a low rumble. You got so used to it that if you were on the street you just automatically started raising your voice. But when you were waiting for it to come so you could get somewhere, you felt relief at that sound.

I was not feeling relieved. I was thinking that if I don't pull my legs out in time I will have to go around on crutches for the rest of my life with my stumps dangling below me and I would never be able to play stickball again or walk with Dorothy.

But if I pulled them back Buster would think I was a chicken.

I kept them there. The train was about five seconds away from reaching the end of the station. We were in the middle of the station. I could see the engineer through his window. He was shaking his head. No horn. What's the point? Just more stupid kids doing stupid things.

The train was at the edge of the station. It would be here in three seconds.

"One, two," I thought, quickly. I counted faster than I usually counted when trying to count seconds, then pulled my legs back and rolled onto my back.

Buster was already away from the edge.

"Chicken," I shouted.

"I came off the same time as you," he said.

"Did not."

"Did so."

We stood up and watched the people getting off the train. It was the beginning of rush hour and lots got off. They pushed past us because they were in a hurry.

"Want to do it again?" asked Buster.

"Naaah. That's boring. Let's go read comics."

Delivering the News

School is what school always is, confusing: "All you need to know about Africa is ABC," said Miss Johnson, "A black continent." She did not laugh or make any other comment. "As for the Low countries, the people are very clean."

She held up a picture of a woman scrubbing her front steps. "They clean their steps every day in Holland. And they wear wooden shoes."

This was mindboggling. Wooden shoes would be impossible to walk in and cleaning every day would be impossible to do. Besides, I've never seen Mrs. Kreuscher scrub the front steps.

"And now we are going onto current affairs," said Miss Johnson. "Do any of you know what's in the news?"

"The Dodgers are doing well, Miss Johnson," said a kid in the back.

"Yeah, they might get a pennant," said another kid.

"Don't be crazy," said a girl. "The Dodgers are never going to win."

Then everyone was talking. It was not like this at other times. No one talked, but now everyone was.

"They are."

"They can't."

"Will."

"Won't."

"Stop!" shouted Miss Johnson.

Miss Johnson raised her voice? She only did that when the Russians were attacking. We stopped.

"That's better," she said. "We were talking about current events."

"The Dodgers are current," said Dorothy.

We loved the Dodgers, but now I loved them more than you could ever begin to tell. I loved them more than life or stickball or maybe seeing Vanessa naked. Before this I didn't know Dorothy liked them. She had not sat outside the bar on the sidewalk watching games.

"But the Dodgers are just sports. We should talk about things that are important, like Winston Churchill stepping down."

There was silence in the classroom. We were back to things from different worlds. We knew what was important in the news. Miss Johnson did not.

"Mickey Mantle hit his one hundredth homer in the summer," someone said.

"Boooo." There was an onslaught of boos. Mickey Mantle may be the best hitter in the history of baseball, but he was a Yankee and no one in Brooklyn or Queens would ever say anything good about the Yankees.

We knew about the play, *Damn Yankees*. None of us had ever seen it, but we heard about it and we knew what they were talking about.

One guy hated the Yankees so much that he sold his soul to the devil so that they would not win the pennant. They always won the pennant and this guy wanted just once to stop them. A soul is nothing compared to seeing the Yankees lose.

The other thing about the play was it was the only time we were allowed to say "Damn" around adults and no one said anything.

"But that is not real news," Miss Johnson said.

One kid in the back raised his hand. There were kids talking now who had never talked before.

"But it's in the newspaper, so it must be news," he said.

A boy on the other side of the classroom stuck up his hand but started talking before he was called on. "There's a newspaper in Brooklyn that said we shouldn't call them 'Bums.'"

"Dos Bums," shouted kids from all over the classroom and everyone started laughing.

"Dos Bums don't never win," said a couple more kids.

We knew the lines. We knew what the men said when they would stand on the corner at nine at night when the first editions of the *News* and the *Mirror* would be dropped off and they would flip the papers over so they would see the back page first.

"Lost again, dos Bums," they would say while standing under the street light with the train going overhead.

"Wad you say? I couldn't hear you," another man would say who was drinking a can of beer that he got from the deli. The can was in a small brown paper bag because it was against the law to drink in public, but if you hid the can no one said anything.

We knew he wasn't a real fan because who would spend time buying beer before finding out if the Dodgers won or not?

"Dey lost, dos Bums," a guy with the newspaper would repeat.

"Dos Bums," said the man with the can and then he took another swig to ease his pain.

Sometimes the men would see us hanging out on the corner about seven o'clock and they would ask us to go down to Lefferts Boulevard to get the papers. That was the first place they were dropped off, at the Stand.

"You two kids, you wanna get the papers for us?" said one guy another night. "The *News* and the *Mirror*. Here's a quarter."

He flipped Vinnie and me the coin.

"Keep the change. But you better get back here before the trucks or I'll wring your necks and squeeze the quarter out of you."

That was a good deal. Fifteen cents tip for only an hour of walking.

There was a sign over the paper, and smokes and a beer shack saying MEET ME AT THE STAND. It was a small building with a Long Island Rail Road trestle going right over its flat roof. There was only about one foot of space between the roof and the trestle so it was very noisy when a big passenger train went overhead. And over that trestle was the El, so you had two trestles passing right over the newsstand with sometimes two, and sometimes four trains going by at once.

"What'd you say?"

"I said you want to get a Coke while we wait for the papers?" I shouted at Vinnie who was standing next to me.

"The papers aren't here yet," he shouted back, but then the trains were gone. He didn't hear the Coke part. Being under the tracks is harder than being on the wrong side of them.

"I said," I started to shout but then didn't. Sometimes you felt stupid shouting when there were no trains. The trucks were still noisy, but they were just raise-your-voice noisy, not shouting noisy. "I said, do you want a Coke while we wait?"

"You crazy? Suppose the papers come while we're drinking and we wait to finish our Cokes before we leave and the truck gets to our street before we do. Suppose that, huh?"

Right. If we didn't get back before the papers were delivered to our street not only would we be dead, but we would never get this job again and then we wouldn't get the fifteen cents tip again. Fifteen cents was enough for two small Cokes, even Cherry Cokes, which cost six cents each. Or we might get a Vanilla Coke, but that you only did when you were with a girl. I don't know why.

But with the mixed drinks, you had to drink them there because you had to sit at the counter and get them in a Coke glass. If we got a bottle to go it was ten cents and then we had to split it, which was okay so long as no one took more than they should.

A truck pulled up at the curb. It said the *News* on the side. Right behind it was the *Mirror*. A couple of large guys riding in the back of each of them started throwing bundles of papers onto the sidewalk and one of the guys from the Stand was out there with a pair of tin snips cutting through the wire around the bundles. There were lineups of people waiting to buy them and they didn't want to wait until the guy got the wire off. They grabbed papers and pushed the coins at the poor fellow who was trying to move the papers away from the curb.

There was little news on the radio, and no evening news on the TV, even for those who had TVs, except for a guy who would sit behind a desk and smoke Camels and read the newspaper stories. So why wait for that when you had it here in your hand?

We grabbed a paper from each stack and went inside and got a bottle of Coke and left with a nickel change. Then we started walking. It was eighteen blocks back and if we walked really fast we could do it in twenty-five minutes, although that would mean some running and we couldn't do that and drink our Coke. It was all under the El but we still managed to talk. There were fewer trains at night.

"Where do you think the bottle came from?" Vinnie asked.

"Don't know. And we can't tell 'til we finish it."

"Yeah, but where do you think? I want to save one from every state, but my mother keeps throwing them out."

Coke bottles were reused over and over until the word Coke, which you could feel even in the dark, was worn out. But on the bottom of each bottle was the name of the state where it came from.

"I got New Jersey," Jimmy Lee once said when he turned it over to see, but the bottle was open and his Coke ran down on his shoes.

"You goof," we said. "That wasn't worth Jersey, everyone gets Jersey."

"Yeah, well I once got one from Florida," said Joey. "I don't know how it got here. I bet it was a truck driver."

"Where's Florida?" asked Jimmy Lee.

"It's in the south somewhere, because it's warm. You can swim all year round," said Joey. "My mother said my uncle bought some property there but it was swamp land."

No one said anything for a moment as we tried to picture what a swamp was.

"So what happened to the bottle?" I asked.

"My brother peed in it," he said, "so we had to throw it out."

Vinnie and I passed the bottle back and forth as we walked.

"How many drinks did you have?" he asked.

"Four. How many you?"

"Four. There's only one drink left," he said. He was still holding the bottle.

"Well, take half a drink," I said.

"I don't know if I can take half a drink. It might all go down my throat and I can't stop it."

"Then I'll take it," I said.

"No, I'll take it."

I grabbed for the bottle. "No, you will drink it all."

We had a tug of war and I dropped the newspapers just as a truck was going by on Jamaica Avenue under the El with the closed-up furniture warehouses along the sidewalk and the wind from the truck had nowhere else to go but straight at the *News* and the *Mirror*.

"No!"

The papers started blowing down the sidewalk and we dropped the bottle and it broke and we ran after the sheets of separating news and sports. Vinnie grabbed some and put his foot on some other pages. I grabbed some and they crumpled in my hand. Another truck went by and some of the other pages took off flying away from us.

I ran and jumped on them and held them under my shoes right under a billboard that said "DON'T DRIVE A DEATH TRAP." The sign was put up by an auto fix-it shop. I liked it because I always thought if I ever have a car I'll make sure it's not a death trap by going to that shop. Some things in life were so simple.

The billboard next to it said, "don't let your kids get polio. keep them away from dirty water and crowds."

I sure didn't want to get polio. The sign had a picture of a kid on crutches like Richard French and another kid in an iron lung. No matter what, I would not drink dirty water.

We had all the pages now, but it was hard to tell which ones went together. The *Mirror*, we were told, was the name of that paper that because it was a mirror of the *News*, the only thing different it had was Walter Winchell, and different sports writers. But we didn't know who they were.

We stuck the pages back together so at least both papers opened again and nothing was upside down.

"Hope they don't notice," I said.

Jackie Robinson: Few have played better or lived braver.

"They just want to know about number forty-two," said Vinnie. "It doesn't matter what page they find him on."

Number forty-two was Jackie Robinson, the saviour of the Dodgers and the world we knew because that's what everyone said.

When we got to the bar, we handed over the papers nervously.

"What's this?"

"Your papers."

The two men opened them, going from page to page.

"They have holes in them. They look like they've been stepped on."

Vinnie and I looked at each other with shock.

"I'm going to call up the papers and tell them off," said one of the men. "How can they print papers like this?"

That was truly a gift from heaven.

"Yeah," Vinnie said. "People were just grabbing the papers when we were there. We just got these two and left."

"You want your change back?" I asked.

"No, of course not," said one man. "Rotten papers." He opened it and scanned down a page. "Jackie got two hits." He was so happy he was giggling.

He lowered the paper and his face was beaming. The world was okay.

We crossed the street and walked over to Matty's.

"Want to split a Three Musketeers?" I asked.

We spent our remaining nickel and walked down the block eating and pulling a three-way gooey, chocolate-covered bar apart two ways. It was hard to get anything better.

"My mother says I have a guardian angel," said Vinnie. "I think she helped us with the papers tonight."

Setting the Pins

"Hey, you want to make some money?" Joey asked.

Money? Of course I wanted to make some money. Then I could buy things like Cherry Cokes and candy and comics. The twenty-five cents my mother gave me each week was not covering it all.

"My father told me the new bowling alley is looking for pin boys."

"I could be a pin boy," said Vinnie.

"My father says it's real tough work," said Joey.

Vinnie shrugged. "Tough work is my middle name."

I wanted to ask, but I was afraid to ask, but I wanted to ask so badly so I asked, "What's a pin boy?"

Joey looked at me like I was stupid.

"I don't know," he said. "I thought maybe you knew."

He said we should go to the bowling alley and find out and maybe we could be pin boys and make some money. None of us had ever been in the bowling alley before. It was a couple of blocks away and we didn't know how to bowl and it was lit up and there were a whole bunch of reasons we did not go. Most of all, it looked scary. This was not like climbing on a roof or going to Matty's. This was a grown-up's world.

We walked in and it was noisy, and grown up. It was filled with smoke and people drinking. Crowds of people. It was right under the El, but there was so much noise that I could not hear any trains. There was crashing and banging and people talking and many of the people looked like they knew each other.

We saw people rolling huge balls down the wooden lanes and most of the balls looked like they were gliding, not rolling. Then crash. The pins went flying. We could see the pins rising after that and getting set up straight. It was easy to figure out what a pin boy did.

"You kids want something?" said a big man with a giant stomach. We did not see very many men with big stomachs, even the ones in the bar. They all said they had beer bellies, but they were not huge like this one.

"We want to be pin boys," said Joey.

"Ha, white boys, I don't think you're strong enough."

What the heck was that? None of us had ever been called a white boy before. He pointed to the side of the alley and told us to go down there and see Charlie.

"Wad he mean by dat?" said Buster. He talked fast.

"I don't know," I said. "I'm strong enough for anything."

"I mean the 'white' part," said Buster. "Of course we're white, what does he think we are?"

We walked alongside the last lane and saw a ball going by us, then crash. The pins went flying again. We figured out the game before we got to the end, but then we saw some black arms come out of the blackness at the end of the alley. Black hands grabbed two pins each and stood them up on spikes that came out of the wood. Then the hands went down and grabbed four more pins and put them up on the spikes.

Then the ball came down the lane where we were watching. Crash.

The same black hands came out and swept away the pins that were knocked down but were still lying on the alley.

Then a ball came down the other alley where the pins had just been set up. Crash.

The black hands, the same hands, swept away the two pins that were on that alley.

Then a ball came down the other alley where the hands had just left. Crash. The black hands came out and started to set up the pins. Then a ball came down the alley next to us. Crash. The hands were still setting the pins in the other alley.

"Hey." And after that came a nasty, face-slapping, insulting, painful word that we no longer say, not even in memoirs. It was the only word they used and it hurt the one who had to listen to it. "Hurry up."

The shout came from a group of men who were standing at the end of the alley where we had met the man with the stomach. The hands finished the pins in the other alley and then suddenly appeared in the alley next to us. But just as the hands were putting up the pins, a ball came flying down that alley before the hands could get away. Crash.

"Owwww, owww, man, that hurts."

The hands had still been holding the pins when the ball hit. The men burst out laughing.

"No tip for you," one of them shouted. "You're too slow."

Then a ball came down in the other lane and smashed down all the pins.

A great shout went up. "Strike! You're the best," someone shouted.

"Hurry up with those pins."

We got to the end of the alley. A black kid about our age was holding the fingers of his right hand under his left arm. He was wearing a white t-shirt which made him look even blacker. He looked at us but said nothing.

Another ball came down the alley and smashed into the remaining pins in front of him. He covered his face with his hand as the pins went flying.

It was noisy, it was scary and I didn't want to be here.

The black kid slid over a low wooden barrier to the other lane and started putting up the pins.

"Hurry up, kid, or we'll get you fired."

We could hear the shouting from the end of the lane.

He finished that side then came over the wooden barrier closer to us and stepped on a metal bar. A set of pins, like nails, came out of the end of the alley and he started picking up the wooden pins and setting them on the spikes. The wooden pins each had a small hole in the bottom.

But before he finished with this side a ball smashed into the pins on the other side and the slamming and noise started again.

"Hurry up, we said," someone shouted.

He finished on our side then went back to the other, but before he got there a ball hit the pins he had just put up. One pin bounced off the ball and hit him in the back as he was climbing over the barrier.

"Ugh," he groaned. But he kept setting up the pins on the other side.

"Tough job?" asked Joey.

"Not tonight," said the kid. "I've only got two lanes."

"What do you mean?" Joey shouted over the noise.

"Sometimes I get three, that's busy."

We had never talked to a black kid before. Maybe we did somewhere in a store or something, but none of us could remember. We saw black men walking along the street sometimes, but we didn't talk to them.

There were no black kids in P.S. 54. Miss Johnson always told us about how the South was segregated and coloured people could not ride in the front of buses and they had to use separate toilets and they couldn't even drink out of the same water fountains that white people did. But it did not make much impression on us because we almost never saw anyone who was coloured.

They lived in South Jamaica and in Hollis and lots of them lived in Bedford-Stuyvesant in Brooklyn. But not in our neighbourhood. They stayed in their area and we didn't go there.

"We're thinking of getting a job here," said Joey.

The black kid looked up from his pins.

"I don't know no white kid who could do this."

While he said that he took his eyes off the pins and didn't see the ball that was thrown down the lane before he got the pins up. That must have been a joke. The ball hit and we could see horror all over his face. He was not ready for this one.

The pins exploded and came right at him. One slammed into his face. He screamed. Blood came out of his nose. He dropped the pins that were in his hands and grabbed his face.

He made some sounds; we thought he was almost crying. Then he lowered his hands and started putting up the pins.

"Hurry up [that painful word again]," someone shouted.

Vinnie said, "Let's go. I can't do this."

We walked back down the edge of the lane. At the end, the man with the big stomach was waiting.

"You want the job?"

"How much does it pay?" asked Joey.

"Twenty-five cents a game, plus tips, but this kid won't get no tips tonight. He's too slow."

"We'll think about it," said Joey.

We walked out of the bowling alley and a train was going by overhead but it seemed quiet compared to inside.

"That black kid is stronger than any of us," said Joey. "I think he's stronger than all of us together."

"Blacks are born stronger," said Vinnie. "My fadder told me that. That's why we have to stay away from them."

We walked back to our street under the El.

"That's mean, the way they do things in the South," said Buster.

"Yeah, would you drink out of the same water fountain as them?" asked Vinnie.

Buster did not answer. We were all wondering about the answer.

"I'm glad they're not in Rocky's gang," said Buster.

We might not know if we would share a water fountain, but we did know for sure that we did not want to fight them.

Poison

"It's neat if you break it. You can do lots of things with the mercury. But I don't want to break it."

Vinnie was holding a thermometer while we were alone in the lunch room.

"Where'd you get that?" Tommy asked. "And let me see it."

He held out his hand. We all knew you couldn't see something unless you held it. You couldn't just look at it. Unless it was in your possession it might as well have been on the other side of the world.

"No," said Vinnie. "I got it from Miss Johnson because she said we were going to do a science experiment this afternoon."

Tommy was still reaching for it, trying to pull it out of Vinnie's hands.

"What kind of 'speriment?" I asked.

"That's not how you say it," said Vinnie. 'Miss Johnson said it's got an x in the front."

That was confusing. X's aren't in words. They were only in

Xmas which we knew you only used if you were Jewish. On the other hand, we were told that X was okay because that was Latin or Greek or something for Christ, so it didn't matter if you used X.

"What kind of 'speriment?" I asked again.

"To see if it's colder down here."

"Of course it's colder down here," I said. "This is the basement."

Vinnie held on to the thermometer and Tommy kept grabbing for it and Vinnie held it up and he was taller than Tommy.

"Get out of here," said Vinnie and pulled it away, but Tommy jumped up and snatched it like a ball going by second base.

"Got it," said Tommy, but only for a second, because after he pulled the thermometer out of Vinnie's fingers it kept on flying. Sometimes a ball or a thermometer did that. You never could be sure of what you had in your hand until you tagged the guy out. Sometimes you would tag and shout, "Got you," and then you would see the ball bouncing down the street. It was just like now with the thermometer bouncing off a bench then bouncing on the floor. Then it shattered.

"Now you've done it. Miss Johnson's going to send me to Miss Flag," said Vinnie, "and it's not my fault."

Tommy was down on his knees scooping the mercury into a puddle.

"Look at this stuff. This is better than the temperature. Look. It's like water but it keeps rolling around."

He squeezed the sides of his hands together and some of the mercury popped up into his palm. He moved his hand around and the mercury rolled like a ball.

"Neat stuff," he said. "Look, I'll put it on my tongue and see what happens."

He dropped what was in his hand into his mouth and made his tongue into a cup and we looked.

"Looks like mercury on your tongue," I said.

"But isn't it . . . " He tried to talk but in moving his tongue he swallowed the silver ball.

"Agggh," he said. "I didn't want to do that."

"I think you're going to die," said Vinnie.

Tommy suddenly looked frightened.

"I don't want to die."

"I heard once that if you get mercury poisoning your brain rots and then you die," said Vinnie.

"Noooo," said Tommy. He grabbed his head. "I don't want my brain to rot."

"Better get it up," I said.

Tommy bent over and started trying to make himself throw up. He stuck his finger down his throat and gagged.

"Can't do it," he said.

"You better or you'll die," said Vinnie.

Tommy stuck his finger further down and this time it worked. He made some awful sounds and some liquid came up, but not the mercury. We would have seen that.

"What's going on over there?" someone shouted.

It was Miss Flag.

"I heard you down here and you are supposed to be in class."

"Tommy swallowed some mercury," I said.

"What?! That will kill him," she said.

That was when Tommy stuck half his hand down his throat and kept pushing harder. This time he gagged like I had only seen one person get sick before. I remember my father getting sick a couple of times, and he looked like Tommy looked now. But I never thought my father wanted to be sick with his face in the toilet and then gagging again when more came up, but Tommy wanted to be sick.

Tommy was trying to get sick and that was kind of fun to watch, except I knew that he might die, which I really did not mind because then he wouldn't bother Dorothy anymore.

"I'll get the school nurse," said Miss Flag. "You two go to your classroom and Tommy, don't worry, the nurse will fix you up, you won't die. But later I want to know how come you swallowed it."

Vinnie and I looked at the white face of Tommy. He was not feeling well.

"Don't worry, you'll be okay," we said. "But we gotta go."

But before we left, both Vinnie and I got some paper and scooped up some mercury. If you don't swallow it, it was fun. We had never seen this before. I folded the paper like a little bag and then grabbed the broken thermometer and we walked away.

"We'll tell Miss Johnson that it was an accident and we'll tell her you probably won't die," we said to Tommy.

On the way up the stairs we both opened our little treasures.

"What can we do with this?" asked Vinnie.

"If we show it to Miss Johnson maybe she can tell us about mercury and that will get us out of whatever it is she is talking about," I said.

"Well, let's just show her one of them," said Vinnie.

Vinnie was smarter than any of us thought.

We started talking as we entered the classroom because if we waited for Miss Johnson to ask us anything we would be in trouble.

"The thermometer broke. Tommy may die, but Miss Flag says he'll be okay. The nurse is going to fix him. It was an accident. We didn't mean to do it. I mean, Tommy didn't mean to do it because it wasn't our fault, it just broke."

"Stop," said Miss Johnson. "What's wrong with Tommy?"

"He ate the mercury," said Vinnie and I held up the broken glass tube and the plastic backing.

"What! He could die from that," she yelled.

Now we were scared. We didn't really think he could die, Vinnie just said that, and I was wishing it, but now Tommy might really die.

"I'll be right back," said Miss Johnson. "Everyone take their seats and get out a book and don't make a sound."

She left and everyone jumped up. "Is Tommy really going to die?" a bunch of kids asked. "What happened?"

But most of all we were asked, "Do you have any mercury?"

"Right here," I said.

I opened the paper and slid the sliver drops out on the floor. There was fighting and pushing to see it, but there was also a lot of ohhhs and ahhhhhs as we rolled it around and it broke apart then came together.

"Can it really kill you?" someone in the circle asked.

"You heard Miss Johnson," Vinnie said. "This stuff is dangerous. It's more dangerous than poison. One little drop and you're dead."

"Is Tommy dead?"

"Not yet," Vinnie said. "Miss Flag and the nurse are saving him."

"Let me try," someone said and pushed through the circle and put his hand down over the fluid.

But he hit it with the heel of his hand and it splattered and now there were only tiny drops. We tried to push them together but they were too small. The door opened and Miss Johnson stepped in.

"I thought I told you to be quiet and stay in your seats. I may have to keep all of you in. But just for your information, Tommy will be alright. The nurse made him regurgitate and he is resting."

A shuddering thought went through many heads. Regurgitating sounded like an operation or at least something very scary.

"And I want to warn all of you, mercury is very dangerous. You should not let it touch your skin or your clothes or even your shoes because you might touch your shoes with your hands and then it could get into your blood and cause serious problems."

Basically every pair of shoes lifted off the floor. Everybody straightened away from the backs of the chairs.

"Now where is the leftover mercury?"

No one said a thing.

"Well, come on, I have to put that in a safe place."

Nothing.

"Vinnie, where is it?"

"Everywhere," he said.

"What do you mean?"

"Everywhere on the floor and my hands and Mickey's hands and some other kid's. Everywhere."

This was something else that was not taught in teacher school. She looked at a class of frozen students.

"Alright, two at a time I want you to tiptoe out of the class-room and go to the toilet and take your shoes off and then wash the bottoms of your shoes and wash your hands and then line up outside in the hallway. You two first." She pointed at the first two kids in the first row.

We all got cleaned up and all stood in the hallway and we made no noise. When we were done, she said she would go back inside and get our coats and we would sit in the auditorium until three o'clock.

"But if you go in there you'll get it on your shoes," Vinnie said.

"Don't worry about me," she said. "I want you all to grow up to be smart young men and women, and learn to be careful."

She got our coats and told us the janitor would mop out the floor and it would be alright for tomorrow.

"But the janitor will get sick," I said.

"That's okay, we'll warn him and he knows how to take care of things like this. Janitors know a lot more than we think."

All the way home we said to each other "you can't hit me. I

maybe have mercury on my clothes and then you'll get it on your hands and die."

We passed by some tough kids, not ones from Rocky's gang, but other tough-looking kids that were hanging out under the El. Suddenly we felt invincible. They looked at us with mean stares. Sometimes kids would come into the neighbourhood and shake down a lone kid or two for their money, even if it was just a nickel.

They looked like the kind of kids who would do that. But we kept walking right towards them. On another day we would have crossed the street to give us room to run if we had to, but not today.

"If they touch us they'll die," Vinnie said to me.

We both smiled, not the smile of funny, but the smile of power. And maybe it was the way we were walking, or maybe they had heard about the mercury or maybe they weren't after our money, whatever it was, they stepped back when we passed. They were bigger than us and they stepped back. That had never happened before.

Vinnie and I got half a block past them and broke out laughing.

"Did you see that? They stepped back. They moved out of the way."

It was hard to believe, but it happened, and it happened to us. Vinnie was so excited he hit me.

"You might die from that," I said.

"I'm not going to die," said Vinnie. "I'm never going to die. That mercury is making me stronger."

That did not make any sense, but I felt the same way. So I hit him. Then he hit me and I hit him and we had the best walk home of any time in my life, except the time when I kissed Dorothy.

Laundry Day

"**M**rs. Belimeyer hung out her sheets."

Vinnie was like a little kid when he said that. He was twelve years old so he wasn't a little kid but he was like one when he saw laundry on a line, especially sheets.

When the sheets came out on the clotheslines, we would play run through the laundry, and since he'd loved getting hugged a lot when he was small, he could pretend he was little again and have arms wrap around him. It was a cool game that was also warm.

We were playing stoopball, wondering if anything was ever going to happen to end our boring day. Then Vinnie told us about the laundry. Stoopball was for anytime. Laundry was when you got a chance.

I remember once seeing my uncle help my aunt when she was hanging out clothes, but that was different. That was when my uncle was the toughest guy on his street. I knew that because he drove a bus and you had to be strong to do that. That was a lot of people he was hauling around.

He also liked football. He played football when he was younger and told me about tackling other guys and I couldn't imagine how you did that. You had to throw yourself at their legs and bring them down. If I tackled someone I figured my face would hit the street and that would be the end of the game for me.

He also mowed the grass in cemeteries when he was really young. But he did not have a power mower. He used a hand mower and pushed it back and forth, so I knew he was strong.

But he would not do laundry. How could he do laundry? He had to fix some lamp or polish some shoes. Laundry was for women, like his wife.

Then one day, while I was visiting them, my aunt had hung out her underwear on the line. She put the clothespins on the line and strung out the things that she wore under her clothes, the kind of things we laughed at when we saw them, except I didn't laugh when they belonged to my aunt.

She was putting the last pin over the last unmentionable when the hook that was screwed into the wooden window frame, which hung onto the pulley for the clothesline, came out of the wall. It just gave out, like things do after fifty years of holding on.

"Help, Ed, help," she yelled.

He jumped up from his lamp or his shoes, it doesn't matter which, but when he heard his wife yelling he was almost there already helping.

"What's wrong?" he asked. He saw her leaning out the window.

"The line's come out," she said. She did not turn her head around.

"Let me get it," he said.

"No. I can't let go."

He could not get past her to reach out the window.

"Just let it down. We'll pick them up and I'll fix the line," he said.

"No, I just washed them and I don't want them to get dirty."

They lived on the first floor. It was only a few feet to the ground.

"But I can't get past you to grab it," he said.

She pulled harder trying to hold the clothes off the ground.

"I can't let them get dirty."

"But I can't do anything if you are there."

"I'm not moving," she said.

He turned and walked away. I had never seen him leave anyone with a problem, much less his wife. But there he went; I thought he was mad and was going to show her a thing or two.

But he did not stop walking. He headed straight to the front door, opened it and went outside. Then I saw him through a side window walking through the alleyway to the back. In a moment he was standing below the line.

"Let it come down," he said.

I could hear laughter and if I pressed myself against the window, I could see a group of men next door in the backyard laughing at him.

"Going to pick up the little lady's underpants?" one said.

My uncle said nothing. He reached up and took the first piece of frilly whatever it was off the line. The laughter grew louder. He took the next lacy thing off the line and put it on his shoulder on top of the first frilly thing.

"Panties on the shoulder, looks nice," one of the men said.

My uncle was very strong. I wanted him to go over there and punch them. But he kept unpinning the undies and piling them on his shoulder.

"Did you wash them too?"

I thought he was going to throw down the underwear and walk over and punch them all. He was going to show them. You don't say things like that to my uncle who can beat up everyone.

But he kept putting the frills on his shoulder and telling my aunt to lower the line a bit more.

"Hey, you look cute," said one of the men.

My uncle took the last piece of clothing and my aunt let the rope of the line fall on the ground. Then he walked straight back through the alley, past the men.

They said nothing more. He said nothing. Please say something, I thought. Please hit them. Please beat them into the ground and then come home with the underwear. Please.

He walked past them.

When he came into the apartment, I said, "Those men were not very nice."

He looked at me and smiled. "They have problems. I hope they get better."

Then he took the underwear off his shoulder and placed it alongside the kitchen sink and told his wife she could hang them up inside.

The men outside were talking and laughing and opening beer. My uncle was fixing the clothesline. I wanted to be like my uncle.

But that had nothing to do with Mrs. Belimeyer's sheets that were rising in the wind like waves. They almost touched the ground when the wind died because they were so wet. The rope line was ten feet up, but the sheets filled the entire space from just above the cracked concrete to the clothesline. Perfect.

"Ready," said Vinnie. "Get set."

He was rocking back and forth on his legs waiting for the right breeze to lift the sheets. That one was too small. He rocked, we waited, he rocked.

The wind came again. A good wind that lifted the sheets toward Vinnie. He waited and waited, then he headed for Mrs. Belimeyer's clothesline. He hit the sheet and his arms went up and he looked like a ghost. That sheet stopped rising while the others went up beside it.

"You shouldn't do that," said Dorothy.

"But it's fun," said Vinnie. "And besides, we don't hurt anything."

"You sure get her mad," said Dorothy.

"Ahhh, she gets mad at everything," said Vinnie. "You coming?"

I wanted to do it, but if Dorothy wasn't going to, I wouldn't, but I was hoping she would because it was fun, and maybe we would get stuck together behind a sheet and then maybe we might touch.

"I don't think so," said Dorothy.

"Come on," said Tommy.

"Come on." Vinnie was waving to her.

"No."

"You coming, Mickey?" Vinnie asked.

"No, I don't think so. That's for little kids."

Joey came back with Vanessa who was just walking down the block looking for anyone to hang out with. By the time we were eleven and twelve the word "play" was fading unless it was playing stickball or something. Mostly we just wanted to hang out.

"You going through the sheets?" Vanessa asked Dorothy. "I am."

Dorothy laughed sort of a sweet little laugh that I knew was laughing at herself. I was getting to know Dorothy's laughs.

"Okay," she said.

"What about you, Mickey?" Joey asked.

"Yeah, sure, yeah, I got nothing else to do."

We all lined up to go through the sheets. Vinnie got close to me.

"You like Dorothy, don't you?"

"Do not," I said.

"Then why'd you change your mind about the sheets?"

"Cause. Just because."

"Just because you like Dorothy."

I think that was the best part of the day, even better than the sheets.

"Wait for the big one. Wait. Go." We all said that same thing. We were all coaches.

The little kids were in front of us. They were heading for the clothesline just as the sheets were rising and heading for them. They timed it perfectly. They hit the sheets just as the cloth was going up and the wet cotton went across their faces and continued up into the sky as they ran underneath.

"Wow. That was neat," said one of them.

"I'm going next," said Tommy.

He ran to the other side of the yard and waited until the sheets were at their height. Then he stood like a racer at the starting line, though I had no idea what a racer at the starting line looked like then. He stood up sideways rocking back and forth ready to run. The sheets flapped in the wind then started to come down.

Tommy rocked and the sheets came down further. He rocked again as they fell, then the wind hit them again and one more rock and he was off. He ran like the police were chasing him. He hit one of the sheets as it took off and slammed into it, held up his hands and kept going until he came out the other side.

"That was fun," he yelled.

Me and Dorothy and Vinnie and Joey ran over to where Tommy had started from. We all rocked and waited. But the wind had died. The sheets just hung. The little kids ran through them and Vinnie shouted, "Hey, you kids, you're ruining it."

But they did not care. They ran through and then turned around and ran back.

"Come on," said Vinnie. "Wait 'til the wind comes."

But the little kids didn't listen. They ran through the sheets again.

"I'm going to beat you up if you don't stop," yelled Vinnie.

"Can't catch us," one of them said.

Then the wind came. It was a giant wind that sometimes came down between the row of houses and the hill of the railroad tracks. It came out of nowhere and lifted the sheets like kites. I should also not say kites since none of us had any idea of what kites were except for the picture we saw in school of Benjamin Franklin flying a kite in a storm to prove that electricity was real.

None of us had any idea how flying a kite in the rain proved anything except that you would get wet, and if you got hit by lightning you would die. We were told we should never stand outside in a lightning storm and we had plenty of those. We could watch the lightning from under the overhang at the front of the bar or from under the stairs of the El. But we knew if we stepped outside and a bolt came down it would kill us. So why was someone as smart as Benjamin Franklin standing outside in the rain with lightning and why didn't he die?

We asked Miss Johnson, but she only said he was proving electricity was in lightning.

"So why didn't he get killed?"

"Because he was doing an experiment."

"Do experiments keep you alive?" we asked.

"No. They can be dangerous, and he was brave to do what he did."

"So can we stand out when there's lightning?"

"No, you'll be killed."

School was so confusing.

But the sheets reached as high as they would fly and then started down. Wait. Wait. It was falling. It would only take a second or two but if you ran too soon you would miss it. You would go right underneath it before it fell and then everyone would laugh. Wait 'til they fell, wait 'til just before they started up again.

"Go," yelled Joey.

We took off. Only ten running steps but the timing was everything. Ten steps and we hit the sheets just after they fell and one second into them rising again. We hit them and the bottom of both sheets wrapped around us and made us look like wet blobs in a world of white.

The cool of the water was wonderful on my face. It slid over my skin and wrapped around my bare arms. My t-shirt got just a bit wet and when I came out the other side I could feel the freshness on my chest.

Dorothy came out right behind me along with Vanessa, Tommy and Vinnie. I would have little chance of getting lost alone in the sheets with her, but it was still fun.

"Where's Joey?"

"Here!"

He raised the other sheet over his head. He had two hands on it and pulled it down to wrap around his head like a hat and a scarf. Then the wind came up again and the sheet buckled out and before Joey could let go, the clothespins snapped and the top end of the white bedcover fell down into the only muddy puddle on the ground.

"No!" shouted Dorothy.

The little kids saw what happened and took off running. We were left holding the crime, the evidence and the conviction.

"Poor Mrs. Belimeyer," said Vanessa.

"We better get out of here," said Tommy.

"No, we can't," said Dorothy. "We messed up her sheet and we have to fix it."

The boys looked at her like she was saying something

impossible because this was impossible. Sure, she could come up with hooks for fishing, but this was a muddy sheet.

"She's right," said Vanessa. "We have to fix it."

Fix it? Vinnie tried to wipe it off but it smeared further. Fix it? "How?" I asked.

Vanessa said we needed a pail and some water and soap. Johnny said he could get a pail. There was a hose behind the house that someone used for washing their car. Soap was a problem. No kid could try to sneak out of the house with soap. Suppose he was caught?

"Where do you think you're going with that soap?"

"Uhhhhhh. Washing something?"

Right there would be an unexplainable problem since no kid at home wanted to wash anything, not the dishes, not himself. It was not like being caught sneaking out with a rat trap or a jar of peanut butter.

"Nothing, just hunting rats," or "just sharing lunch."

But soap? Never.

"I'll try to get some," said Dorothy.

She was an angel, and she could probably get away with it.

"I'm going out to do some girl stuff with the other girls," she might say to her mother, or something brilliant like that.

In five minutes, Johnny came back with a pail filled with sand and cigarette butts and Dorothy came back with her blue jeans' pockets filled with powered detergent. The sand was dumped out and the pail rinsed out. Then the soap went in and a corner of the sheet went on top of the soap and then we poured the water on top.

"I'll do it," said Vanessa. She looked so pretty scrubbing I thought for a minute that she was even better than Dorothy, but then I saw Dorothy holding the rest of the sheet so it would not touch the ground and I liked her better again.

When I was older I learned that love is fickle, but I was not fickle then, I was just admiring them both for saving us all and they both looked very nice, especially when they moved.

"I'll do it now," said Dorothy. She shoved her hands in the pail and Vanessa held the sheet, letting the dirty end drop into the water. It got scrubbed then Vanessa pulled it out, piling the rest of the sheet on her shoulder and I saw the water dripping down on her pants.

I thought for a moment of marrying both of them.

"Mrs. Belimeyer's coming down the street," a little kid yelled. He ran into the alley. He had seen her at the other end of the block. Considering he was fast and she was slow we had about four minutes to finish.

Dorothy and Vanessa held up the sheet. It looked very good, almost no brown at all. They stretched it out and said, "Put the water on it."

Tommy aimed the hose that was attached to the faucet and hit the sheet but the water bounced off and hit the girls and me and Vinnie and Joey.

"Keep going," said Dorothy.

The water hit the sheet some more then Joey said, "Enough."

He grabbed the end and threw it over the line. He made it. Tommy and Vanessa took one end and started to pull. I jumped up and grabbed the end that was hanging over the line and pulled it down on the other side.

It came out straight. How did that happen? There were no clothespins on it, but it was hanging on the line and now blowing in the wind just as the back window opened and Mrs. Belimeyer stuck out her head.

"What's going on here?" she said.

"Nothing, Mrs. Belimeyer," said Joey.

"I know something is," she said. "I don't know what it is but it's something."

She started to pull in the line. No, don't, we thought.

She reached out and touched the sheet. "How did this get wet?" she said with a very nasty voice.

"Don't know," said Vinnie. "We were just playing."

"And where did my clothespins go?"

"Don't know," said Joey.

"Well, you kids did something and someday I'm going to catch you and you are all going to go to hell for being so bad."

Then she pulled herself inside and closed the window.

"Did you hear that?" said Joey. "She doesn't know what we did."

We all started laughing and walked down the alley together. "She didn't know."

We laughed some more. Vanessa and Dorothy were the heroes, although heroes who were girls were called heroines then, but we couldn't say it. The word was too big.

"Thanks, you two," said Joey. "You saved us."

We left the alley and put our arms around each other's shoulders, including Dorothy's and Vanessa's. I held Dorothy. That was very nice.

"Sheets is fun," said Vinnie. "Hope we can do it again soon."

Size Doesn't Matter

"You got a skate?" Johnny asked.

"Yeah, I got a skate, but just one," said Buster.

"So let's go skating."

Johnny and Buster were sort of loners, except Buster was really a loner and Johnny was sometimes a loner. But on the other hand, Johnny could do anything so it did not matter that he stayed by himself a lot.

I know why he stayed by himself. He told me and told me not to tell anybody ever and I never did. You don't get a secret and tell it or you're no good. But I can tell it because his secret wasn't true.

He had a small penis. That's why he stayed by himself because if we ever had a peeing contest and he was there he would have to go into the contest and everyone would know his secret and laugh at him.

He said he would never be able to get married and never have kids and he wanted kids so he could teach them to make things.

Johnny and Buster went skating, coasting on one foot and

269

pushing with the other. Most kids skated that way because it was impossible to keep two skates without one of them getting lost or stolen or the wheels on one of them getting so rusty they would never turn again.

That always happened when you put the skates away after it was raining and you put them in the basement because you were not allowed to keep them in your apartment. And you put one skate on top of the other so they would not get separated and then you came back two or three weeks later and the bottom wheels would not turn.

We knew that 3-In-One oil did not help. It made your fingers slippery, but the wheels still would not turn.

But then Johnny said he could do something. Every kid across the country heard about scooters that you could make from an old skate and a two-by-four and an orange crate. Every kid had heard about it, but not many really did it.

Except for Johnny. He became like a scooter factory one night. We had found some two-by-fours behind a factory and we could always get the wooden crates from in front of the grocery store on garbage day.

Johnny took apart some skates, oiled them, then nailed the front part with two wheels into the front of a two-by-four and nailed the back part with two wheels into the back of the wood.

Then he nailed the crate on the floorboard and even nailed some pieces of broomsticks at an angle on the top of the crate for steering.

It was so simple, but no one else had done it. We rode and raced and yelled and went over the cracks in the asphalt and got out of the way of cars and crashed into each other and had the best night of our lives.

Johnny also liked boats. That's because his big brother was in the

Navy. We never saw his big brother, but there were lots of pictures of him in a sailor uniform and in front of ships.

"I'm joining the Navy, too," said Johnny.

But until he was old enough, he had his own Navy, though mostly they were just Popsicle sticks that he would float along the edge of the gutter after a rainstorm. The water came off the street, hit the curb and ran like a river to the sewers.

When there was a big rainstorm, the gutter ran with rapids. Put a stick in and you could barely keep up with it, running, picking it up when it got stuck behind a tire and then racing to the mouth of the sewer, trying to grab it just before it got sucked into the black hole of the bottomless pit that swallowed goldfish.

"It's also called Davy Jones' Locker," said Johnny.

"What's that?" asked Vinnie.

Johnny said he asked his brother one day when he was home on leave after his brother told him that he was lucky to have escaped Davy Jones' Locker.

"It's death, Johnny. It's a funny word for when your ship gets torpedoed and you are swimming in the ocean and the sun is burning overhead and there are sharks and your shipmates say they see mermaids way off toward the horizon."

"He said 'then they swim away and you never see them again,'" Johnny said his brother told him.

"That sounds worse than being in the Army," I said. "At least in the Army you just get shot and you're dead right there. I don't ever want to drown."

Johnny was sharpening the end of a Popsicle stick with his pocket knife so it had a bow.

"I don't care if I drown. I have a picture of my uncle steering a landing barge on D-Day. He wasn't afraid and I'm not either," Johnny said.

Sometimes Johnny tied two or three sticks together and sailed them. Sometimes he put a cigarette butt in front of his ships and let them try to catch it. The butt was the enemy submarine surfacing and his ship was the sub chaser.

"The sticks are like Corvettes, except America didn't have any Corvettes," he said. "But Corvettes were the fastest. The Canadians had lots of them. They were supposed to protect the convoys."

Johnny knew a lot about ships. But one day he was alone and soaked after a storm – he had been out all day during the rain trying to get his ships going, first with a trickle of water, then with a torrent – when out of nowhere came a boot that kicked his Popsicle stick into the curb.

Johnny looked up in disbelief. No one had ever kicked his ships before. That's not the way the gutter Navy works.

"I want this spot," said Stan.

Stan was big, almost six feet. Johnny had not seen him since the kick-the-can incident. Stan had long, wet hair and wore a black motorcycle jacket. He was about five or six years older than us and lived in one of those apartments on the corner next to the El.

All we knew about Stan was that he had joined the Army, but he was back before basic training ended. We heard it was a medical discharge, but we didn't believe it because there was nothing medically wrong with him.

He was just mean. Even after the night with kick the can, he was still mean. People don't change after one game. We figured he was too mean even for the Army.

"I want your boats," he told Johnny.

"Make your own," said Johnny.

"I want yours, so get out of here."

Johnny knew he could not fight Stan. But he also knew he was not going to back down and go away. His brother had told him you never back away from a fight, not in the Navy. And now the Navy was up against the Army.

"You're going to be sorry," said Johnny.

"Yeah? What are you going to do?"

Johnny stood up, leaving his sticks on the ground and said, "I'm just telling you, you're going to be sorry."

Stan made a fist. "Any time you want to try."

Johnny went farther down the street. The water was running faster now and was almost two inches deep along the curb. He got half a block away. He could just see Stan squatting down getting ready to launch Johnny's ships.

Johnny scooped up some dirt and gravel from under the water by the curb. His fingers got scratched and then a piece of glass cut him. The pain did not come until a moment later because of the cold water. The blood started oozing out. He thought of the billboards with the kids in iron lungs and knew that you could get polio from dirty water. Then he thought of Stan taking his ships and he shoved his hand back into the water and scooped up more pebbles and gum wrappers and cigarette butts and packed them into a dam. He hid it behind a tire then put some more dirt on top and wiped his hands on his pants.

The water hit the dam and made a right angle out into the street in the path of the delivery trucks.

Stan was running down the sidewalk at the edge of the curb trying to keep up with the Popsicle sticks. Johnny bent down between two parked cars just beyond of the dam and waited.

When Stan's ships hit the dam, they changed direction in front of him and took off like torpedoes. Stan tried to grab them, but he was way too slow. The ships shot out into traffic and the aim and the timing were perfect, even if there was no aiming or timing beforehand. The ships went straight in front of the tire of a truck coming down the street and were crushed in an exploding, shattering instant that was too fast for Stan to stop.

Stan looked bewildered. Johnny stood up from three car lengths in front of him and gave one giant "Ha!"

"What did you do?" Stan shouted.

"That's how the Navy takes care of the enemy," Johnny shouted back. "My brother taught me that."

Stan started to run around the car to hit him, but Johnny stood his ground and raised both his fists. Blood was running out of one of them.

"I'll show you what else my brother taught me," Johnny yelled.

Stan looked at the fists and the blood and the soaking wet kid standing in front of him and waved his hand down like he wouldn't bother to fight him and turned around and walked away.

Johnny just stood there and watched him go. He could not wait to join the Navy.

He told me about Stan and I said once again, like I often did, as a joke to tease him, "Show me your penis."

"No," he said. "It's small. And you probably are going to tell someone if you see it."

"Will not," I said. "When you're in the Navy you'll have to take showers with everyone and . . . "

His face went blank. Before I finished talking I could see he didn't think of that.

"So show me. Let's have a peeing contest. Mine's not so big either and maybe yours is the same size as mine."

His face was still blank.

"Let's go around the corner in the alley behind the garage behind Mrs. Belimeyer's house and pee."

Still blank.

"Come on. You'll have to do it when you're in the Navy so do it now and I'll tell you."

He walked. But he didn't talk. He walked like someone going to the electric chair. I always figured I knew how people walked to the electric chair because two years earlier my uncle tried to get me into the Cub Scouts – one evening, I was with a bunch of kids in the church basement for the meeting and there was a big picture of Jesus on the wall when someone said, "Julius and Ethel Rosenberg were just fried."

The Scout leaders cheered.

We knew the Rosenbergs were supposed to be spies for the Russians and gave them atomic secrets, but every kid also knew that the government never really proved they did that. We heard the stories that they were innocent and stories are always true, or almost true.

But some of the boys who were waiting for the Scout meeting to start began walking under the picture of Jesus pretending they were going to the electric chair. They waddled back and forth because their legs were in chains.

Then they sat down on the hard metal chairs against the wall where the picture of Jesus was hung and they turned on the electricity and shouted, "Zap. Agghhh. Agghhh, again." And they squirmed and jerked in the chairs until the Scout master said, "Stop that silliness. They got what they deserved. And now get up and act like Scouts."

Except for the chair, that's the way Johnny was walking now.

"Come on. I bet you've never been in a peeing contest."

He shook his head.

We got behind the garage.

"Take out your thing," I said.

He shook his head.

"We can't have a peeing contest if you don't take out your thing," I said. "I'll take mine out first."

I unzipped and pulled out my penis. He watched.

"Now yours. I'm not going to do it for you."

He unzipped, slowly. He reached in and I saw his face go up to the sky as he pulled out his penis.

"That's almost the same size as mine," I said.

He looked down. His eyes went from mine to his, back to mine, back to his.

He almost smiled.

"But you said yours was not so big and mine's smaller," he said.

"Well, it's different sizes all day long, you know. It depends on if I'm running or scared or thinking of Vanessa undressing."

I felt like a teacher. I was giving a lesson to Johnny but I was thinking how could anyone not know that?

"We got to pee now. Who can get the furthest over that line. You got to pee?"

"A little," he said.

"Well, try."

I squeezed and my pee came out over the line on the concrete and then Johnny's came out and went further than mine.

"If yours goes further it means yours is stronger," I said.

I looked to see if he heard me but on his face was a look of horror. Then I saw what he saw, Mrs. Belimeyer coming down alongside the garage, which was our only escape route.

"I caught you, I finally caught you, you sick, rotten kids. You are homosexuals. That's what you are. I'm telling everyone."

She was shouting. We were trying to stop peeing and put our penises back but it was impossible to stop peeing that quickly and get them back inside and get zipped up and I was peeing on my hand while my hand was trying to push myself back inside and I could feel the pee running down my leg.

"I saw you two going in here. I knew you were up to no good. Now I'm telling your mothers."

Johnny looked like the electricity was going through the chair and he was sitting on it. I looked down and saw the stain on his pants was down to his knee. I was still trying to pull up my zipper. Nothing could be worse than this minute.

"Owwww," I screamed. I caught the skin of my penis in my zipper.

"Owwwww!"

I screamed again, louder because it hurt more the second time when I realized what I had done, and Mrs. Belimeyer shut up.

I knew what was going to happen next because this had happened before. When I tried to pull the zipper down it would hurt even more. That would last for a second before I was free but I could not stand more pain, even if it meant less pain. And I could not pull it up past this spot like you do when a zipper is caught on your coat because then I would not have a penis. And I could not just stand there, bent over, screaming because it was hurting worse than anything I could describe and I had do to something.

"Stop your screaming. That's not going to get you out of this mess you're in," shouted Mrs. Belimeyer louder than I was screaming.

I pulled down on the zipper and screamed again, now louder than she was shouting.

"Oh, that hurts," I said after I was free and knew the pain would go away.

"You two come with me," she said. "I don't want homosexuals doing dirty things behind my garage."

"We're not that," said Johnny. "We were just having a peeing contest."

It was easy to get past her because she moved aside, not wanting us touching her. She even pulled her hands back when we moved.

"We're not homo-sex things," said Johnny. "I don't even know what that is."

We got free and started to run, but it was hard because our pants were sticking to our legs.

"You are going to hell," she shouted as we hopped and limped and half-ran down the alley.

"What's a homo thing?" asked Johnny.

"It's when two guys do something together, but I don't

know how they do it," I said. "So don't worry, we're not whatever it is."

Johnny later served two hitches in the Navy then moved to Florida where he was last based and opened a construction business. He and his wife had three girls, and there were always a bunch of kids hanging around his garage where he taught them to make things, like old-fashioned scooters and boats out of Popsicle sticks.

The Arms Race

"The Dodgers are on a streak."

"Are not," said Vinnie.

"Almost every game," I said.

"They're bums," he said. "They're gonna lose."

We were swimming. We had come up for a serious talk about baseball and were resting on top of the ocean.

"Look at all the Greeks," said Vinnie. "It must be hot in those clothes."

The Greeks were wearing heavy white North Pole-type coats that had hoods with fur lining, which they wore because they worked in the freezer making ice cream. Their pants were thick and heavy. But on their coffee breaks they looked odd sitting on milk crates in the sun.

It was early spring, probably April because a lot of people had ashes on their foreheads for Ash Wednesday. That was important because the Jewish kids had to be on time for school and we didn't. But we didn't want to go to church either because we had not been swimming all winter and this was the first time the ocean was getting filled up.

So we went in the water and talked about the Dodgers and we could be late for school. All we had to do was get some dirt from the street and rub it on our heads and the teachers said nothing.

"Why do you think Greeks have so much hair?" I asked.

"To keep them warm in the freezer."

"But they were born that way. How'd they know they were going to wind up working in a freezer?" I asked.

Vinnie crawled across the top of the boxes and I followed until we got to the edge by the fence and we could look down on the men in the thick white winter coats.

"Look, you can hardly see their faces," said Vinnie. "That's because they're Greeks."

We crawled out of the ocean. The easiest way was to swim down almost to the ground to a hole in the fence that had been there for years. That way when we came out we did not mess up the boxes which would have happened if we got out through the open end where they threw the boxes in.

We did that a couple of times last year and they got mad at us and yelled things, but it was in Greek so we didn't know what they were saying. But once we started using the hole, they just smoked their cigarettes and drank their coffee and watched us. It was funny that we never saw them eating ice cream.

On the way to school, Vinnie and I passed an empty store when some arms reached out and grabbed us. They pulled us into the dark doorway and pushed us up against a wall. There were four of them.

"Rocky wants to settle this once and for all."

We said nothing.

"You hear?"

Nothing.

"You better talk and say you heard us or we'll give you a knuckle sandwich and you'll never talk again."

"Okay, we heard you," said Vinnie. "What do you want? I mean, like what'd you mean?"

"We mean a war, with guns. Zip guns tomorrow after school."

"We can't do that, we don't have any," said Vinnie.

One of the guys laughed. "Well then, you've got a problem because we're coming after you and we're shooting to kill."

"You got to give us an extra day to get ready or it's not fair," said Vinnie.

"Rocky said tomorrow. We'll meet you between you and us, up on the tracks, right after school."

Then they let us go and they ran away.

"We better tell Joey," I said.

We hurried to school. Zip guns were dangerous. Only once did I see one and that was when a kid brought it to school to show off. We all knew how they worked. His was like a pistol, one piece of wood, one by one inch by eight or nine inches long. That was the barrel and another piece nailed to it that was the handle.

A thick rubber band was held at the end of the barrel with a nail and you stretched the rubber back to the handle and hooked it over a headless nail that was sticking up where the hammer on the gun would be. Then you put a piece of square linoleum in the rubber band, aimed, and with your thumbnail slid the rubber band up over the nail. Zap.

With a strong rubber band the linoleum could go thirty feet. If you used a little piece of sheet metal instead of old flooring, you could get forty or fifty feet. But most of all, if you made a rifle that was three or four feet long and used a sliced strip of inner tube you had something that would fire more than a hundred feet, well across four train tracks.

"And it could put out your eye," said Vinnie.

We told Joey just as Miss Johnson was talking about the Civil War. But a train was going by and all we could hear her saying was,

"I hate to talk about war but . . . " Then the train passed and we weren't sure why she did not like war.

But we sure knew what Joey was thinking when Vinnie leaned out of his seat and whispered it in his ear.

"What?" said Joey. "I can't hear you."

"I said Rocky wants a zip gun war with us tomorrow."

Miss Johnson stopped talking.

"Vincent, you know you're not supposed to talk when I'm trying to teach. But what did you say about war?"

"Nothing, Miss Johnson. We were just talking about how bad war is."

"You said zip guns. Are you making zip guns?"

"No, Miss Johnson," said Vinnie. "We don't have any."

She closed her book. "Zip guns can kill you and put out your eyes and you will be blind forever and do you know how bad life will be then? You'll bang into walls and you'll spill food on yourself and you'll never be able to go to a movie. Now I hope you don't make any zip guns."

"No, Miss Johnson. We won't."

But there was nothing else on my mind, or Vinnie's or Joey's for the rest of the day. We knew we had to get home, find wood, get Johnny to help us put them together and then get some linoleum or sheet metal and get it all done before we had to go in and pretend we were doing our homework.

Miss Johnson may have talked about war, but she never had to get ready for it. And if we didn't do our homework it was because soldiers, real soldiers, don't have time for that.

The day went slowly. Three o'clock was the starting line. We ran home. By then every kid in the school knew there would be a zip gun war tomorrow and most of the kids said they were glad they didn't live on our block. All of the kids in Rocky's gang went to Holy Rosary school. It is good to have your own gang in your own school and on your own block. That saved on fights in school.

"You gotta help us, Johnny. You gotta."

"But I'm sick. I have the stomach flu, that's why I didn't go to school today."

Joey looked at him straight in the eyes. Joey never looked scared, but this time I think that was the look on his face.

"Johnny, you gotta help us. You can make anything."

"But I have diarrhea."

"So we'll make them in your basement," said Joey.

"But the bathroom's upstairs."

Vinnie moved alongside Joey. "Help us this once and we'll do anything in the world for you."

"I don't want anything except to stop going."

Then he groaned, an awful sound, and turned and ran upstairs to his apartment. "I can't make it," he shouted.

"He'll be okay," said Joey. "Let's find the wood and get some inner tubes and we gotta find some ammunition."

Linoleum was not hard to get. When it was worn out, most men just ripped it up off the floor and took it around the corner of one of the factories and threw it out. Then they bought some more and tried to measure it and lay it down themselves. That is why most apartments had big gaps between the end of the linoleum and the beginning of the sink or the stove.

At first I thought that was the way it was supposed to be with the worn-out black wood showing around the edges of stoves and sinks. Then I went into Johnny's kitchen and it looked so neat.

"Who put in the linoleum?" I asked.

"I did," he said.

But today he had to make zip guns.

We got back to his basement with a pile of wood and an old inner tube and Johnny got a hammer and nails and a saw and started putting together some guns. They were not hard to make, just a few nails and some handles at the end of the wood. But

Johnny made them look good. He even put rifle butts on them so we could hold them against our shoulders and aim them like real rifles.

The inner tube was harder. We made thin slices with a razor blade then sliced the slices in half because they were still too thick. They had to be strong, but they had to be thin enough to stretch at least double their length.

Johnny nailed the two ends of a rubber strip together at the front of the rifle right where the bullet would come out, then stretched the looped end more than three feet back to the tiny stub of a nail right below where our aiming eye would be. Vinnie and Joey and Buster and Jimmy Lee and I were cutting squares out of the lino as fast as we could.

We test-fired one piece in the first rifle that Johnny made. The lino went snugly between the rubber straps and Joey aimed it at a wall and pushed the band up over the nail.

Zap. It fired faster than we could see and hit the cinder-block wall and tore a chunk out of it.

"Wow," said Vinnie. "That would hurt."

"I gotta go to the bathroom," said Johnny.

He ran upstairs and we went on cutting up lino and Jimmy Lee cut some small rubber strips for one of the pistols. They were for close fighting if Rocky's guys got over the tracks.

In two hours, we had seven rifles and four pistols and more than a hundred rounds of ammo.

"Tomorrow we will slaughter them," said Joey.

"I wonder how many guys they'll have," asked Jimmy Lee.

"I think maybe ten," said Vinnie.

"We only have six, or seven if we can get Buster," I said.

We said nothing for a while.

"Don't be sick tomorrow," said Joey to Johnny after he came back looking pale.

Then we all went home and tried to do our homework.

World War

"You're not going to fight with zip guns, are you, Mickey?"
Dorothy looked worried.

"Don't worry. We can handle them."

"But you can lose an eye."

"If we don't we lose everything. We won't even be able to come out of the house."

We were walking to school and I never expected Dorothy to be walking with me.

"I waited for you," she said.

What?!

"You did?"

"I don't want you to get hurt."

There is no way to tell you this without sounding like I was going to explode with happiness, so I won't even try. But I felt very big. "I won't get hurt. We just have to keep them from coming over the tracks."

"When is the fight supposed to be?"

285

"Right after school."

We walked for a minute without talking. We passed the cardboard ocean and the Greeks who were taking their morning break. They were sitting on crates in the sun drinking coffee from Thermoses. I did not know how they got up so early and got to work before we even had breakfast. They had it hard, I thought.

I could see they were turning their heads as we walked by and I thought I saw a couple of the men smile when they saw me with Dorothy. I don't know if they knew what I was thinking.

"How many do they have?" she asked.

"Vinnie thinks ten and we have six, if we can get Buster. And seven if Johnny is not sitting on the can."

She said nothing. We walked past the Bungalow Bar trucks getting loaded with ice cream and past the dry ice that was steaming in boxes on the ground.

"I didn't see Johnny this morning. I think he's still sick," she said.

"He'll be alright," I said. "He said he'd be alright so he has to be."

We walked under the El and the morning rush hour trains that came one after the other were thundering overhead.

"You can't call it off, can you?" she shouted.

I shook my head. Of course not, she knew that.

School took forever that day. Miss Johnson seemed to talk in slow motion. The whole day went by and it was only lunchtime.

"We're going to beat them," said Vinnie.

"I hope there aren't too many of them," I said.

"Don't be scared. You only die once."

I thought that was true and it was a good thing because I would hate to get killed by a zip gun and then have to get hit by a car later on.

Three o'clock and I had an hour and a half to live. It might be less. Fights after school always started at five after three. But this was bigger so it would be later. But we had to be there when they attacked or they would come right over the tracks and be on our street, and then they could take over the street, and us.

I thought the couple at the deli would miss me tonight when I did not come for hot dogs. They would wonder what happened and then hear I had been killed in a zip gun war. They would not know I died before I got to tell Dorothy what I thought about her.

Tommy, Vinnie, Jimmy Lee, Joey and me knocked on Johnny's door. His mother opened it.

"Can Johnny come out and play?" we asked.

"Johnny's sick," she said. "I even had to stay home today because he was so bad off. I thought I would have to take him to the hospital."

We walked underneath the El on our way to school. This is where I tried to talk to Dorothy about the zip guns but when one train went over another train no one could hear anything. The ice cream factory was behind the truck on the left.

None of us could think of saying anything. We couldn't say that the guns that her son made were still in her basement. She started to close the door.

"Does that mean he can't come out?" said Vinnie.

She opened it halfway.

"Of course he can't come out. I gave up a day of pay. Do you think he's going to come out now? I'd kill him," she said.

She closed the door and we went down the steps to the sidewalk.

"You think we could talk Rocky into waiting a day before we tried to kill him?" Vinnie said.

"Are you kidding?" said Joey. "When he hears we don't have any guns, he'll be over the tracks and shooting us in the face."

I thought that would hurt.

"Maybe we can break into Johnny's basement and get the guns," said Jimmy Lee.

We looked down the alley alongside his building. The windows were only seven or eight inches high. They were made to put a coal chute into and were right above the empty coal bins. We could not open them, we could not fit through them and if we could, then we would wind up in a storage space upside down and stuck between piles of junk.

"I don't think so," said Joey.

"Let's knock on the door again and tell his mother we have to get something out of the basement," said Jimmy Lee.

"That's crazy," said Joey. "She'll be mad if she has to open it again for us."

Silence. I was thinking it is a tough choice, getting killed by Rocky's gang or getting Johnny's mother mad at us.

"I'll go," I said.

I went back up the stairs and knocked. Then I waited. And waited. And a lot of time went by.

I started to knock again but the door opened.

"I thought I told you Johnny was sick," said his mother.

"We're sorry to bother you, but we left something in your cellar."

"What?" she asked.

I looked back at the desperate tiny gang standing on the sidewalk then said to Johnny's mother, "Just some things."

"Well, I can't have you traipsing through my basement. Tell me what it is and I'll get it for you."

What? That's crazy. Worse than impossible. If I told her we needed guns she was not going to say, "Okay, just wait a minute and I'll get them for you."

She would scream and rant and tell us we were ruining her son's life and we should go away and never come back and what guns were we talking about and she was going to call the police. So I said, "Some sticks."

"What do you need sticks for?" she asked.

"Making something?" I asked. Why did I ask when I said that? I wasn't sure. It was the first thing that came out of my mouth and it was true, sort of, but I didn't say it, I asked it.

"We need them for a school play."

That was Dorothy saying that. Dorothy was not part of this. I turned and there she was, all smiling and friendly and she was a girl talking to a mother just like girls do, which is different than boys. Mothers listen to girls.

"Johnny helped us make them in your cellar and we need them to practise with."

I halfway believed her even though I could not believe this was happening.

"Well, okay, you come and get them. But just you," said Johnny's mother.

Dorothy passed by Joey and I heard her whisper, "Where are they?"

"Against the wall on the opposite side from the furnace," he whispered. "And you got to get all the linoleum too."

She smiled and hopped up the stairs like a little girl. Johnny's mother let her through the door, then returned to the open space and stood there in case one of us tried to rush the opening.

"Since when are you kids doing a school project?" Johnny's mother asked.

"Oh, we love school projects," said Vinnie. "This is an after-school project."

In three minutes, Dorothy came out with all the guns and the linoleum squares in her hands and stuffed in her pockets.

"What kind of project is that?" asked Johnny's mother.

"It's a science project about moving things," said Dorothy.

"Oh," said Johnny's mother. "Well, don't break anything."

Then she closed the door.

We could not believe Dorothy did that. She dropped everything on the sidewalk.

"Why didn't you put the lino in a bag?" she asked.

We started picking up the guns.

"I'm taking one, too," she said.

"You can't," I said. "This is not for girls."

Dorothy grabbed one of the rifles. "I got them for you. Without me you wouldn't have them. And besides, this is my street, too."

Once again we couldn't believe what she was saying. I know I couldn't believe it and I know what everyone else was thinking because no one could believe such a thing was happening. We were now six. Six against ten or twelve was not good, but it was better than five.

"I'm going with you, too."

We looked behind us. Vanessa was standing there looking so sweet.

"You can't," said Joey.

"If Dorothy can, so can I."

"But supposed you get killed?" Jimmy Lee asked. And he asked it in a way that we had not heard him talk, ever. He really meant it.

Then I thought, I didn't say that to Dorothy, and I wished I could turn back time, again.

"Well then, give me flowers on my grave," she said.

Seven, which included two girls, but that was not bad.

"We better go now or we won't have the tracks to keep them away," said Tommy.

We walked down the street, half-running, half-excited, half-frightened, half-terrified, half-feeling like we were invincible and half-wishing we were doing our homework.

"Where did you come from?" Dorothy asked.

Johnny was standing at the fence that separated us from the tracks.

"I thought you were sick," Joey said.

Johnny's face was sick. He looked terrible, like he was in pain.

"I am sick. I don't think I can hold it, but I can't let you fight by yourselves."

"What'd you mean you can't hold it?" Vinnie said.

Dorothy moved in right next to Johnny like she was his mother. "It means he can't hold it. Like he's sick and he can't hold it. You know what that means, don't you?"

"Well, what are you going to do if you can't hold it?" Vinnie asked.

Johnny looked like he did not have the strength to answer.

"Forgetaboutit," said Joey. "He'll hold it. He's a real friend. You too, Dorothy, and you too, Vanessa."

We all walked to the fence.

"But your mother's sure going to kill you," said Vinnie. "That is if you live through this."

We threw our rifles over the fence and started climbing. A

train was coming at the top of the hill. In a moment it was racing by with the big wheels flying. We could see it was mostly empty going to Manhattan to pick up the rush hour crowd going home, which meant we might get this whole fight done without many people watching us.

We climbed the hill and as our heads got to the top, just level with the tracks, zap. A piece of linoleum went flying just over us. Then another, and another.

We took cover, laying flat on the hill. When I looked up, I saw an army. There were more than twelve. I don't know how many. Maybe fifteen. Oh, God. Zap, zap, zap. The sharp squares were flying overhead. We could not even get up.

I loaded my rifle and tried to poke it up and fire, but I know my shot was very high. I know that because I wasn't aiming at them. To do that, I would have to point the gun at them and that would mean I would have to get up high enough to see them and if I did that, I would have only one eye.

Zap, bang. Some of their shots were hitting the tracks right in front of us. Joey and Vinnie were getting up on their knees and shooting, then falling back down to reload.

"Owww."

That was Jimmy Lee. Then I saw him get up and shoot anyway.

I got on my knees and fired again, but this time I saw they were coming across the tracks. They had little need to hide since we were only firing a handful of times.

Bang, zap, bang, "owww."

This time it was Vinnie. He was holding his face.

Dorothy and Vanessa were together. They both got up, shot, then got down.

"I want to help." The voice came from behind us. I looked down the hill. It was Buster.

"Get one of the guns," I said.

In a minute he was laying beside me, loading, then popping up and firing, then dropping down and loading again and jumping up. He looked like some soldier I had seen in a movie once. He didn't look like he was afraid of anything.

"Owwwwww." That was me. "Owwwwww." I grabbed my stomach. "Owwwwww." I meant it. That hurt. It went right through my shirt and was stinging like crazy.

I put another piece of lino in my gun and this time I took careful aim. The pain in my stomach made me want to hit someone. I eased the rubber up over the nail and watched it go.

"Owwwww."

I got somebody. Ha. But my stomach still hurt.

And now we had a problem. "Fire faster," said Joey. They were in the middle ground between the two sets of tracks. They were only about twenty-five feet away and they could crouch down now in the hollow of the ground.

We were firing. They were firing. Then we could hear another train coming from our left and heading for Manhattan.

"Load up," Joey shouted. "When it passes, everyone shoot at once."

"What happens if they attack after that?" Jimmy Lee shouted back.

"We hit them with our guns," Joey shouted, but suddenly it was quiet. The train had gone. We had not loaded up fast enough. Dorothy and Vanessa stood up and shot, but now they were coming.

For the first time, I was really scared. I pulled my rubber band back, hooked it over the nail, and put one more piece of lino into it. This would be my last shot. Then it was hand to hand and we didn't have a chance.

"I'm coming, I'm coming!"

I heard the screaming from behind us.

"I'll show them what we do in the real Army."

It was Stan. Stan, who was rotten and mean and miserable and big and strong and older and crazy, was running up the hill.

At the top, he grabbed some of the rocks by the side of the tracks and started throwing them.

"Owww, owww, owww!" He was hitting them with every one. "Owww, owww!"

"This is how I threw hand grenades," he yelled as he scooped up more rocks and threw them so fast he had no time to wind up. He just fired them.

"You can't use rocks," we heard Rocky yell. "Rocks are not in zip gun wars."

Stan heard the voice and his aim was a lot better than most of us who had really good aim.

"Jeeeze, owwww!"

Rocky was hit. Then Stan threw another one. Same target. "OWWWW!!"

I don't know where he hit him, but I could hear that it was a hit and that was better than I had done.

It took a moment for us to get over our shock at having Stan with us, but we loaded up and fired, then I grabbed some rocks and I saw Johnny standing up throwing rocks and Buster was throwing them faster than I could believe.

Jimmy Lee was still shooting, but he was standing now and taking careful aim and zap, hit, "owwww." Zap, "owwww." Hit. He scored again.

Rocky's gang was retreating back across the tracks. We could hear a train coming from the other direction, from the city with the first of the rush hour commuters going home. Rocky's guys either had to stay where they were and get hammered by us, mostly by Stan, or try to get back across the tracks before the train came. They had only a second to move or it would be too late and they would either be killed by us or really be killed by the train.

We kept throwing. They turned away and ran. God. That was close. They all made it before the train came.

Then we saw someone still in the hollow lying on the stones on this side of the tracks.

"Don't shoot. I give up."

We could barely hear him. The train had not finished ripping by yet. But we could see his hands up, surrendering.

Rocky? Is that him?

The train passed. Rocky was on his knees with his hands up.

"I give up. Don't shoot. You won."

Rocky? Really?

"Don't," pleaded Rocky.

Stan was standing ten feet away with a rock cocked back in his arm.

"Don't," said Dorothy.

"He's a prisoner of war," said Stan.

"Let him go," said Joey.

Stan lowered his arm.

Another train was coming on our side. We backed up.

"Go back to your own street," shouted Joey.

Rocky got up and after the train on his side passed, he crossed the tracks in retreat just before the train came from our left in front of us. We stood at the top edge of the hill just three steps back from the giant wheels. The wind was scary and fierce, as always.

We said nothing. We couldn't say anything because we couldn't hear anything we might have said if we did say something. But we all wanted to say something.

Then the train was gone. "Did you see that? Did you, huh?"

"We won. They lost."

All our voices were mixed together.

"Why are you here, Stan? And thanks, Stan. You saved us, Stan."

We said everything at once. Then we heard from across the tracks, "It's not over. We'll get you next time."

Darn, just when we thought everything would be good.

"You try it," shouted Joey. "We're better than you any day."

Then we sort of climbed, but mostly fell and rolled down the hill and climbed the fence, just in time to hear the sirens.

"Hurry," someone shouted and we did. "Forget the guns, just leave them," said Joey. "Go home, and good luck, Johnny."

Everyone scattered and by the time the first police car got to the end of the street, no one was there.

"Where have you been? What have you been doing? How'd you get so dirty? Where'd you get those cuts? Why are you hanging around with those rotten kids?"

The same questions in every house, except Stan's. His mother just asked if he had a good day.

He nodded. She was happy.

I looked at my stomach behind the closed bathroom door. I had been cut right through my shirt, which was ripped. I had a big, red welt right above my belt. I put some soap on it so I wouldn't get polio and it stung even more.

We would trade stories the next day. Vinnie had a scar on his face for the rest of his life.

But that night there were smiles in every house, even when we were being yelled at. And once our hearts stopped pounding, which was not until long after we lay down, everyone said they had incredible dreams.

Them Wonderful Bums

"The Bums are still winning," I said to Jimmy Lee.

"Can't last," he said.

We were swimming, just the two of us. Fishing had been bad. We hadn't caught anything worth talking about for a long time and it was getting dangerous arguing with the drivers who wanted to park over our sewers.

"Can't park here," I'd say. "We're fishing."

One day, a driver got out of his car and said, "I'm not even counting to three. I'm just backing up. If you're still there, I'll say I didn't see you."

He got in and we heard the gears grind as he put it into reverse. Then he started backing up.

"You think he's really going to kill us?" Jimmy Lee asked.

"Naaah. He's just bluffing."

He wasn't. The car came back without a brake light and we both jumped, Jimmy Lee onto the sidewalk, and me onto the street. The two bumpers clunked together.

"Hey, you bum, you coulda killed us," I shouted.

He stuck his head out the window. He had a cigarette in his mouth. "Where'd you come from?" he said in pretend shock.

I hated him even more.

"I didn't see anyone back there. Were you hiding on the street? Cause that's what I'd tell the cops, you were hiding and I checked in the mirror and there's no way I could have seen you."

Then he laughed.

So we went swimming. No one was going to kill us here in the ocean.

"What do you think the ocean's really like?" asked Jimmy Lee.

I shrugged. "Like this, with ice cream factories and trains. I think everywhere's like this."

We looked down at the snowmen in their parkas having coffee and cigarettes. They were staring at us. We stared at them. We were not going to be out-stared.

"Hey, Jimmy Lee, did you see him?"

"Who?"

"The one staring harder than the others are staring."

"Yeah," he said.

One snowman was smoking and staring.

"You think he wants us to come down?"

I looked down. He was still staring, then he stood up, put his Thermos back into his lunch box, flipped his cigarette out into the street and walked back into the factory. He took one last look at us before he walked inside.

"They're kind of scary, especially him," said Jimmy Lee.

"I know they're strong, but they couldn't catch us in here," I said. Then I dove down into the hard boxes with edges that jammed into my sides.

"This is great," I said underwater to Jimmy Lee.

"I can dive better than you," he said. Then he went down and I went down chasing him.

"Hey, you guys, hey, I want to tell you something."

It was Vinnie standing outside the boxes. He knew we were here because he could see the boxes moving. We swam over to the fence and grabbed the chain links and stuck our faces up against it. But we were about ten feet up and Vinnie was almost five feet below us.

"What'd you want?" I said.

"Come on down lower so I can talk to you," he said.

"Naah, you climb up here. I'm tired of swimming," I said.

The truth was that swimming through the boxes was the most wonderful thing in the world, but it also was the hardest. Pushing the boxes aside to crawl through them was okay when you were trying to escape with chocolate wafers or were following Dorothy, but it was not worth it just to talk to Vinnie.

"No, you come down here," he said.

Vinnie had the news, whatever it was, and he did not want to climb the fence to tell us.

"You come up here," Jimmy Lee said.

"No," said Vinnie. "If you want to know what I'm going to say, you got to come down here."

"No," I said, "If you want to tell us, you got to come up here."

But I knew I would go down there because news was more important than swimming. And besides, Vinnie was heavier than any of us and so climbing the fence was harder for him. It was because he had pasta every night, and he had pasta for breakfast. That was the leftover pasta from the night before. And then he had pasta for lunch.

"I could eat pasta every day," he said.

"But you do eat pasta every day," all of us said.

"Pasta is my favourite."

"Don't you like potatoes?" we asked.

"Sure I like potatoes. Sometimes I have them with my pasta, but mostly I like pasta."

We had no idea that potatoes and pasta could change the way you looked. We only knew that Vinnie was bigger than all of us and he had pasta every day. And because he was bigger, he did not like climbing.

"I have a secret, a super secret and the only way you're going to hear is down here."

"Don't care," I tried one more time just in case he would climb up. "And what's the big secret anyway?"

"The Dodgers are moving."

He shouted it up to us.

"What!"

That was impossible.

"Moving where? When?" I asked while trying to kick my way down. I was now surrounded by boxes, but this was terrible news and I had to know.

Vinnie shouted into the cardboard, "Los Angeles," he said.

"Where's that?" I shouted through the boxes.

"California."

I pushed two boxes aside and suddenly was face to face with Vinnie. That was scary because either I had to swim to the hole in the other end of the fence and then I had to find the hole, or I had to swim all the way up because I was almost at the bottom.

"Where's California?" I asked.

"It's as far as you can go. It's way past all those other states."

"Where are they going?" That was Jimmy Lee who had finally caught up to us.

"California," I said.

"How did you know?" Jimmy Lee asked me.

"Because Vinnie just told me."

"Why they going?" Jimmy Lee asked.

"Cause they don't like Brooklyn no more," said Vinnie. "That's what my fadder said."

"What's wrong with Brooklyn?" asked Jimmy Lee. He was

trying to get his footing in the boxes but kept slipping and now was below me sort of lying twisted like a pretzel around the boxes so I didn't feel so bad about myself.

"I don't know," said Vinnie. "But my fadder said we could go to Ebbets Field before they go and maybe see Jackie Robinson and that would be the most famous thing we could do in our lives."

We stopped talking. See Jackie Robinson? On the TV in the bar he was a speck. In the newspapers he was a picture. But see him? For real?

"My fadder said he's getting old and he won't be around forever."

See Jackie Robinson? For real, in front of us?

"They're playing at home tomorrow and Friday," said Vinnie. "We could skip school and see him."

We could see number forty-two? With our own eyes we could see him and then we could say we saw him and we could tell others we saw him and there would be nothing else in life that we would want. Nothing, except maybe Dorothy, who now had the same bumps as Vanessa.

I did not think Dorothy would go to the game because she would not miss school for anything, but I also worried about how I was going to skip out again. They said I would be held back if I played hooky any more. But it was the Dodgers and it was Jackie Robinson so there must be a way.

We got out of the boxes faster than ever. We went out through the opening where they threw the boxes in and all the boxes that we knocked out while we were getting out we threw back in so the Greeks wouldn't get mad.

"You going?" Joey asked me.

The word had spread faster than we had heard it. In fact, Jimmy Lee and me were the last to know about the trip.

"We couldn't find you," said Joey. "Why'd you go swimming without telling us?"

"Why are you going to see the Dodgers without telling us?"

"We did tell you," said Vinnie. "Right now."

Jimmy Lee was steaming. "If you didn't find us, would you have gone without us?"

"But we're not going until tomorrow or Friday," said Tommy, "and why'd you go swimming without us?"

Then he pushed Jimmy Lee. I was not going to let him get away with that, so I pushed Tommy back. Then he pushed me and I hit him, and he hit me.

Jimmy Lee pushed Vinnie. You really should not push Vinnie. All that pasta made him squishy yet hard, like a rock made of spaghetti. Vinnie did not move when Jimmy Lee pushed him, but he did hit Jimmy Lee who had never been hit by Vinnie before.

"What are you doing lying on the ground?" I asked Jimmy Lee when I looked down after I was hit by Tommy.

"Vinnie hit me. Do you know how hard Vinnie hits?"

"Well, are you coming to see the Dodgers?" Joey asked. He was leaning against a car not doing any pushing or hitting.

"Of course," I said.

"What'd you think we don't care about Jackie Robinson?" asked Jimmy Lee.

The Dodgers were playing Boston on Thursday. That was tomorrow. It was a 2 p.m. game. We could go to school in the morning and then just slip away at lunch. They would only miss us for half a day and we would only get in half the trouble, except I knew

I would be in deep trouble because of my earlier attempt at homeschooling.

Before I went to bed, I told my mother that I might be home late because of a game after school.

"That's not lying, is it Joey?" I asked.

We got on the train heading to Manhattan and all of us paid a dime, except we didn't really all pay. We could squeeze two of us through the turnstile together so it only cost a nickel each, except for Vinnie, since he was too big to share the space.

"Why do I have to pay a dime when you guys only spend a nickel?"

"Because you eat too much pasta," said Joey.

That was that. No arguing. We got on the train, which went through Brooklyn on the way to the city.

"We gotta change trains at the East New York station," said Joey.

"How do you know that?" I asked.

"I asked my father."

"Didn't he know why you wanted to know?"

Joey smiled. "He asked, I told him and he said 'go ahead, but don't let your mother know I told you.'"

"Gee, you're lucky," I said.

Joey nodded. "My father said everyone should see Jackie Robinson."

The stations went by and I lost count and I was lost but I did not say anything. No one was going to know I did not know where we were, but the truth is I had not taken a subway ride since my mother sneaked away from my father.

I walked to the department store to go shopping when my mother asked, and I walked to my aunt and uncle's house, and I walked to school. There was nowhere else I wanted to go. Our street was all I needed or wanted or cared about and all the geography I had to know, our street and the ice cream factory around the corner.

But now we were riding and then riding some more. It took over an hour.

"Are we there yet?" I asked Joey.

"I don't know. My father said we had to change at East New York. That sounds dangerous."

I did not ask why. We changed trains and rode more and the train went underground and that was exciting. We walked through the cars and then we took turns riding between the cars with one foot on the platform of each car. Light bulbs went flashing by along the walls of the tunnel and there was wind and noise. This was wonderful. We all wanted to ride the trains forever.

Then it was there, the station signs flashing in front of us as we pulled in. Flatbush Ave. This was like the first time jumping into the boxes. We climbed the stairs and we were in Brooklyn across from Ebbets Field.

"It looks just like it looks in the newspaper," I said.

We each had $1.25. That was enough for a cheese hero, made with American cheese, a bottle of cream soda and entrance to the bleachers.

"Why's it called the bleachers?" I asked when I bought my ticket.

"Cause you sit in the sun and bleach," said the man selling me the ticket.

We sat in the sun. It was hot. We ate and drank even before the game started.

"There he is. Number forty-two."

He was in a lineup along the first base line. All the players held their caps over their hearts. "The Star-Spangled Banner" played but I didn't know where the music came from. I only knew I was looking at Jackie Robinson for real, right there, right in front of me.

We did not sing. We just stared. The three men in front of us did not sing either. They kept chewing their cigars and blowing smoke back into our faces, which we tried to duck because it stunk.

Vinnie kept eating his sandwich while the music was playing. I thought that was wrong, but I didn't tell him because he would have hit me and then we would have had a fight and I did not think you were supposed to fight during the national anthem.

"He's right in front of us," said Tommy.

"Shhhh, I know," I said.

"Right there," he said again. He could not believe it.

"I see him," I said.

"But can you see him? He's right there, for real."

Jackie Robinson had trotted out to second base and the game began and we sat in awe. Roy Campanella was catching, but we could not see him because of the catcher's mask and also he was too far away.

Don Newcombe was pitching, and we could see him, but we did not care. He was not Jackie Robinson who was right in front of us.

Duke Snider was even closer, in centre field, but we only said, "Hey, there's Duke Snider, but can you see Jackie Robinson?"

And there was Pee Wee Reese. He was different. We liked Pee Wee Reese. He was brave and he had a name that made you like him.

"Hey, Pee Wee, got any white friends?"

That was one of the cigar guys in front of us.

"Hey, Pee Wee, you want your sister to marry one?"

Ebbets Field: A sacred place to those who loved the Dodgers. It is now a high-rise, low-income apartment complex with no room to play ball.

We said nothing. We just watched them and tried to make the space between us and them get further away. We did not think you were supposed to yell at baseball players, especially Dodgers, and especially friends of Jackie Robinson.

"Hey, Pee Wee . . . "

Crack. A ball was hit to shortstop and Pee Wee grabbed it on one bounce and fired it to first. We had never seen a ball thrown that fast or that hard before.

"Hey, Pee Wee, do you drink out of the same cup?"

It took a while for us to figure out what was happening, but then we got really mad. There were many blacks in the stands and most of them were sitting in the bleachers.

There was no way on earth these three guys were going to start insulting Jackie Robinson and go on living.

But Pee Wee had once put his arm around Jackie's shoulders when players on another team were calling him names. That was a long time ago, when he first started playing. But we had heard about it for years. We knew Pee Wee was a good guy.

"Hey, Pee Wee, does your momma know who's your friend?"

It went on for three innings. We sat and watched the game but we could not cheer because they took the fun away. They drank more beer and relit their cigars and shouted more insults at Pee Wee.

There was no way we could watch the game. This was not the way baseball was supposed to be. And there was no other place where there were five seats together. There was nothing else we could do.

"Hey, Vinnie, don't push me," I said.

"Well, don't push me."

"You want to fight?" said Joey.

The men turned around. We were doing nothing but sitting in our seats. Crack. Another ball was hit and Jackie grabbed it and threw out the runner at first. That was the first time we had seen him in action. It was thrilling.

"Atta boy, Jackie," we shouted.

"Humph," one of the men said, half turning around. "Lucky catch, he's getting so old he can't move."

He said that to the man next to him but he wanted us to hear it. "If Pee Wee wasn't there to back him up, he wouldn't be so good at all."

"Hey, don't push me," I said.

That was Tommy.

"I told you not to bother me."

That was Vinnie.

The men turned around. We were sitting. They looked like they did not understand.

Jackie was up at bat.

"He's in a slump," said one of the men.

"Hey, Pee Wee, you gonna hold your friend's bat for him."

Jackie swung, and missed.

"See, he's no good," said one of the men and he blew cigar smoke up and it went back to us.

"If you hit me again I'm gonna knock your head off."

That was Vinnie.

"You just try it."

Jimmy Lee.

They turned around and we were sitting.

The pitch and Jackie connected to right centre field. We jumped up and cheered.

"Lucky," said one of the men.

"I'm going to pour my soda over you," said Tommy.

"Yeah, well I'm going to pour my soda over you!" said Jimmy Lee.

All the men turned around. "Hey, you kids. You better watch it or we'll get you thrown out of here."

"We're not doin' nothin'," I said.

"Well, you better not."

They turned back to the game.

"I told you, I'll dump my soda over your head."

Joey.

They turned around again. We were sitting still.

They turned back to the game.

"I'm going to punch your teeth out if you do that again."

Jimmy Lee.

One of the men stood up and turned around.

"Okay, I don't know what you kids are up to but I'm going to get you thrown out of here."

He walked away toward one of the ushers that patrolled the stands. We saw him pointing at us. We turned our heads back to the game and sat with our hands folded on our laps.

I sneaked a peek at the usher and saw him shrug. The man came back and said to us that we were going to be thrown out if we did one more thing. When he turned back to the game Johnny said, "That does it, you guys. I'm pouring this soda over all of you."

All three of them turned around. We were sitting still.

"Let's get out of here," said one of them. "These kids are crazy. They shouldn't be let in."

They got up and moved out of the aisle and down the stairs and took the only three empty seats that were left, right in front of a row of black fans.

We jumped up and shouted, "Yeah, Jackie. Yeah, Pee Wee."

Then we sat down and looked at each other in disbelief. We had won. The Dodgers won. We left with the crowd, took the subway home and talked every minute of the way about the game, about how Jackie made the greatest hits and greatest catches we had ever seen and how Pee Wee also made the greatest hits and the greatest catches.

At home, I walked into the kitchen. My mother had already eaten a TV dinner, the latest thing to come into our lives. We did not have a TV but she could buy TV dinners and just put them into the oven and in twenty minutes take out an aluminum tray with aluminum foil on top, peel off the foil and there were three compartments, one with meat, one with peas and carrots and one with mashed potatoes. It would make life so easy.

"Before you get mad I have to tell the truth," I said, saying it as fast as I could. "I went to see the Dodgers today and they won and we saw Jackie Robinson and Pee Wee Reese and we sat in the bleachers and we saw the game and they won."

She was about to scream at me when I walked in, but when I finished talking she said, "You saw Jackie Robinson? For real? What was it like?"

"It was neat, Mom. He was at second base and Pee Wee Reese was at shortstop and we saw them, mostly we saw their backs because that's all you can see in the bleachers, but we saw them."

She sat down and I had never seen her like this. She went from mad to nice all at once.

"I always wanted to see Jackie Robinson," she said, "but your father hated him because he was black so we never went to a game. Tell me about it. Tell me everything. I'll cook you a TV dinner."

It was one of the best meals I ever had, even though I was still hungry after I finished it.

Changing the World

*J*ackie was really in a slump now. The men on the corner with their newspapers at night said this might be his last season.

We knew we were lucky to have seen him. We knew when we were old, people would say to us, "You really saw Jackie Robinson play?" And we would say, "Of course, we went to all the games."

The sun was hot. We had gone for another swim, but you couldn't come out of the boxes and sit on the roof because the black tar was too hot. Dorothy said if she had a bathing suit she would sit up there on a towel like they do at Coney Island. I could hardly breathe thinking of Dorothy in a bathing suit.

We climbed down the fence and walked up the block to the El. There was shade under the tracks, but it was still hot. Then we walked to the other end of the block and when we got there we said, "What are we going to do now?"

So we walked back to the other end.

"You think when we grow up we're just going to walk up and down some street?" asked Jimmy Lee.

"This is what they do in the Army, that's what my fadder told me," said Buster.

"I thought your fadder was in jail," said Vinnie.

"That was after he was in the Army," said Buster. "First he was in the Army and he was a hero and he got shot a couple of times and then he went to jail."

"How do you know that?" asked Vinnie. "I mean, about getting shot."

Buster kept walking and didn't say anything.

"How do you know?" asked Vinnie again.

Buster shook his head. He didn't want to answer so Vinnie asked him again. "How do you . . . "

"Cause I saw a picture of him with his rifle and he probably got shot a lot of times. I saw the picture in my mother's drawer."

"What were you doing looking in your mother's drawer?" asked Dorothy.

Buster looked embarrassed, said nothing and looked away.

"That's not right," said Dorothy. "You wouldn't want her looking in your stuff."

"She does, that's why I did. She took my father's dog tags back from me."

"Why'd she do that?" asked Dorothy.

"Cause she wants to have everything that was my father's and I don't got anything, except his rifleman ribbon so I know he was a good shot."

We walked for a minute while each of us was thinking about Buster's father firing a rifle and killing someone. We had lots of thoughts like that when we heard war stories.

"How'd you get the ribbon?" Vinnie asked.

"I stole it from her drawer, but she didn't notice it, or at least she didn't find it because I put it in the box that I keep my soldiers in."

"You still play with soldiers?" asked Vinnie.

"No. I just keep them."

Then we went on walking, me thinking, and I know Vinnie and all the boys were thinking of the soldiers that we still had, the little plastic ones that were throwing grenades and lying on their stomachs while shooting and one looking back and waving to others to come and attack. But we didn't say anything.

"I still have my dolls," said Dorothy.

"That's different," said Buster, who was trying to sound tough. "Girls are supposed to have dolls but we only play with soldiers when we're little."

We kept walking, this time down the block, stepping up over a big crack and a rise in a concrete slab of the sidewalk that once had a tree root under it.

"Can you imagine how strong that tree was?" Joey said. "It pushed the cement right up."

We stopped to admire this feat. There was a square patch of dirt next to the broken sidewalk where a tree had once been. We could almost make out the stump, but it had been stepped on so many times that it was hard to know where the dirt ended and the living thing had started.

"What do you think happened to it?" Dorothy asked.

"Probably got sick and died," I said. "Look, it could only get water from this little spot. And trees need a lot of water."

"Want to go swimming?" Dorothy asked.

Wow, suddenly I saw a connection between two things. One thing led to someone mentioning something else that was the same thing. I felt my brain grow. I had never felt like this in school. Plus I thought Dorothy was going to crawl through the boxes and maybe I could touch her.

"How long will it be before your father gets out of jail?" she asked Buster.

"Five years, with good behaviour," he said. "By then, I'm going to join the Marines and make him proud of me."

We turned the corner and the last of the white Bungalow Bar pickup trucks with bungalows on the back were getting packed up. Some of the drivers were ringing the bells which had to work or they wouldn't. A couple of the drivers were picking up their empty cardboard boxes and walking across the street to throw them into our ocean.

When all the trucks left there was nothing left on the street, except . . .

"Do you see that?" Dorothy said.

It was steaming in the morning sun, a large cardboard box left alone and steaming. We knew what was in it and we ran. You don't find things like this very often. In fact, we had never found anything like this, not this much.

"I can't believe it," said Vinnie.

"You know what we can do with it?" asked Johnny.

There was some silence. No, we did not know what we could do with it. If we were lucky we found little pieces of dry ice, maybe about the size of a finger or smaller, that had broken off when the trucks were getting loaded. Those we tossed back and forth to see how long we could hold them or put them in our mouths and pretended we were smoking.

But this was twenty pounds of dry ice. Some poor driver must have put it down on the other side of his truck, then loaded up the cooler with ice cream and driven off without remembering. That was awful. He would learn about it in about an hour at lunchtime outside some school.

Meanwhile, we had everything we had ever dreamed of having, except we had never dreamed of twenty pounds of dry ice.

"What do we do with it?" Vinnie asked Johnny.

"Well, you know what happens when you put dry ice in water."

Vinnie nodded. I nodded. Joey nodded.

Dorothy smiled. I knew then she was making some kind of

connection with what we could do with it that I had not made, but I also knew she was smarter than me, or anyone.

We had heard about dry ice in water from some of the drivers who said never put this stuff in water or it will fill up the whole room with fog that can kill you if you breathe it, but first it will freeze you to death.

So we got a paper cup and put water in it from one of the nozzles where they attached hoses to wash the trucks, then scrounged around until we found a couple of pieces about the size of our fingernails.

Ploop. Fizz. "Holy mackerel, look at that."

It bubbled up and over the cup and we put it down on the sidewalk and watched in mesmerizing fascination.

"I'm going to stick my finger in it to see if it freezes me to death," said Jimmy Lee.

"Well, don't breathe it," said Dorothy.

He put his finger into the fog then quickly pulled it out. He bent his finger.

"It still works."

Then he got on his knees and leaned forward.

"Don't, you'll die," said Vinnie.

"I wanna see," said Jimmy Lee.

He stuck his nose in, sniffed, and pulled it back.

"Wow, that's cold."

"You didn't die," said Vinnie.

"Naah, the drivers just say that so we won't steal it," said Jimmy Lee.

Dorothy folded her arms while we looked at the big steaming box.

"I know what we can do with it."

This mental connection stuff was happening everywhere. Why did we bother going to school when you could learn everything on

132nd Street, I wondered. But I still did not know what we could do.

"What?" asked Joey.

"Johnny knows. I know. Think about it," she said.

"We can have fun," said Johnny.

"We drop these down the sewers and see what happens? Maybe it'll reach the street," said Joey.

Dorothy nodded. She figured that out before he said it.

There were two sewers between Jamaica Avenue and 88th Avenue, at the edge of the factory. Two sewers with black, ugly water stagnating below the street. Two chances to change everything.

It took all of us changing hands every few seconds to carry the box from the ice cream factory around the corner to our street.

"Owww, golly, that's cold," said Vinnie.

"I can do it," said Jimmy Lee.

He got ten steps before he put it down.

"I can't hold it," he said.

"Don't drop it," shouted Johnny. "We don't want them to break."

We tried to push it with our feet, but we couldn't because the ground was too rough and the box too heavy.

I opened the box and tried to drag it with the flipped-open flap but a few feet later the bottom of the box was worn through and slivers of dry ice were being sliced off and left behind on the asphalt.

"Now what are we going to do?" asked Vinnie.

"We need someone's shirt," said Johnny.

"No way," said Dorothy. "No one is going to get away with that at home." Then she added, "Wait. Don't do anything," and she ran back to the ice cream factory.

She came back with another cardboard box from the ocean. She was so smart and I was hopelessly, totally in love.

We laid the new box on its side and tilted over the broken dry ice box into the open end of the new box and then lifted it and the ice slid into the new box. It was bigger and thicker than the one the ice had come in.

"Dorothy, do you want to be our teacher?" asked Joey.

Now with three of us, we could pick up the box by the flaps and carry it about ten feet, then put it down and pick it up again and move it and put it down.

"It's not that heavy or cold," said Vinnie.

But it was both. We needed everyone. This was not going to be something anyone could miss out on. "Stan, go get Stan," said Johnny.

Buster ran.

"And Patrick, that kid who lives with his mother next to the El."

I ran.

"And Vanessa, and those other girls who were at the party who never come out."

Dorothy ran.

Johnny pushed the box under the front bumper of a car to keep the sun off it. In five minutes, kids were coming from both ends of the block.

I rang Patrick's bell, but there was no answer. Luckily someone was going through the door and I ran in with him.

"Hey, kid. I can't let you in here."

"I won't be long," I shouted as I ran up the stairs. I had no idea which apartment it was, but there were only four on the top floor, and two were on the train side, so there were only two choices.

I knocked on the first door. Nothing. Knock again. I'm not going to wait. I ran a few steps down the hallway and knocked on the other door.

I could hear the bolt move behind it. The door opened a tiny crack with the safety chain holding it tight.

"Oh, it's you," said the woman who was Patrick's mother. "Wait a second."

She closed the door. I could hear her taking the chain off, then she opened it.

"Come in," she said.

"No, no, I just want to see if Patrick's home because we're doing something and we don't want him to miss it."

"Patrick's not home," she said. "Why don't you come in?"

She was wearing a tight sweater and tight pedal pusher pants. Her feet were bare. Her hair was falling down around her face. She took my hand.

"Come in," she said.

I could see her bumps under the sweater. They were mountains. She had a pretty smile. This is not possibly happening. This is what happened in the book in Tommy's cellar. This is not happening. Not now. Not when there is dry ice down the street.

"Come on, I won't hurt you," she said.

I knew something was happening behind my zipper. This was impossible and it was happening.

"I can't, I've got to see the dry ice," I said, and turned around and ran down the hallway and down the stairs and out the door and past the window of the bar and down the street until I saw all the kids around the sewer and I did not stop until I was in the middle of them.

"Did you get Patrick?"

"He wasn't home."

But suddenly all the running had felt so good behind my zipper and as I stood in the middle of all the kids trying to catch my breath, and I wanted to run some more but all the kids were standing around looking at the dry ice. Sex is a very strange thing.

"We break it into two parts and some of you go up near

Jamaica Avenue and the rest of us stay here. When I wave my hand, everyone drops it all down together."

Johnny was like the boss. But unlike the bosses we heard the men at the bar talking about, everyone was listening to him.

This was more than twenty pounds, we guessed. There were four large slabs, each one about five pounds. We divided ourselves up without choosing sides. I just wanted to be with Dorothy except I also wanted to be at Jamaica Avenue under the El next to Patrick's mother's apartment.

We dumped out half the ice. The rest was in the box and a bunch of guys and girls picked it up and ran toward Jamaica Avenue. It was easier to carry now.

Dorothy stayed here, so I did not move.

In two minutes we were in position. We could see each other although the elevated train was coming by and a Long Island Rail Road train was going behind the apartments, so there was no point in shouting.

Johnny raised his hand, looked north, whatever that meant, then dropped it like a signal.

Dorothy and I and Johnny and Vanessa and Buster kicked our ice down the sewer. We looked up toward Jamaica Avenue. The guys there were jumping up and down. They had done it.

We looked down into our sewer.

Blurp. blurp, blurp. White bubbles were rising, coming up through the blackness of the putrid air above the stinking water. Blurp. The bubbles kept coming. The bubbles were not bubbles, they were solid foam, rising both slow and fast.

It was slow because it wasn't speeding. But it was fast because we could see it and it was getting closer and closer. "Here it comes," said Johnny.

The white fog reached the bottom of the steel sewer grating and then wrapped around and over it. The grating disappeared.

The fog spread out through the holes in the grating, then started creeping out over the street.

The sewers were more than a hundred feet apart. There was no way this fog was going to last long enough to really do anything.

"Do you think it's going to cover the street?" I asked.

Johnny was standing over the sewer. The fog hid his feet. He looked at me and then at Dorothy and Vanessa and Buster then down at his feet again and smiled.

It kept coming. It was flowing out to the middle of the street. It was an inch deep at the highest point in the street, almost as high as the curbs. Now two inches deep in the middle, it crossed over the hump in the middle of the road and was sliding down to the opposite curb and more was rising from down below. The blackness was all whiteness now.

"Look," said Dorothy. She pointed toward Jamaica Avenue. The fog was coming our way.

The street was slightly downhill, which we did not know until then, and our fog was going away from us but theirs was coming.

A car came up from the factory. It was going to ruin everything. We started shouting and waving at it to stop, but it must have been something on the street that made the driver go faster.

We got out of the way and it raced by. We could see the driver gripping the top of the wheel with both hands, and he looked terrified.

"Ha, did you see that?" Buster said.

The fog was pushed aside by the car, but it came back almost as quickly, filling in the path cut open by the wheels. And now the white cloud was growing higher. Three, maybe four inches deep.

And what was more wonderful, the Jamaica Avenue fog was just about to join our fog in the middle of the block.

"Look, there's that old man who never comes out," said Vanessa, pointing at an old man who was standing by his open door.

We watched windows open and heads leaning out. Then

a truck turned off Jamaica Avenue, heading for the factory. It stopped. There was honking behind it.

Then we saw another truck coming up the street from the factory. It was amazing that we had this much time without traffic, but it still had been fun.

"Wow, wait, look," shouted Buster.

The truck had come halfway up the street into the fog, but now we could see through the windshield the driver, who looked like he was Puerto Rican, making the sign of the cross. Then he did it again, and again.

It was a panel truck with a giant windshield.

"Look, he's climbing up on his seat."

I don't know who shouted that. But we had power. We were doing something. We were changing things, sort of what Johnny said. This was wonderful. Except for the times when I thought about Dorothy and seeing Jackie Robinson and that feeling behind my zipper when I ran down the street, this was the greatest moment in my life.

The horns stopped as drivers behind the trucks rolled down their windows. We could see a lot of pointing and gesturing and some hands squeezed together in prayer. More apartment windows were opening. And except for the El and the Long Island Rail Road, the street was quiet. Between the trains it was almost silent. It had never been like this before, without cars and trucks, except maybe at 3 a.m. when I got up after a party to look for cigarette butts to smoke in the morning.

A little girl of about four or five came out the front door of a house with her mother. I had only seen her a few times since she wasn't old enough to be interested in watching stickball.

But it was quiet enough that I could hear her say to her mother, "It looks like a fairy princess world."

And it did. We made a fairy princess world. And then the fog started going down even quicker than it had come up and it began disappearing. I tried to wish it wouldn't but I didn't know how to do that.

"I wish it wouldn't go," I said to Dorothy.

"Me too," she said.

Wow. Dorothy wished the same thing as me. That was better than getting the fog wish granted.

Then the sign-of-the-cross truck driver started his motor and began creeping ahead; from the opposite end of the street, the other truck started up and came our way, slowly. In two minutes, trucks and cars were passing like nothing had happened. Except it did happen. And we made it happen.

We gathered in one large group over the sewer where Johnny had started it all. There had never been a group this big on the street since the basketball game. It was neat to have friends. We started laughing and slapping each other and talking about what we had just done and how wonderful it was.

Then Mrs. Belimeyer leaned out of her window and shouted, "I saw what you kids did. I'm reporting you to the police, and you are all going to get in trouble."

She closed the window. The fog was totally gone.

We were quiet. Mrs. Belimeyer was making all the noise. We looked at each other and started laughing and laughing.

That's when we heard the police car.

No sense in running away. We would look guilty and since there was nothing here now, there was nothing wrong and no way could we get in trouble.

Two cops we had never seen before got out of the car.

"Alright, we just want some answers now," said one of them, the biggest one.

"What happened and what did you kids do?"

Joey spoke, then Dorothy, then Tommy, then I did and Vinnie.

"It was scary," said Vinnie.

"We don't know what happened," said Dorothy.

I added, "It was white. I think it was from outer space."

"It was here then it was gone," said Joey. "Do you know what it was?"

The cops looked us up and down. Then they looked up and down the street. They were not going to be fooled, but there was nothing here to arrest us on and take us away to jail, or at least to threaten us with.

"We're going to investigate," said one of them. "If we find you kids did anything wrong, we will haul you down to the station house."

We looked so innocent. It was good to look innocent. We'd learned that when we were two.

Then the cops got back in their car and left. We waited until they turned the corner and we laughed like the best comedy show we had ever seen, except, you know, we had never seen a comedy show. But this was plain funny.

"I hope the ice cream guy found out before his ice cream melted," Vanessa said.

"You sound like one of those religious people who are always hoping for good things," Vinnie said. "Just imagine if he didn't. He would open his cooler and he could sell milkshakes."

That was enough to make all of us laugh, including Vanessa.

The World Series

The seventh game. The Bums might, could, couldn't, no, impossible, not Brooklyn up against the damn Yankees. We could say "damn" and get away with it. We could say "Damn Yankees" and the guys on the corner would slap us on the shoulder instead of the side of the head.

"Damn" – it sounded so good. A real curse word but it was sent to a real devil, the Yankees, and now the Yankees were up against the real angels, the Dodgers who never won, and this was the seventh game and that never happens and the impossible was possible.

"That's impossible," said Tommy. "Brooklyn can't win, they're Brooklyn. And besides, we can't see it, we can't hear it, we can't nothing."

He looked so despairing, but he was right. We could not skip another day from school, even for the seventh game. One more day, just one I was warned, and I would be in the same grade next year and then everyone would be younger than me and they would know I was too dumb to move on. So not even one more day, even for the seventh game.

"The game will still be going on when we get out," said Vinnie. "We can make it to the bar if we run real fast."

"Are you kidding?" said Joey. "The bar'll be packed. Even the men will be standing at the door."

We knew we had the radio. We didn't have to say that. But the radio was not fun when you were alone, not for baseball. For *The Lone Ranger* and *The Cisco Kid* and especially *The Shadow,* the radio was great when you were alone. You could sit and close your eyes and see everything. You didn't want anyone yelling then.

But for baseball, you had to have cheering and someone else's face to look at while waiting for the pitch. The problem was none us could bring all of us home to listen so the bar was the best place, even if we couldn't see or hear the game. At least outside the door we could hear the men cheering and shouting and they would tell us what was happening and it would be like being at the game with a lot of big guys sitting in front of you.

We passed the cardboard ocean and walked under the El and tried to talk but the trains were still busy with rush hour. Then we got up to where the Long Island Rail Road trestle went under the tracks of the El. It was like the Stand except there was no stand to buy papers from and so no one ever just stood there. You walked under them but it was neat to be there when trains on both levels were going by at the same time.

Once, and only once, did we walk under them when four trains went by overhead all at the same time, two Long Island trains and above them, two trains on the El. That was a great moment.

Four trains at once. We talked about that almost every time we walked under the trestles, because that doesn't happen every day, or even twice in a lifetime. Amazing things you never forgot, like the seventh game of the World Series when Brooklyn was playing the damn Yankees and we would miss at least half the game, and then we would go home and listen to it alone.

"It's not fair. If Brooklyn and the Yankees play next year, I'm going to take off even if I get left behind," said Jimmy Lee.

"Me too," said Joey.

So I said, "Me too."

Then Dorothy said, "I'll come with you."

Did she say that to me, or to us? I didn't care. She might have said it to me.

"Yeah, that'd be great," I said. "We could go and the heck with school. We could see Jackie Robinson in the World Series."

"Do you think he'll still be playing next year?" asked Joey.

"I don't know, but he might," said Dorothy. "But his batting average is slipping, you know."

Just like the boys, Dorothy knew his average.

Then a pair of trains went over our heads and the talk should have stopped. It always did, but this was about the Dodgers and Jackie Robinson so we went on shouting, "I think the Bums will win."

"What?"

"I think the Bums will . . . " then the trains passed and Vinnie finished the sentence with, "WIN!"

We laughed. Trains made talking fun. We went on walking but as we got closer to school, we talked less and less. We walked with our heads down into the classroom. It looked the same. It always looked the same, every classroom in every public school in the city looked the same. The same desks with the same initials carved into them bolted into the same floor. We knew it was a different floor in other classrooms, but they all had the same worn-out wood and we knew the initials were different, but with so many initials carved from so many kids, the letters were always getting repeated. If you read any one desk you knew eventually everyone sat there.

And there were the letters in capital and lower case printed on squares of paper and stuck above the blackboard. The teacher's desk was always at the front close to the windows.

Nothing different to distract us.

"I have an announcement to make," said Miss Johnson.

This would be bad.

There was nothing to distract us. We sat down. Nothing new, like talking about the game or listening to the lineup and listening to the commercials that said, "Hey, getyourcoldbeer."

For the first two years I heard that, I did not know what they were saying. I thought it was, "Hey, get your cobia." And I did not know what a cobia was, but I was too embarrassed to ask. So I said, "Hey, getyourcobia" along with everyone else.

And we could not listen to "The Star-Spangled Banner," which we did know the words to. Those were drilled into our heads. During the War of 1812, a guy named Francis Scott Key was a prisoner on a British ship and he saw the cannons shooting all night at an American fort and in the morning the flag was still there.

We had a lot of problems with this. First, it was hard to keep up with the wars: the Revolutionary War, the French and Indian War, the Civil War, the War with Mexico, the Spanish American War, the Indian Wars, World War I, World War II, the Korean War and the Cold War. We were always at war.

"Those other countries want to beat us because we are a peaceful nation," said Miss Johnson.

And then there was the War of 1812 with Francis Scott Key. We figured they ran out of names when they got to that one.

But most of all it was Francis Scott Key and his song that confused us. It's a strange name, we said. Nobody is called by three names, and if he was a prisoner of the British, how come he could stand on the deck and watch the cannons? Prisoners were kept in prison, below decks, and they did not have paper and a pen which he had to dip into an ink bottle.

Miss Johnson said he was a special prisoner and was treated kindly. We knew this was baloney because we had heard stories of the British prison ships in the Revolutionary War that were anchored in New York's harbour and they were filled with thousands of American soldiers who were left there to starve and rot and die of thirst.

So we did not trust this story of the guy with three names. But we still learned the words because we had to sing them every week in the auditorium with Miss Flag playing the piano and if anyone wasn't singing, he was pulled out and brought to Miss Flag's office and when she came back from the assembly he had to sing them, or stay there until he learned them.

And we also learned the Pledge of Allegiance, but that we learned in the first grade and said it every morning. Except this year we had to add, "Under God," in the pledge. President Eisenhower wanted "Under God" so we wanted it too. Because anything Ike wanted, we wanted, especially Eisenhower jackets which only came down to your belt. We got those at the Army Surplus store and our mothers all said they were useless because our bottoms would get cold, but on the other hand, if this was what Ike wore it must be good because Ike saved us from the Nazis.

But the thing we wanted even more than an Eisenhower jacket was a picture of the salute to the American flag from before the war. The first time Joey saw it cut from the front page of a magazine and hanging in the back of a closet, he couldn't believe it.

In ten minutes, he had called every kid on the block in to see it. We walked out of the closet in disbelief.

"It couldn't be."

But it was.

They were giving the Nazi salute to the American flag. And this was in an American classroom. We could tell because it looked like ours, with no distractions, except for the salute.

We asked Miss Johnson.

"They changed that when I was in school, before any of you were born. In 1942, we were at war with the Nazis and their salute looked like our salute," she said.

She told us the pledge back then started with their hands on their hearts, but on the last line everyone raised their hands out to the flag.

"We weren't going to look like the Nazis," she said. "So we stopped doing that and everyone was told to throw out all the pictures that showed it."

We looked at Joey.

"What happened if you still had the picture?" Jimmy Lee asked Miss Johnson.

"People thought you were a traitor or a spy and you probably were."

We looked at Joey again.

"Do you know where one of those pictures are?" asked Miss Johnson.

We looked back at her, so guilty she could read the answer.

"No, Miss Johnson. We just heard about it."

We all talked at once.

"Never saw one, not once."

Joey's father might have been a spy and a traitor, but Joey wasn't and we knew the Nazis' kids always turned in their parents when they suspected them. We were not going to do that to Joey. But it made us know how you don't know anything even when you think you know everything. That was one of those lessons you don't get in school, and we could talk to Joey later.

"So long as we are asking questions," said Miss Johnson, "would you like to tell me, Mickey, how it is you say you go to the Mediterranean in the summer when you clearly have never even been to Manhattan?"

"Because that's where we go," I said, wishing I could say I had been to Manhattan. "And my mother goes to Manhattan, every day."

"But not the Mediterranean. And if you don't tell me the truth, I will have to send you to Miss Flag's office for the rest of the day again."

Might as well, I thought. The Dodgers were going to play the Yankees. I could not hear it. I could not see it. I could not imagine it because this would be the greatest day in history and I would have to tell everyone I spent the first couple of innings, maybe right up to the seventh inning stretch when we could hear the crowd on the radio singing "Take Me Out To The Ball Game" in the big chair outside of Miss Flag's office looking at the wall with the pictures of Washington and Lincoln.

"But we do swim in the Mediterranean," I said.

"Alright, go to the office," said Miss Johnson.

"But that's where we go. You said so," I said.

"Me? I never . . . "

"Yes, you did. You were teaching geography last year and you said you were going to tell us about Greece. That was when a train went by and we didn't hear anything you said after that, but we know Greeks, lots of them."

I was bubbling. I was telling the truth.

"They have long mustaches and big eyebrows and they work in the ice cream factory."

Miss Johnson was shaking her head. "Those are not the Greeks I was talking about. I was talking about the classical Greeks who gave us the modern world."

A train was coming so we both stopped talking. Then we each tried to start ahead of each other as it was passing.

"The Greeks gave us culture," said Miss Johnson.

"The Greeks lived by the Mediterranean, you said," I said, trying to say it before she said something else.

"Yes, I did. The Mediterranean Sea is next to Greece."

"Well, our ocean is not a sea it's an ocean and it's next to the Greeks so it's the Mediterranean Ocean."

"What ocean? The Mediterranean is a sea." Miss Johnson was so confused she almost looked like I always looked when she said something that I did not understand.

"The ocean we swim in," I said.

"Coney Island?" she asked.

"No, the cardboard ocean. The boxes next to the ice cream factory. The Greeks put the boxes behind the fence, so that's the Mediterranean."

She said nothing. It was good to be a teacher, I thought, since that was me now.

"Cardboard boxes?" she asked.

Teaching was hard. I nodded.

"Cardboard boxes that you swim in?"

I smiled and nodded again. Joey put up his hand.

"We swim in them all summer," he said. "We have two weeks to go before they close for the winter."

The Cardboard Ocean was along this wall. The cardboard was behind a fenced-in area and piled right to the roof. Now the factory makes pipes and there is barbed wire where we used to dive from. The fence is gone, the cardboard is gone—it's like looking at an ancient dried-up ocean.

She looked at Joey like he was speaking another language, but I know she understood him because he was speaking English even though he secretly might speak German at home.

"Don't you swim in the real ocean?"

She looked at me, and Jimmy Lee and Vinnie and Dorothy and Tommy and Joey and Vanessa and Johnny and Buster.

We looked back. We said nothing. She said nothing. This was the showdown in P.S. 54. The moment of truth. The awakening. The moment when we realized we were together and Miss Johnson was from another world that knew nothing about our world.

"No," Vinnie said.

"No," Dorothy said.

"Never?" asked Miss Johnson.

"Never seen the ocean," said Vinnie.

"But it's at the bottom of Brooklyn. It's not far."

"Never been there, Miss Johnson," said Vanessa. "But we've heard of it."

"Not even once?"

We all stared back. If anyone had ever been there they didn't say so, but we didn't think anyone had.

"In cardboard?" asked Miss Johnson, and then a train started coming and at last the showdown was over because the noise had taken away the shootout of disbelief. We swam in cardboard boxes and that was all there was to it and the boxes were our ocean and the ocean was named the Mediterranean because Greeks worked in the factory and Miss Johnson said Greece was next to the Mediterranean. What was hard to understand?

"Mickey, you will not go to the principal's office today."

Then Miss Johnson said she had a treat for us. We did not get treats except at Halloween, and once I got a whole box of Cracker Jacks from an old man in the lobby of an apartment building and that was the greatest moment of my life, except when I saw Dorothy and Jackie Robinson.

"I know how much you want to hear the start of the game today," she said.

Then she turned her back on us and picked up a bag that was behind her desk.

"I know I am not supposed to do this, but I thought you deserved it, especially when you all tell the truth."

She put down the bag and put her hands into it, pulling out a radio. We sucked in thirty-six breaths. The last thing she brought to show us was the celery and she wanted everyone to know that.

"I don't want you to tell anyone," she said.

This was impossible. Not impossible to keep a secret, but impossible that she was asking us to keep a secret. She was a teacher. Teachers did not act like real people who told secrets. And teachers did not bring radios into the classroom when they were not supposed to because that was against the rules and teachers did not break the rules.

"Do you mean we can listen to the game?" Dorothy shouted. Dorothy never shouted.

Miss Johnson smiled.

"Really? Honest?" thirty-five other kids shouted.

"Shhhhhh," said Miss Johnson.

She put the radio on the windowsill and plugged in the cord. She started turning the dial until she heard the voice of Red Barber.

"This will be a game you will never forget," he said.

We knew the voice. It was the voice of the Dodgers for years until it became the voice of the Yankees, the damn Yankees.

The men in the bar said he was a traitor, but it was the same voice and he said, "Back, back, back, that ball is gone," in the same way.

We stared at Miss Johnson. The game was almost ready to start.

"And now our national anthem," said the Old Redhead.

"We should all stand," said Miss Johnson.

Thirty-six kids got out of their seats and with music from the radio we sang "The Star-Spangled Banner." A train was coming.

" . . . the bombs bursting in air."

It was hard to hear the bombs bursting in air.

We got louder.

"Gave proof through the night . . . "

The train got closer. We raised our voices.

" . . . that our flag was still there."

The train was at the edge of the building.

"Oh, say does that . . . "

The train was right outside the windows, blotting us out.

" . . . star-spangled banner . . . "

We fought back and yelled the words.

" . . . yet wave . . . "

The train filled the room.

"over the land of the free . . . "

We could hear us. The train was there, but we could hear us.

" . . . and the home of the brave."

We won. We could hear ourselves. We beat the train. And then the train was gone which would have left the room quiet except Miss Johnson started clapping and the people on the radio were cheering and we started clapping and cheering.

"Shhhh, we don't want Miss Flag to hear us."

Miss Johnson held up both hands and for the first time I could remember we got quiet, instantly.

We sat, we listened, most of us staring at the radio but seeing the batters, hearing Red saying, "Mister Reese, or Mister Hodges was up at bat." We called every man mister after we heard it from Red.

Jackie wasn't playing today. He had played in three games before this, but he was injured, and older. We understood. But we sure wished we could hear, "Mister Robinson is up next."

A train passed. We leaned toward the window, pressing against the desks, trying to scoop away a couple of inches of noise, but it didn't work. The train was loud, louder than the words and when it was gone we heard, "What a play!"

Groan. Thirty-six times.

We could hear now. We knew every player, every statistic. We listened and saw the swing and "crack." We heard it. "Did you hear that?"

"Did you hear it?"

The crack of the ball in the seventh game of the World Series with the Dodgers playing the Yankees, the damn Yankees, and we heard it, right there in P.S. 54, a moment never to forget. Except it was a Yankee hit.

"Back, back, back, back, back . . . "

"Nooooo." Mouthed, thirty-six times.

"Caught by Hodges at the warning track."

"Phew." Thirty-six times.

Three o'clock. The bell. We did not move. Two minutes passed. Another windup, another pitch.

"Do you want to wait for the end of the inning?" Miss Johnson asked.

Nods. Thirty-six times.

Twenty after three. "He's out."

"Go," said Miss Johnson. "And pray for the Dodgers."

We all hit the door at the same time. Some squirming and elbowing, then pop! We came out like peas from a pod, except we never had peas except from a can, but we heard about pods. A few burst through and the rest followed like spaghetti that slipped out of a pot and went down the drain before you could stop it. That we understood. We all had spaghetti.

Miss Flag was standing in the hallway.

"Children, what is going on here?"

"Dodgers, the Dodgers are up next."

"Stop," she said. "Tell me why were you all kept in?"

Some stopped. Some slowed but kept walking.

"I said stop."

"It's the World Series," said Dorothy. "It's going on right now. We got to get to the bar."

"The bar?! You can't go to the bar," said Miss Flag.

"But the game is on," said Vinnie. "We gotta hurry."

Miss Flag crossed her arms underneath her large bumps. We did not actually think of her bumps as bumps. They were more like giant lumps that kept her from crossing her arms where you were supposed to cross your arms.

"Don't anyone move," she said. "I demand an explanation. What is going on here?"

"The game," whined Jimmy Lee. "The game. We're missing it and it's after three and school is over."

"It is over when I say it is over," said Miss Flag, "and my school is not a zoo but you are acting like monkeys. Now, all of you go to the auditorium while I find out what's going on."

Miss Johnson looked out of the doorway and we could almost see her swallowing her surprise.

"Why are these children here after three?" asked Miss Flag. She was not gentle when she asked.

"We were . . . " Miss Johnson said, but then paused. She was not allowed to bring a radio to school. She knew that. We knew that. Miss Flag knew that, but what she did not know was that Miss Johnson did that. At least she did not know it yet.

"We were listening . . . " said Miss Johnson.

But before she could go on Dorothy said, "We were listening to Vinnie tell us about the time his father played with the Brooklyn Dodgers."

I was in love, again.

But before I could finish thinking that, everyone was saying, "Yeah, yes, Vinnie's fadder was a Bum."

Miss Flag jerked at that last remark, but Miss Johnson said that was a term of endearment. Then she told Miss Flag that we had been extremely quiet and attentive that afternoon and had been so good we did not notice the bell.

"In that case, you may go. But be quiet on your way out," said Miss Flag.

We walked out, hands by our sides, saying nothing but squeezing our lips together so we would not burst.

Outside: "Did you see her face? Did you hear her? Did you see what happened? Did you hear Dorothy?"

I said that.

Dorothy was surrounded by a group hitting her shoulders and saying she saved our day and she saved Miss Johnson. I tried to get in, but the crowd was too big around her.

Then someone said we better run, and we scattered, kids from each neighbourhood breaking off to run home to the game.

The 132nd Street gang ran under the El and past the steel girders and past another bar that had the game on and no one standing outside. That was probably because it was under the tracks and no one outside could hear anything. But you probably could see it from the door.

Didn't matter. We wanted our bar. We jumped curbs and raced across Jamaica Avenue, hardly looking for cars. No, that is not true. We could see sideways. We did not need to turn our heads when we were in a hurry.

The bar was filled past the doorway. It did not matter. We were there and Brooklyn was playing, even if this was Queens, it was next to Brooklyn and it was the BMT that ran over our heads and that stood for the Brooklyn-Manhattan Transit, so we were almost Brooklyn. We had to get to Brooklyn to get to Manhattan, so Brooklyn came first.

"What's the score?" one of us shouted.

"One nothing."

"For who?"

"For Brooklyn, you dumbski. Brooklyn! Brooklyn is winning."

Brooklyn had not won in the last five series they were in. And it had not won the last four times they played the Yankees. They had been ahead a couple of times, but not won.

"We're winning! We're winning!" Vinnie shouted.

Then he told me that what Dorothy said in school was true. His father used to be a Brooklyn Dodger, long ago, when he was young.

"Did not," I said. "She just made that up."

"He was," said Vinnie. "I never told anybody, but he was. Then he got hit by a bad pitch."

Dorothy stood in front of Vinnie with her back to the bar.

"I know, Vinnie. I know," she said. "That's why I told Miss Johnson."

Vinnie said nothing. He looked at her while everyone else was jumping around them and he looked and said nothing. Then he said, "How did you know?"

"I just know."

Dorothy turned around again and faced the open door and started clapping along with us kids and the men at the door and the men inside and the German couple in the deli across the street who had come out on the sidewalk and Matty who came out of his candy store and we were all clapping and cheering and shouting, "Go, Dodgers, go."

Vinnie stopped clapping. Then he tapped Dorothy on the shoulder. She turned.

"But really, how'd you know?"

She gave him a smile. I wished she was smiling at me. Her hair flopped around on the back of her head. Sometimes she wore a ponytail. Today it just flopped.

"Because your father did everything, I know. So I know he did this."

She was not making fun of him. I could hear that. She was

saying his father did everything like it was one of those things you learn in school or church, like it was true. It did not matter if it sounded crazy. It was true. And Dorothy said it was.

I wanted to be Vinnie. I wanted Dorothy to be my lawfully wedded wife. I wanted to kiss the most wonderful girl in the world.

Vinnie grabbed her and kissed her.

"Phooey." Dorothy pushed him away.

"Watch the game, silly," she said.

The bottom of the ninth came and went and the Dodgers became the champions of the world. If there was an atmosphere in the bar it was so thick it was one solid thing. You could not squeeze into it a fingernail or a doubt or any prayer that was not praying for the Dodgers. There are a few things that are remembered in life because they are so overwhelming: the Dodgers winning, a president killed, and a kiss.

Later in life, in another country, I learned how others laughed at the idea of World Champs. No, not the world, just Brooklyn, and Queens, and two or three million people who never really believed this day would happen and there was dancing in the streets. I saw it. I grabbed Dorothy and we went round and round, me holding her hands and looking at her face and swinging around with our arms holding each other from falling backwards and thinking the Dodgers were the best thing that ever happened in the world, but she was better.

And then, and then while her face was in front of mine and the world was spinning and the Dodgers had won, I leaned forward and kissed her. And she smiled.

It went on forever. It is still going on for everyone who believes that the Bums can win against the giant, overpaid, nose in the air, damn Yankees. I don't remember having dinner that night. But I did remember the kiss.

<h1>Last Chapter</h1>

"So is your mother or father a spy?" I asked Joey.

We were treading boxes, which meant you had to keep moving your feet because the cardboard would sometimes collapse under your weight when you didn't expect it and suddenly you would sink up to your neck and then you had to search around for something to push yourself up on.

"No," he said, then some boxes collapsed under him and he had to scramble and we laughed because that was always funny.

"How do you know?" I asked when he came up. Even though we were laughing I was kind of afraid to ask because if they were spies Joey might be a junior spy and I knew from what I heard that they could stay hidden for years and then suddenly kill, and we were alone in the boxes and no one would ever find me.

"I asked my mother. I said I saw that picture and asked her what it meant."

He didn't sound like a spy.

"What did she say?"

Joey pushed down with one foot, rose up like he was rising up with a wave, then he shifted to the other foot and sank.

"She said that's the way she learned to salute when she came to this country. She said she loved that flag and she didn't like it when they changed the way you saluted."

"So she's not a spy?"

"No. But I was worried too," he said. "I asked her why she hid it and she said she was afraid they would take it away like the Fascists and the Nazis were doing."

"Is your father a spy?" I asked.

"Are you kidding? He can hardly read. He just looks at the comics and then tells the stories to Junior . . . "

Joey had brought Junior with him today, for his last day at the beach. He was down on the sidewalk playing with the boxes that were spilling out of the open end of the enclosure.

"My father spends hours with Junior. He doesn't have time to be a spy."

I felt so much better I told him I was going to swim down to the bottom and look for crackers for both of us. But just as I was going to dive down, Vinnie and Dorothy and Buster were coming around the corner.

They said they wanted to make sure they got one more swim in before the factory closed for the year. They had called Vanessa and Jimmy Lee and everyone and they were on their way. It would be one last beach party like we heard they had in places where there were beaches.

In ten minutes, there were nine of us diving and swimming and jumping in and wishing this could go on forever.

Bang, bang. Again, bang. I was under the boxes but I knew it was the sound of a metal pipe or something hitting the fence. I thought I knew who it was.

"We want this."

I knew the voice. Rocky had come to ruin our day again.

"Come out and fight or we are going in after you."

I didn't want to fight. I was tired of fighting. I had lifted the dumbbells, but I didn't think I was any stronger. I looked in the bathroom mirror and my muscles weren't any bigger. And the last big fight with Rocky's gang had hurt. I was bruised and sore for days.

"You're a bunch of chickens," said Rocky.

Okay, we can't let him get away with saying that, so I climbed straight up. That was the hardest way to go. Going up at an angle was easier, but slower. But I had to get to the top fast to see what was going on.

"You're chickens, cluck, cluck."

I heard that near the top of the boxes.

We knew that was the way chickens were supposed to sound. But mostly we knew that unless we stood up to the "cluck, cluck," we would be called chickens for the rest of our lives. But what was worse, the cardboard was ours, it was our vacation, it was our fun, and if Rocky took it over we would never be back here, and there was nowhere else to go.

I pushed aside the top boxes over my head. There was Joey and Tommy to my left looking down. And Vinnie and Dorothy were to my right. I could just see Buster and Vanessa and Jimmy Lee coming to the surface. I knew Johnny was coming up.

I crawled to the fence.

"Uh oh."

I said that to myself. There were at least fifteen guys down there and it looked like they all had pipes or baseball bats or sticks.

I said nothing. I was scared.

"You're not taking our boxes," Vinnie shouted down to them.

"Come out and fight," said Rocky, "or are you chicken?"

"It's not fair that you have bats."

"Tell that to your undertaker."

Some of them started laughing, some banged on the fence with their weapons.

"We got to go fight them," said Joey. He was talking to me and Tommy and everyone.

"We're going to lose," said Buster.

Joey said nothing. There was nothing he could say. He was our leader. He was the strongest. He knew we could not win against that many, especially when they had pipes and bats and we had nothing.

"We are coming down. Don't hit my brother," Joey shouted.

Rocky looked up, then he looked over at Junior who was holding a box over his head.

"If he gets in the way, tough luck, unless you want to take him home, then you'd be out of the fight," said Rocky.

"I'm staying, but you better not hurt Junior," said Joey.

We all looked at Joey. He was hung between two worlds. We knew he would not leave us, but we knew he would do anything to keep his brother from getting hurt. That is, anything except leave us.

Joey and Tommy and I climbed over the top of the fence and then started going down on the outside. Buster and Dorothy and Vanessa and Jimmy Lee were near the open end of the fence and worked their way out with the boxes falling down behind them. Johnny was near the hole in the bottom of the fence. He dug through the boxes and then pulled himself out onto the sidewalk. You had to crawl out of that and as soon as he did, one of Rocky's guys kicked him.

We saw Johnny yell and roll over. That was enough to get Joey really mad and he jumped the last six feet off the fence and fell on the kid who kicked Johnny. Then the bats started swinging and the pipes were banging into the fence and the sidewalk and our arms and backs.

Junior shrieked and ran to help his brother but someone hit him in the stomach with a baseball bat and Junior fell screaming.

He grabbed his stomach and yelled and yelled and Joey grabbed the kid that hit him by the shirt and threw him into the street.

I had never seen such strength. But then something hit me in the face and I saw blackness, then redness then coloured stripes before I felt the sidewalk under the side of my face. I tried to get up but someone kicked me in the ribs. I tried again, but this time I got kicked on the other side.

I opened my eyes and saw Vanessa being grabbed by two guys who were trying to grab her bumps, while she was screaming and kicking them.

"Stop!"

I heard the word, but I got kicked again.

"STOP!"

I heard it louder this time but then I got kicked in the rear and my head went into the fence.

"STOP! Or I will kill you."

The voice had an accent, which I knew was Greek. Then I was kicked again.

"STOP! NOW!"

I looked up. There was a giant man wearing a white snow coat with long eyebrows and a moustache that covered his mouth standing near us. He was holding up a rounded ice pick.

"Stop fighting."

It wasn't really English. It was guttural, but they were the best words I had ever heard since Dorothy said that Vinnie's father was a Dodger.

"Stop now I say."

We all stopped, even the kid who was kicking me. Even the kids who were grabbing Vanessa.

"No fighting," said the man in the snowsuit.

"But we want this spot," said Rocky.

"No fighting," he said.

343

"We're going to fight until we get this spot for ourselves," Rocky shouted at him.

"No."

"You can't stop us," said Rocky.

Joey was holding Junior who looked like he was in serious pain.

"You will have a race," said the snowman. "The winner gets to stay."

"No, we will fight," said Rocky.

The snowman took two steps toward Rocky and held his ice pick at his face. It was just the curved side that Rocky was staring at, the point was facing back at the snowman, but there must have been something in the snowman's eyebrows that made Rocky change his mind.

"Okay, we'll race. From where to where?"

The snowman pointed at the boxes. "From the top to the bottom, and back."

He told us each to pick one kid to race and he would meet them at the top, then he opened a door into the factory and went inside.

We picked Joey, of course, and they picked Rocky.

"It doesn't matter what happens, after the race this is ours," Rocky said to us.

The Greek snowman stood on the roof looking like a white giant against the sky. No, he did not look like a giant, he was a giant. We could just see his chest and his head. The boxes hid the bottom half of him. His hood was pushed back, but he still had a knitted hat on, the same kind of knitted Navy surplus hat that we wore in the winter.

"Come up here," he said. "You," he pointed at Rocky, "come up here." He pointed to the boxes on his left side. "And you," he pointed at Joey, "you come up here." He pointed to his right.

Joey and Rocky climbed the fence. When they got to the top

the snowman said, "You both go down to the bottom. Then you come up. The first one up stays here. The others, you go."

Rocky laughed. Joey looked serious. Then Joey looked down at his brother who was sitting on the sidewalk still holding his stomach with one hand. But with the other hand Junior was waving to his big brother.

"Ready, now, go," said the snowman.

Joey and Rocky pulled themselves over the top of the fence and then fell into the boxes. Both went down head first. Joey was strong, we knew that. He was pulling himself through the cardboard faster than we had ever seen him.

But something was bad at the other end of our ocean. Rocky was going much faster than Joey. We couldn't see either one, but we could watch the boxes moving and Rocky's boxes were getting pushed aside much faster than Joey's.

"Ha, we're gonna win," said one of Rocky's gang. Then he spit on the ground. We didn't spit, none of us spit, at least not after Dorothy said that was disgusting. Then he spit again and pushed me.

I turned around to hit him.

"No fighting," shouted the Greek who was a snowman. I remembered Miss Johnson saying it was always warm in Greece, so I didn't know how they knew how to work in the cold.

"No fighting, just racing," he shouted again.

But the race was bad. Rocky's boxes were moving at the bottom, and Joey's were only getting pushed aside halfway down.

"We're never gonna let you back here," said another one of Rocky's guys. "Never, never, never."

It hurt. It hurt a lot because we knew it was true. Next summer would come and we could walk up and down our street, but we could never go around the corner. We could see the edge of the boxes from our street, but we would just watch them swimming in them while we walked back and forth.

"Hurry, Joey, hurry," we shouted. We got close and banged on the fence. "Hurry."

Vanessa crossed her fingers.

Rocky's gang spit more and hit each other. "Ha. Say goodbye to this."

"Hurry, Joey," said Vinnie. "You're stronger than even my fadder."

But Rocky was starting to go back up while Joey still had not reached bottom. Once they claimed this for their own that would be the end. It would be theirs. We might sneak in while they weren't there, but it wouldn't be any fun because we would know that any minute they might come down the block and if they caught us it would be another fight and you can't have fun if you are worried about fighting.

We saw Rocky's boxes moving as he was going up. He was five feet off the ground and Joey still had another couple of boxes to get through before he could turn around.

"Hurry, Joey."

Then, suddenly, Rocky's boxes started moving backwards. He was going down again.

We stared.

"Hey, Rocky, go the other way," one of his guys shouted.

We heard a muffled yell from Rocky, but no one could ever hear words from inside the boxes.

Joey got to the bottom and started back up. We knew how tough that was. You try to grab something and step on something and pull yourself up, and push the boxes aside from over your head, but sometimes your foot goes inside a box, and sometimes it flips over and the edge bangs into your shin and sometimes the whole box collapses. But he was climbing.

Rocky was going up again, but about five feet up, just about up to our heads, the movement in the boxes suddenly reversed and it seemed like he was swimming down.

"Go, Joey, go."

More muffled yells came from Rocky.

Joey was moving up. Rocky was rising, but then went down again.

Then Junior yelled. It was more a squeal than a yell. It was a box-piercing squeal and for a moment Joey's boxes stopped. Then, like Superman was suddenly in there, Joey's boxes moved like he was running up through them.

Rocky's boxes moved up, then down again.

Joey's arm stuck up through the top of the boxes and then he pulled himself high enough to get his head and chest out of the cardboard. He looked down and we were cheering. Junior got caught up in the action and was clapping.

The Greek leaned over the edge of the roof and grabbed Joey by the arms and pulled him out of the ocean and stood him on the roof.

"The winner," said the Greek and held up Joey's arm. It looked just like the cover of the book I read and I thought maybe somebody up there liked us. I wasn't sure if the up there was on the roof or in the sky.

At Rocky's end, there was a lot of yelling and boxes moving. Then Rocky crawled out through the hole in the bottom of the fence. He was covered in chocolate syrup.

"Not fair," he said. "It's not fair."

In a minute, Joey and the Greek came out through the factory door.

"It's a do over," said Rocky. "This isn't fair."

The Greek did not laugh. He did not smile. But while Rocky was talking he slowly shook his head left then right, then again.

"It's a do over," said Rocky again. "Either we have another race, and Joey goes on this side, or we fight."

"No fight," said the Greek. "No race again."

"You can't tell me nothing," said Rocky as he wiped his hands on his pants.

The Greek took his ice hook off his neck.

"You can't tell us nothing," Rocky said again.

The Greek reached out with the hook and with an aim I could not believe, he slid the point under Rocky's shirt and then he pulled the hook back and lifted it, with Rocky getting lifted with it.

Rocky tried to swing his fist, but the Greek lifted him higher with one hand, and the chocolate-covered Rocky with his chest held up by the hook of a giant in a white parka looked very funny.

"No fighting, or I fight you," the Greek said to him.

"Let me down."

It looked like the Greek could hold Rocky in the air as long as he wanted. He must have lifted a lot of ice in the freezer because now he was smiling as he held Rocky. Then Rocky's shirt ripped and he fell to the sidewalk.

"You ruined my shirt. You owe me a shirt," yelled Rocky.

"You ruined my coffee break," said the Greek. "One shirt for one coffee break."

Rocky got up and said, "We'll be back and you'll be sorry."

He was saying that more to us than to the Greek.

"You come back and I will hook more than your shirt," said the Greek. "You never come back. Never. You hear me? Now go."

Sometimes just the right tone and an ice pick and a thick moustache and long eyebrows can make a point that parents and teachers never achieve.

Rocky started walking away, dripping chocolate behind him. He turned around a couple of times and his friends were spitting a lot on the ground as they left, but they did leave. The Greek said nothing to us. He turned around and went back through the door and back to the freezer.

Joey made sure Junior was okay and gave him a box to play with. Then we climbed the fence and got back on the roof. We could just see Rocky and his gang turning the corner under the El. The chances of them coming back were small. No. They would never be back. A gang was not as strong as an ice hook in the hands of a Greek.

"Hey, look at this," shouted Johnny.

Johnny did not often shout. He was standing on the roof above where Rocky had gone down. We ran over the tar and gravel and saw what he was pointing to. It was an empty five gallon can of chocolate syrup.

"The Greek fixed the race," said Joey.

"But why?" asked Jimmy Lee.

"He likes us," said Dorothy. "He always watches us."

We said nothing. It was like something really important had happened to us. It was like one of those miracles they told us about in church of walking on water or feeding a lot of people with just a couple of bottles of wine and few loaves of Wonder Bread.

"Someday I'm going to Greece to swim in the real Mediterranean Ocean," said Dorothy.

"Can I go with you?" I asked.

"Sure, everyone can come."

That wasn't as good as going alone, but I was still happy she said I could go.

We spent the rest of the day and all the next day and the next day swimming. Then the summer ended and the factory closed and the Greeks got laid off and the boxes got taken away and not replaced. Then winter came, and the years went by.

Last, Last Chapter

orty years after I watched the great basketball game in my mind, the one where we all played and the hoop got flattened, I walked around the corner to the ice cream factory. It now made long, black steel pipes. There were a couple of abandoned and stripped-down cars, no wheels, no seats, no doors.

The fenced-in cardboard enclosure was gone. A stack of pipes about twenty feet long were strapped together and piled up on the sidewalk.

The street was greasy and oily. Men in coveralls were loading pipes on flatbed trucks farther down the street.

I had learned that Dorothy had gotten married to someone from another neighbourhood, had three kids and then was abandoned by her husband. She lived a hard life.

Vanessa had become a nun. That almost made me feel bad about wanting to see her naked.

Buster went to Vietnam with the Marines and was killed.

Tommy married someone from another neighbourhood named

Dotty, for Dorothy, and moved to California to drive potato chip delivery trucks for his uncle. He was never heard from again.

Johnny joined the Navy, then moved to Florida, got married and had three kids. He taught the neighbourhood kids how to build scooters and boats made from Popsicle sticks.

Jimmy Lee, as I told you in the chapter called "Gone Fishing," got married when he was seventeen, had two kids by the time he was nineteen and died of a heart attack while he was jogging when he was twenty-two. Amazing how life is not fair, and also amazing how, to me, we are still fishing together on the street over the sewer.

Vinnie disappeared, at least from my world.

And Joey did too. I tried to find him but even with Facebook and Google it was useless. Then two years ago, I got a note from my cousin, the one who moved out into the hallway when my mother and I moved in. He said he read in a newsletter from a tire company he once worked for that a longtime employee, Joe Colacioppo, had died.

He said a dozen years earlier he and Joe had been talking and they discovered they had a common link, me. Funny. Then it passed. One of those things you hear, then forget about, until you are reminded.

Back on the street, the elevated train had been taken down and now had many trees planted on it.

I saw one boy, mixed with a bunch of races, riding a bicycle.

"Hey, I used to live here," I said to him.

He stopped, then with his feet on the ground, backed away from me.

"I just want to know what you do here? For fun, I mean."

"Just play video games," he said. "I gotta go."

He got on his bike and quickly rode away.

I looked at the place where the cardboard used to be. Because this is now the computer age, I looked up Bungalow Bar on Google. You can do the same. It was started by a Greek who escaped from Europe right before World War II.

"Thank you, Mr. Greek," I said. "Let me repeat that: Thank you."

This photo of a Bungalow Bar Ice Cream truck abandoned at Broad Channel in Jamaica Bay was taken in 1973. I possibly, probably, washed that very truck for twenty-five cents. It is the right year, 1953—you can tell by the back fenders. They used those trucks for about three years. It was beautiful then and it still is.